Reason, Freedom and Religion

Toronto Studies in Religion

Donald Wiebe, General Editor
Trinity College
University of Toronto

Vol. 6

Published in association with
the Centre for Religious Studies
at the University of Toronto

PETER LANG
New York · Bern · Frankfurt am Main · Paris

Lorne L. Dawson

Reason, Freedom and Religion

Closing the Gap Between the Humanistic and Scientific Study of Religion

PETER LANG
New York · Bern · Frankfurt am Main · Paris

Library of Congress Cataloging-in-Publication Data

Dawson, Lorne L.
Reason, freedom, and religion.

(Toronto studies in religion : vol. 6)
Bibliography: p.
Includes index.
1. Religion—Study and teaching.   2. Religion
and sociology.   3. Hollis, Martin.   I. Title.
II. Series.
BL41.D38   1988   200′.1′8   87-17055
ISBN 0-8204-0600-7
ISSN 8756-7385

CIP-Kurztitelaufnahme der Deutschen Bibliothek

Dawson, Lorne L.:
Reason, freedom and religion : closing the gap
between the humanist. and scientif. study of
religion / Lorne L. Dawson. – New York; Bern;
Frankfurt am Main; Paris: Lang, 1988.
  (Toronto Studies in Religion; Vol. 6)
  ISBN 0-8204-0600-7

NE: GT

© Peter Lang Publishing. Inc.. New York 1988

Printed by Weihert-Druck GmbH. Darmstadt. West Germany

Table of
Contents

Preface

This book was written with two ends in mind: (1) to examine the methodological context, nature, strengths and weaknesses of an unconventional approach to the explanation of human action: 'the argument from rationality'; (2) to argue the possible advantages of introducing a modified form of this unconventional mode of explanation into the social scientific study of religion. The study focuses on the innovative presentation of this alternative method of social science made by the British philosopher Martin Hollis. The argument from rationality proposes that in the explanation of human actions consideration must be given to an asymmetry in modes of explanation: nonrational actions are subject to causal analyses, but rational actions are their own explanations. A rational action, that is, is a free action; and the social scientist is under a methodological obligation to discover whether an action is free prior to formulating a causal explanation.

The argument from rationality is suited to the needs of students of the social scientific study of religion because its development and legitimation ameliorates two points of antagonism between the scientific and the religious worldviews. The argument from rationality directly curbs the reductive thrust of scientific accounts of religion by giving methodological voice to the freedom of will asserted by the great religious traditions. Indirectly, the epistemological framework of the argument indicates that references to the transcendent are a conceptual a priori of 'talk of religion,' just as rational human agency is for 'talk of human action.'

There are three parts to the book. First, the parameters of the problem of human freedom are established through discussion of the two sociologies conflict (i.e., sociologies of social system versus sociologies of social action). the positivism-humanism debate, and the struggle of determinists and libertarians. Second, the epistemological and methodological legitimacy of the argument from rationality is argued through a critique of positivist and conventionalist alternatives and the specification of the analytical constituents of what I call Hollis' qualified idealist perspective. Third, the argument is applied to the debate over reductionism in religious studies and defended against the charges of vacuity and decisionism by proposing that the rationality of an action is a question of 'degree' and hence open to empirical investigation. Through these arguments the basic epistemological framework is set for a more humanistic social science (particularly a social science of religion). And in the process Hollis' idealist endeavor is placed on the more stable footing of what I have chosen to label an 'epistemic naturalism'.

Every effort has been made in the text of this book to use non-inclusive (i.e., non-sexist) language. Most of the sources quoted, however, including Professor Hollis, employ traditional inclusive language. Therefore at some junctures for stylistic reasons it has been necessary, regrettably, to revert to the traditional usage.

Acknowledgements

I would like to acknowledge gratefully the encouragement and support given to me in the preparation of this book by Louis Greenspan (Department of Religious Studies, McMaster University), Peter Erb (Department of Religion and Culture, Wilfrid Laurier University), and the editor of this series Don Wiebe.

I would also like to note with appreciation the financial assistance provided by a Book Prepartion Grant from the Research Office of Wilfrid Laurier University, Waterloo, Ontario, Canada.

Portions of this work have appeared previously in print. Parts of Chapter VI are drawn from "Determinism in the Social-Scientific Study of Religion: the Views of Martin Hollis and Ernest Gellner," *Religious Studies Review* 10, no.3, 1984: 223-28 and " 'Free-will Talk' and Sociology," *Sociological Inquiry* 55, no.4, 1985: 348-362. Parts of Chapter X are reprinted from "Neither Nerve nor Ecstacy: Comment on the Wiebe-Davis Exchange," *Studies in Religion* 15, no.2, 1986: 145-151 and "On References to the Transcendent in the Scientific Study of Religion: A Qualified Idealist Proposal," *Religion* 17, no.4 (pages unknown at time of publication). I wish to thank these journals for permission to reprint this material.

Introduction

... it seems to me unlikely that metaphysicians attempting to be rational can be dispensed with. Merely to mediate between religion, however mystical, and science, or between widely different religions, or widely different sciences, such as physics and psychology, we must have such metaphysicians.

Charles Hartshorne,
"Mysticism and Rationalistic Metaphysics,"
Monist 59, 1976.

The Problem: Religious Versus Scientific Explanations of Religious Action

Religionswissenschaft is established, but its method is not. In the academic study of religion a humanist majority and social scientific minority contend with each other, and their disagreements echo the traditional struggles between religion and science. The literature of the field is laced with introspective accounts debating the feasibility and merits of applying the methods of science to the subject of study.[1] Yet an increasing number of students of religion are coming to realize that their studies need to be grounded in more explicit insights from the philosophy of science, and even more particularly the philosophy of the social sciences. It has become clear that the old assumptions about religion and science, and their relationship, are no longer serviceable. Hence new thought must be given to what it means to study religion scientifically.

In the past the humanistic bias against the social scientific study of religion was largely justified since the method of science most frequently evoked by social scientists tended to be wholly deterministic and naturalistic. Objecting to the positivist underpinnings of this method, the humanists claimed that the truth of religious experience requires something other or more than social scientific understanding. This claim undergirds what Robert Bellah (1970a) has termed a "nonrationalist" tradition of scholarship in religious studies. The exponents of this tradition reject the reductive implications of the "rationalist" accounts of religion advanced by Auguste Comte, Herbert Spencer, Edward Tylor, James Frazer, Friedrich Nietzsche, Emile Durkheim, and Sigmund Freud. Seeking to guard the specific nature of religion from explanations which in the end explain it away, they turned to such thinkers as Johann Gottfried Herder, Friedrich Schleiermacher, Wilhelm Dilthey, and to some extent Ernest Troelstch and Max Weber; scholars who had displayed a greater appreciation of the central and irreducible role played by nonrational concerns in human society. Stressing the *sui generis*, esoteric, and self-interpreting character of religious beliefs and practices, the nonrationalists favoured a "science of religion" based on a nonreductionist, phenomenological descriptivism (e.g., Rudolf Otto, 1917; Gerardus van der Leeuw, 1938; W.B. Kristensen, 1960; C.J. Bleeker, 1959 and 1975; Mircea Eliade, 1963 and 1969; Wilfred Cantwell Smith, 1959, 1962, and 1976).

Many students of religion, however, think the nonrationalist approach is too self-validating. These scholars are leery of the pejorative language and conclusions of some of the rationalist theories of religion, but the nonrationalist option, they argue, rests on insufficiently demonstrated a priori postulates [2] and fails to distinguish adequately criteria for choosing between competing "descriptions" of religious phenomena. To fashion a true science of religion, these scholars argue, the demands of science (as method) must be given precedence to those of the subject. Therefore, the spectre of reductionism (in some form) probably cannot be avoided (e.g., Hans Penner and Edward Yonan 1972; Donald Wiebe, 1979, 1981 and 1984b; Robert Segal, 1980 and 1983; Michael Cavanaugh, 1982; Hans Penner, 1986).

Most students of religion operate, with varying degrees of awareness, with some hybrid form of these opposed methodological options. But the very uncertainies of this situation reflects the success the nonrationalists have had in shaping the collective psyche of the 'discipline.' A kind of "nomothetic anxiety" has gripped the academic study of religion, leading scholars to retreat "behind the safe bastions of historical particularism and relativism" (Svein Bjerke, cited by Donald Wiebe, 1983: 287). Even amongst sociologists of religion, Roland Robertson suggests, a kind of religious attitude towards religion has emerged. In the face of the charge of reductionism, that is, an almost apologetic orientation has slipped into the supposedly objective study of religion (Robertson, 1974: 46 and 1985: 357).

This tendency is understandable, since the conventional social scientific response to religious beliefs is dissonant: it recognizes the value of, and implicitly commends, religion at the level of general theory, while explicitly rejecting the specific truth of any religious propositions (see William Shepard, 1972: 238 and Benton Johnson, 1977: 368). Yet this situation does not provide an epistemological warrant for simply stipulating the *sui generis* nature of religious phenomena. As with other phenomena, systematic knowledge of religious phenomena can only be purchased at the price of a certain tactical blindness to the full nature of these phenomena. This fact can be taken into account with the appropriate philosophy of science and method of social science. But no matter how this limitation is treated, if methodological respectibility is a concern, then I think that the academic study of religion would be better served by holding to a neo-positivist method of science, than by reinforcing its identification with the nonrationalist perspective.

In light of recent developments in the philosophy of science, however, methodologically informed students of religion might be disinclined to heed this advice. Alternatively, they might seek epistemological solace for an empathetic and internalist approach to the study of religion in the conventionalist (i.e., nonrationalist) philosophies of science of Thomas Kuhn (1970), Paul Feyerabend (1975), and Richard Rorty (1979) (see, for example, Charles Davis, 1984). But this alternative threatens to resolve the problem of devising a method for religious studies by subsuming all knowledge to the endless contingencies and relativities of the hermeneutical circle. In other words, it threatens to permit students of religion to speak meaningfully about their subject at the price of severely curtailing their claim to be scientific in any traditional sense.

But the extremes of neo-positivism and conventionalism, are not the only or best options available. At least two other readings of the epistemological lot of the human sciences can be delineated. Two additional ways, that is, have been envisaged for breaking out (relatively) of the hermeneutical circle of self-validation pinpointed by post-positivist philosophies of science. Reiterating the classic distinctions of epistemology, the two ways are a modified empiricism and a revamped idealism. The former perspective points to new grounds for faith in the inductivist logic of traditional naturalism; the latter points to new grounds for faith in a deductivist logic of science which permits the differentiation

of social and natural scientific methods without fostering an outright dualism. The new empiricist perspective I have in mind is
presented in Ernest Gellner's small and well known book *Legitimation of Belief* (1974). The new idealist perspective is presented in
Martin Hollis' engaging and compact *Models of Man* (1977) (Hollis
actually employs the synonymous term "rationalist," but to avoid
confusion with Bellah's dichotomy I shall speak of a new idealism.)
Both Gellner and Hollis have attempted to reformulate the epistemological traditions in question in a manner which renders them
congruent with the pragmatist insights common to the debates of
post-positivist philosophers of science.

The innovative views of these authors can be correlated readily with the methodological schism besetting religious studies. Indeed, Gellner's ideas have been used by Michael Cavanaugh to criticize stringently the humanistic attempt to found religious studies
on "a kind of technical competence about religion" which could
"rule out extra-religious claim testing" (1982: 110). In the process of providing new reasons for rejecting the phenomenological
method of the nonrationalist tradition, however, Cavanaugh simply reiterates the threat posed to religious truth by the classic rationalist accounts of religion in the guise of what Gellner calls an
inevitable tension between "cognition and identity." True knowledge, Gellner argues, depends upon a mode of explanation which
is inherently dehumanizing (because it is thoroughly deterministic and naturalistic). Therefore, Cavanaugh asserts, students of
religion must squarely choose to be either the promoters of a "disconsolate knowledge" or an "unjustifiable [religious] consolation"
(1982: 114). In other words, adapting the terminology of William
James, Cavanaugh has used Gellner to provide new legitimation
for a *hard* reductionist science of religion. This science categorically rules out any explanatory consideration of the references
made by the religious to the transcendent by blocking the inclusion of any 'references to the transcendent' in the discourse of the
scientific study of religion.

Hollis' ideas have not been applied in the same way. Here,
however, it will be argued that his new idealism points to the
possibility of squaring the social scientific study of religion with
sound epistemological practice without having to choose between
cognition and identity. It does this by providing valuable epistemological and methodological support for programmatic suggestions
for a *soft* reductionist science of religion like those made by Donald Wiebe. Such a soft reductionist perspective not only permits

but necessitates the inclusion, at least intially, of the espoused references to the transcendent of the religious in the complete and scientific assessment of religious phenomena. And it is this soft reductionist conception of the academic study of religion, I will contend, that constitutes the most reasonable and constructive methodological option available.

In fact the argument advanced by Hollis in *Models of Man* and elsewhere, provides a unique opportunity to ameliorate the gap between religious explanations of religious behaviour and social scientific explanations of the same behaviour. This is because Hollis' work demonstrates how students of religion might come to grips with both horns of their methodological dilemma: the problem of determinism as well as that of naturalism. Hollis is not concerned with the problem of making social scientific sense of the references made by the religious to the transcendent. Rather his attention is focused on the problem of making social scientific sense of the pervasive naturalistic claim to human freedom. It is focused on the attempt to devise an active (i.e., voluntarist), as opposed to a passive (i.e., determinist), "model of man" for the social sciences, by developing a new "method of science" based on an ambitious theory of rational action and a priori knowledge. In the pursuit of this objective, however, he performs a double service for the academic study of religion: he assists the student of the scientific study of religion both directly and indirectly.

Hollis argues for a reconceptualization of the nature of social scientific analysis on the basis of two propositions: free actions are rational actions, and all human actions can be systematically assessed for their rationality as effectively as they can be assessed for the cause and effect relations normally associated with scientific analysis. To the extent that he is able to demonstrate these propositions he directly assists students of religion by providing a more satisfactory account of the human context of religious beliefs and practices. In the methodological debates of religious studies attention has focused almost exclusively on the contrast of immanent and transcendent modes of explanation. The methodological resolution of the free will-determinism issue, however, can play an equal if not more instrumental role in the formulation of a method of science for the academic study of religion. A conversion or pact with the devil is religiously authentic, and hence praiseworthy or damnable, both because it involves a relationship with a true transcendent and because it is freely undertaken; the absence of either factor renders the act religiously inauthentic and hence open to naturalistic explanation. By establishing the conceptual identity of free, rational, and religiously authentic acts, Hollis' approach offers a more viable epistemological reason for granting to religious phenomena a measure of the autonomy sought by exponents of the nonrationalist tradition.[3]

Indirectly, though, Hollis' efforts to provide for the social scientific conceptualization of human freedom are perhaps of even greater assistance to the student of religion. There is a marked similarity between the epistemological and methodological difficulties presented to the social scientist by the talk of human freedom and the references of the religious to the transcendent. It should come as no surprise, then, that the line of reasoning developed by Hollis to deal with the former problem might be transferred profitably to the second. Here, as indicated, such a transference of insights will be effected through a correlation of the views of Hollis and Donald Wiebe (in Chapter X).

For this correlation to have the desired impact, however, it is first necessary to demonstrate the viability of Hollis' own undertaking. Everything hinges on finding a workable understanding of what constitutes a rational, and hence free, action. It is this concern, then, that will occupy centre stage. We must deal first with the thorny issue of the direct connection between the explanation of free human acts and the understanding of the human context of religious acts, before tackling the even more prickly and indirect issue of the possible methodological implications of Hollis' alternative method of science for the question of reductionism in the scientific study of religion.

The Solution: Martin Hollis and the Argument from Rationality

Models of Man was written because of Hollis' dissatisfaction with the attitude of resignation or indifference adopted by most social scientists in the face of the disjunction of contemporary modes of self-understanding and understanding of the world. Building his argument on a purposefully simplified dichotomy of "models of man," Hollis proposes that there are sound reasons for holding to our common-sensical and institutionalized notions of "Autonomous Man" and rejecting the "Plastic Man" image generated

by the dominant modes of scientific explanation. Human freedom can be incorporated into the scientific study of our actions
by constructing a mode of explanation based on the rationality
of the subject which complements and extends the causal mode
of explanation which presently demarcates scientific analysis. In
the discussions to follow (extending Quentin Gibson's usage, 1976:
111), this alternative mode of explanation will be termed 'the argument from rationality.'

Taken at face value, the argument from rationality does not
represent an unusual way of thinking about things. On the contrary, the opposite is the case. In simple terms, the argument
from rationality is any argument which adopts the rationality of
humans or a specific actor or actors as its premise and attempts
to draw from this conclusions about the character and causes of
actions undertaken by the actor or actors. In this form, as Gibson
points out, it is "an argument of a kind which is extremely common in the social sciences, and without [which] our knowledge of
human affairs would be very much more limited than it is" (1976:
111). Such an argument is used to produce historical inferences,
explanations and predictions.

As usually employed, the argument from rationality has a
threefold structure: first, the rationality of humans or the actor
or actors in question is assumed; second, a hypothetical rational
argument is formulated to explain the specific actions of the actor or actors; and third, this hypothetical argument is actually
attributed to the actor or actors (Gibson, 1976: 113-114). There
are problems with each aspect of this argument. But what is
most problematic often goes unnoticed: the argument rests on a
metaphysics of human agency which is logically at odds with the
conventional metaphysics of causality. Hollis grasps this fact and
uses it to develop the argument from rationality into a true alternative to the inadequate modes of explanation offered by both
neo-positivist and humanist accounts of social science.

The use of a rationality assumption in the explanation of human action has been explored in diverse ways by such philosophers
as William Dray (1957), Carl Hempel (1962), and Donald Davidson (1980). [4] But Hollis' work is essentially original in the sense
that his position relies neither on theories gleaned from these authors nor on direct criticisms of their ideas (though he is aware
of their well known views). His work provides the most accessible
and comprehensive discussion of the argument from rationality as

a necessary component of all attempts to explain complex social action. He has sought, more specifically than Dray, Hempel, and Davidson, to link the metaphysics of human freedom with a social science methodology which permits the analysis of the individual as the efficient cause of his or her actions.

To this end, Hollis has disputed "not only the positivist doctrines behind orthodox methodology but also empiricism in general." Yet he has not followed "those recent philosophers who therefore reject all traditional epistemology" (1975: 3). Nonrationalist or conventionalist philosophies of science have discredited the traditional criteria of scientific rationality, they have not, he declares, "abolished the need for truth in science" (1977: 179); nor have they exhausted all the ways of introducing an element of necessity into the world, thereby making science possible. In opposition to conventionalism, positivism, and empiricism, Hollis looks to a method of science based on a theory of knowledge which he takes to belong to the rationalist tradition of Leibnitz and Kant.

Commenting on Hollis' position, William Outhwaite observes that his alternative perspective seems to involve two distinct but closely interrelated theses (1983: 13):

> a general philosophical thesis that 'all sciences depend on necessary truths knowable a priori' and a special thesis that 'rationality assumptions are essential to social science.'

Both of these theses will be detailed in the second part of this study. The general thesis and its ramifications will be the focus of analysis in Chapters V and VI, while the special thesis and its ramifications will be examined in Chapters VII and VIII. But a few preliminary comments are in order here.

The general thesis of the argument from rationality stems from Hollis' critique of positivism (Hollis and Nell, 1975, and Hollis 1977). Hollis criticizes the positivists for inadequately appreciating the constitutive function of theoretical ideas, especially with regard to the derivation of causal laws from observed regularities amongst contingent facts. To have science one must be able to tell genuine laws from spurious concomitants. This involves reference to some sort of necessity. On the basis of an analysis of the actual operations of the social sciences. Hollis argues that this necessity comes from reference to the truth of an overarching theoretical insight. Like the later operationalist brands of positivism, in other words, his idealism entails viewing theories as "axiomatic systems on the geometrical model" (Hollis, 1975: 13). Therefore the necessity invoked by science appears to be merely a definitional necessity.

Unlike the later positivists, however, Hollis denies that these "axiomatic systems are optional or empty" (1975: 13). In other words, they are not composed of statements whose truth is guaranteed by logic alone. Rather Hollis argues for the methodological necessity of conceptualizing "the rational prior to the real, or ... the ideal prior to the actual," and he contends that the axioms of theoretical systems "are to be regarded as (putative) necessary truths" (1975: 13).

In the case of the social sciences the necessity of this approach is compounded by the fact that so much of the subject matter is pre-identified in terms of the descriptions of actors and their cultures. Consequently, in contrast to the accepted dogma, Hollis suggests that the attempt to expound 'real' (as opposed to 'nominal') definitions of social phenomena is of the essence of social scientific practice. The derivation of real definitions by transcendental arguments from pre-scientific descriptions is the pre-requisite to law-like explanation. "It can be shown," Outhwaite comments in agreement, "... that most inter-theoretical conflict in the social sciences is fought out at a level which, if it has to be a priori or empirical, must be the former" (1983: 17). Recognition of this epistemological fact in the social sciences can be used to undergird the more specific axiom that "humans are creatures whose behaviour is constituted as free action, just as money is paper that is constituted as currency" (Simon, 1982: 5).

The special thesis of the argument from rationality grows out of Hollis' criticisms of the causal mode of explanation underlying scientific determinism. It represents a logical extension of the general thesis with specific reference to the problem of scientifically conceptualizing human freedom. But it should be noted, as Outhwaite points out, that Hollis proposes that "the special thesis can survive without the general one" (Outhwaite, 1983 : 162; see Hollis, 1977: 186). Finding the account of causality employed even in the natural sciences subject to a number of telling logical "snags," Hollis argues that there is insufficient methodological warrant to abandon the socially institutionalized intuition "that action has determinants unique to the agent-*an-sich*" (1977: 185). Yet he also argues that the familiar humanistic programmes for understanding social action in terms of "purposes," "intentions," or "rules" all fall short of according a true and full freedom to social action. And the freedom which these programmes do obtain for the subjects of social analysis is not open to any sufficient kind of systematic assessment. It is not intentions but reasons, Hollis proposes, that should be substituted for causes as the first principle of explanation of social action. What is important is not the intentional quality of the belief which causes an action, but the rationality of the belief and hence action. Rational actions, he suggests, are free, whereas actions which are not fully rational or are irrational are subject to explanation in terms of determining causes. The overall premise is to complement scientific causal analysis with the knowledge that "rational action is its own explanation" (Hollis, 1977: 21). The special thesis, then, is an argument for a second mode of explanation in the social sciences, a mode which allows for a true human freedom which is open to systematic treatment because it is anchored in a second principle of necessity – reason.

In passing it should be noted that there is a strong affinity between Hollis' special thesis and the theories advanced in two other well known works, R. S. Peters' *The Concept of Motivation* (1960) and A. I. Melden's *Free Action* (1961). Unlike these authors, though, Hollis does not claim that determinism fails to apply in principle (for conceptual and logical reasons) to human action. Rather, he makes the lesser and more defensible claim that determinism does not apply to rational actions. This position is more in line with the arguments advanced in a series of articles by Alasdair MacIntyre (1957, 1962, 1967, and 1971). But here again we will see (Chapter VIII) that there are crucial differences.

As indicated, rationality is the key, and Hollis' approach points out that ultimately human understanding necessititates postulating the existence of some universal (i.e., transcendent) criteria of rationality.[5] Reality is the product of interpretations, nevertheless human sociation requires a "bridgehead" of shared interpretations (Hollis, 1982: 73).

> In upshot there has to be some set of interpretations whose correctness
> is more likely than that of any later interpretation which conflicts with
> it. The set consists of what a rational man cannot fail to believe in
> simple perceptual situations, organized by rules of coherent judgement,
> which a rational man cannot fail to subscribe to.

This set founds the necessary assumption of all human interaction: it is "an activity among rational men" (Hollis, 1977: 186). In turn, this necessity complements the root principle of sociology, namely that humans are nothing without society, with the knowledge that rational and free human agency is a transcendental condition of social action and organization, and thus of sociological analysis as well.

For the present much of this must appear murky. But as Hollis stipulates in the Introduction to *Rational Economic Man*, here we can only say: "since we must first overthrow some renowned theories of knowledge and then present our own, before arguing the merits of the approach, we shall withdraw into enigmatic silence for the time being" (1975: 13). Let us turn then from matters of substance to a delineation of the format and arguments employed in this book.

The Conceptual Context: The Perennial Problems of Social Theory

In *Seven Theories of Human Society* (1981), Tom Campbell proposes that there are three perennial philosophical issues, which from Aristotle to Alfred Schutz, have had a bearing on the choice between competing approaches to social theory: the issues of (1) free will versus determinism, (2) the nature of explanation, and (3) the objectivity of values (1981: 234). In the argument from rationality, all three of these issues are tackled, and each has a particular relevance for a different aspect of Hollis' formulation of this argument. Therefore, these philosophical concerns will be used to sequentially structure a delineation of the conceptual context and content of his alternative method of social science.

In Part One, the nature and significance of the free will-determinism debate in sociology will be examined, with an eye to ultimately demonstrating that the argument from rationality constitutes the most obvious and promising foundation for a humanistic social science. This will entail doing three things: first, outlining and criticising the notion of a conflict between a sociology of social system and a sociology of social action; second, reviewing the debate between positivistic and humanistic conceptions of social science; third, scrutinizing the merits and demerits of the traditional arguments advanced in support of a libertarian or a deterministic understanding of human action. These initial investigations set the stage for the rest of the study by establishing four points: (1) the metaphysical question of free will underlies both substantive and methodological disputes in sociology; (2) it is the viability of a method of science, however, which has had the greatest influence on the determination of the "model of man" predominant in the social sciences; (3) most sociologists, for example, have opted for the Plastic Man model because they think that explicability necessitates that our ideas of freedom presuppose determinism (i.e., causal regularity); and (4) the only real alternative to this state of affairs is to develop a mode of explanation based not merely on the subjective meanings of actions, but their 'rationality.'

In Part Two, the nature of a proper explanation of social action (and hence to some extent religious action) will be examined. As indicated, this will entail doing two things: elaborating the 'general thesis' of the argument from rationality, and detailing the 'special thesis' of the argument. Elaborating the general thesis will first involve preparing the ground for due consideration of the argument from rationality by refuting the presumption that the only viable method of science open to those social scientists opposed to a totally hermeneutical conception of their activities is some form of "soft positivism" (i.e., showing through a critique of positivism that explicability does not necessitate that freedom presuppose determinism). Then, secondly, attention will be turned to the actual task of laying the foundations for an idealist method of science by arguing that the notion of 'natural necessity' underlying scientific explanations is not some kind of ontological fact. Rather the notion of natural necessity stems from our epistemological judgements about what is theoretically true of experience. These steps broadly delineate the rhyme and reason of the theory of knowledge undergirding the argument from rationality and hence the recommendations to be advanced eventually for a new method of science for the study of religion. To more specifically establish the credibility of this orientation, however, a comparative critical analysis will be undertaken of Hollis' views and those of Paul Tibbetts and Ernest Gellner. As social scientists and philosophers, Tibbetts and Gellner have recently attempted to resolve the debate about human freedom in the social sciences by in effect resurrecting an essentially positivistic method of science within different pragmatist frameworks.

Detailing the special thesis of the argument from rationality will involve progressively establishing three things. First, the immediate methodological stage of the special thesis will be set by demonstrating the inadequacies of sociological role theory, with its passive image of humanity. This will entail, simultaneously, laying the groundwork for an alternative mode of sociological explanation by demonstrating how the principle of rationality can be used to fashion an identity for free social actors which remains compatible with our knowledge of the social character of human existence. Second, with the notion of rationality thus inserted into the framework of sociological explanations, more specific philosophical and methodological justification will be advanced for postulating an asymmetry in modes of explanation for rational and hence free actions, on the one hand, and irrational and hence caused actions, on the other. Third, having thus fashioned a logical as well as a methodological space, so to speak, for the argument from rationality, attention will be turned to the nub of the matter: delineating the nature and justification of the specific conception of rationality which Hollis invokes as the prerequisite for the full analysis of social action. The argument from rationality which finally emerges from all of these preparatory discussions is curiously circular and normative, yet nevertheless plausible, for its limitations are not so much its own as those characteristic of all modes of social scientific analysis (even the most positivistic).

In Part Three, having worked through the argument from rationality, attention will be returned to the overarching concern of the book: demonstrating how the argument from rationality could play an instrumental role in reducing the methodological significance of the debate between reductionists and nonreductionists in the field of religious studies. This will be demonstrated, as indicated, by showing how Hollis' views can be used to support Wiebe's efforts to ground the academic study of religion in a 'soft reductionist' approach to the references to the transcendent intrinsic to religious beliefs and practices. In conclusion, however, it will be argued that if the potential of the argument from rationality as a basis for the study of social and religious action is to be realized, then the epistemological foundation of Hollis' theory must be crucially modified. Specifically, if the approach is to be successfully defended against two charges, namely that it is empirically vacuous and excessively value-dependent, then the logic behind Hollis' general thesis must be pressed to reveal the viability of an even more unorthodox epistemological position – one of "epistemic naturalism" (my term).

A Few Cautionary Remarks

The difficulty of the task at hand calls for some qualifications. First, it is not my intention to burden this study with complicated definitions of determinism, freedom, and rationality prior to tackling the issues engendered by the problem of human freedom in sociology. The considerations are too many and too abstract to be surveyed meaningfully in advance. For the present the following definitions will suffice. "Determinism is the general philosophical thesis which states that for everything that ever happens there are conditions such that, given them, nothing else could happen" (Taylor, 1967: 359). In modern terms, determinism is the theory that every event (including human thought and action) has a cause. Free will is the philosophical thesis that at least some events, namely human choices, are not caused, in the sense that people are not inevitably compelled by pre-existing circumstances to think or act in one way rather than another. Here freedom is further being connected with rationality, and for something to be rational means it conforms to reason. And reason, to use Hollis' formulation, is the "portmanteau name for the rules of proof, which aid the mind in securing a priori knowledge, and for the canons of empirical evidence, used in judging the truth of beliefs against the facts of an independent world ... (It has also included whatever intuition is deemed needful to ground the first inference)" (1982: 68). As matters proceed these rather simplistic, static, broad, and absolute conceptions will be replaced with more complicated, dynamic, specific, and relational conceptions of causality, freedom, and rationality.

Second, the problem of freedom confronts the social scientist with a host of logical, epistemological, methodological, ethical, and in our context even theological difficulties. Few scholars possess the full range of expertise to do justice to all of these considerations. Certainly no pretense to such encyclopedic capabilities is being maintained here. Nevertheless, the issue is one which the social scientist must grapple with first hand. It is too fundamental to be left to the philosophical savants and then all too imperfectly absorbed piecemeal into the body of social scientific thought. The question of human freedom transcends academic divisions of labour, and the account which follows will range over at least five different frameworks of analysis: social theory, the traditional philosophical arguments over free will and determinism, the philosophical theory of action, the philosophy of science, and the methodological debate over reductionism in religious studies. Each of these frames of reference will be consulted only to the degree that they help us to understand the potential viability of the argument from rationality. The objective is not to resolve the differences and dilemmas of these diverse fields of discourse, but to secure enough knowledge to help bring about an adjustment of sociological method; an adjustment of particular benefit to the integration of sociology and religious studies.

Third, it is recognized that the subject matter of this book raises the vexed issue of levels of analysis in another more general sense: Is it an essay in method, methodology, or theory? The distinctions themselves are by no means clear. Verbal usage of the distinctions is widely variant, and consequently nothing of great importance is meant to depend on the usage adopted here. But for the sake of foreclosing on certain inappropriate expectations, a few things need to be said about the level of analysis at which this study will be operating. 'Method' will be understood here to mean the specific procedure or procedures used to acquire, organize, and analyse data which have already been determined to be relevant to the issue or subject under study. 'Methodology' refers to an analysis of the assumptions and logical limitations of a method. 'Theory' refers to the attempt to actually explain the nature and/or operation of some specific thing; theories, unlike methodologies entail existential claims. This study is a methodological investigation. It is examining whether there is methodological reason for social scientists to turn to the argument from rationality, and it is examining the logic of that method as it presently confronts us. It is neither advancing the theory that humankind is indeed both rational and free, nor is it seeking to specify the precise method which would successfully operationalize the argument from rationality. It is arguing that there is merit in further developing the argument as a method of social science because it is logically as sound as existing alternatives, it expands the scope of human activity potentially subject to systematic study, and it circumvents certain persistent and perhaps ultimately unproductive theoretical conflicts like the positivism-humanism debate in sociology and the reductionism issue in religious studies.

Fourth, in keeping with this specific orientation, when the issue of how religious references to the transcendent should be treated is raised in Chapter X, it must be kept in mind that this particular phrase (i.e., references to the transcendent) has been employed to place certain controls on the discussion. The appropriate qualifications are detailed in the openning pages of Chapter X, and some readers might well wish to familiarize themselves with these stipulations before proceeding with the analysis of the argument from rationality.

In the end, this study recognizes that in the context of contemporary social scientific concerns, the very decision to support the quest for a method of social science which can take into account humanity's claim to freedom and religion's claim to autonomy, is probably, in the strictest sense, an act of prejudice. But then, it also hopes to show, so is the decision to ignore these claims. If the objective of social science is to fashion an ever more accurate map of the contours of human existence, then such fundamental claims, no matter how recalcitrant to empirical treatment, should not simply be ruled out of consideration. In the face of our relative ignorance, judgements of substance with regard to these claims may well have to be suspended. But if our understanding is to be advanced, then conceptually a place can and should be prepared for these claims in our formulation of the method of social science and the science of religion.

Part One
Free Will Versus Determinism in Sociology

To breed an animal 'with the right to make promises'–is not this the paradoxical task that nature has set itself in the case of man? Is it not the real problem regarding man?

Fredrich Nietzsche,
On the Genealogy of Morals
Second Essay, Aphorism I

I.
The Importance of the Question of Human Freedom

The Nature of the Problem

The British social theorist Anthony Giddens has observed that sociological theorists are involved in two tasks simultaneously: understanding the character of human social activity, and investigating the logical form of social science. Such an observation is equally apposite for theorists in the field of religious studies. The two endeavors of the sociological theorist, Giddens suggests, "feed from a pool of common problems" (1979: 259). And one of these problems, which is as relevant for the student of religion as for the sociologist, is the free nature of some human actions.

The free will-determinism debate constitutes a basic parameter of social scientific thought, though in the practise of the social sciences this fact is rarely acknowledged and weighed. The issue of human freedom also constitutes a basic problem for the scientific study of religion. In fact its importance, as noted, is magnified in this discipline by the traditional identification of the integrity of religious beliefs and practices with the principle of human freedom. If the idea of human freedom can be incorporated into the scientific mode of explanation of sociological theory, then an instrumental step will have been taken towards reducing the degenerative methodological gap at the heart of the academic study of religion between 'religious' explanations of religious behaviour and 'scientific' explanations of the same behaviour.

The question for the social scientist or the student of religious studies, unlike the philosopher, is not whether human beings are, in some ultimate sense, free. If the scholar's objective is to understand the character of human social and religious activity, it is hard to see how he or she could avoid introducing the idea at some juncture. Explicitly and implicitly, social and religious theorists employ the notion of freedom in important ways to define and differentiate their own activities and those of the people they know or study. In most religions, and certainly within the Christian tradition, freedom of choice is the prerequisite for responsibility before

God, true conversion, and the attainment of salvation (whether as heavenly bliss, *nibbana*, or whatever).[1] The distinction when drawn in daily life or religious doctrine may be subtle and ambiguous, but it is by no means inconsequential or irrelevant to the interests of the human sciences. To ignore the human capacity for freedom is to engage in an unnecessarily 'reductive' analysis of religious phenomena even within the confines of a strictly naturalistic framework.

Yet social scientists have not known how to treat the presumption of human freedom. Like the old Viennese professor of Russell McCormmach's *Night Thoughts of a Classical Physicist*, they have simply avoided giving systematic theoretical expression to the idea by clinging to the traditional wisdom "that natural science has recognized limits, beyond which lie freedom of will and the ethical force of European man" (1982: 90). But this cautious obeisance to the limits of science has simply made them determinists by default. By turning a blind eye (as scientists) to the claim to human freedom, they have neither done justice to their subject matter, nor to their obligation to fashion a logic of inquiry which is truer to the character of human social and religious activity. For as McCormmach's old physicist laments, in the twentieth century our perception of the nature of science, and hence its limits, has greatly altered. While society and religion have become the subjects of comprehensive scientific study, the precise nature of science has become a mystery; and in the last analysis neither science nor the ethical force of humanity are adequately protected any longer by a mute accommodation to the deterministic social science attendant on the professor's dated maxim. There is a need to rethink our options, to rethink the fit between the nature of science and the nature of humanity.

In *Models of Man*, Martin Hollis frames the dilemma faced by the social scientist by offering the trenchant suggestion that "every social theory needs a metaphysic... in which a model of man and a method of science complement each other" (1977:3). Traditional social theories (e.g., Aristotle, Aquinas, Hobbes, Adam Smith, Rousseau) were founded on ontological claims about the essence of humanity. But the start of knowledge, contemporary science tells us, is to recognize that there is no human essence. Bound to the canons of empiricism and ethical neutrality, orthodox modern theorists strive to strip the scientific study of human action of its traditional debt to metaphysical conceptions. Yet as William

Kolb has pointed out (1962: 5), the scientific study of humanity requires more than empirical method.

> It requires the presupposition that the world is real, important, and knowable. It further requires some image of man and his status in the world, so that criteria of significance for the selecting and ordering of data can be developed. Such images are in part empirical but they are also in part composed of non-empirical presuppositions and assumptions about the nature of man.

In the very act of rendering human wants and needs dependent variables–functions of social, psychic and biological forces–modern theorists themselves have posited a model of humanity. By making the individual "no longer *causa sui* in the explanation of social action" (Hollis, 1977: 2), the empiricists in their triumph have impregnated us with the image of men and women as the passive subjects of causal processes. The dominant and typical image of humanity which has come to inform the social sciences is that of a being whose behaviour is determined in the same way that other natural phenomena are determined; potentially every human act can be understood as the result of antecedent factors, especially of the sociocultural environment, which operate to make that act inevitable.[2]

Admittedly, it can be argued that the passive conception of humanity does not represent a "model of man." It does not entail a return to essentialism in the sense of postulating an ontology of necessary beings and subsistent attributes. But the basic orientation does entail some ontological and metaphysical assumptions. Minimally, and paradoxically, as Hollis comments: "any claim that [the passive image] has no essence will turn out to be an essentialist thesis, in that it asserts a priori and on epistemological grounds an informative proposition about the stuff of human behaviour" (1977: 7). Similarly, in sociology, the attempt to avoid the pitfall of traditional essentialism or psychological reductionism has implicitly fostered an essentialist presentation of humanity as *homo socius*: individuals as the creations of socialization, devoid of any innate humanness.[3]

Most social scientists do not personally believe, of course, that human behaviour is wholly determined (though there appear to have been exceptions, e.g., B. F. Skinner, 1973; Otto Neurath, 1973; and perhaps George Lundberg, 1968). They defend their deterministic approach to human affairs as a limited operational procedure of clear heuristic value. Under the influence of the legacy of positivism, they argue that in the conduct of 'scientific' inquiry there is no alternative. This position has been representatively stated in a single paragraph note published in the *Journal for the Scientific Study of Religion* under the presumptive title "A Brief Resolution of the Issue of Free-will versus Determinism" (Wilson, 1964: 101):

> Free will is a conscious experience and like all conscious experience must remain forever epiphenomenal to science. It exists.... However, inasmuch as the causal efficacy of free will can never enter into a predictive formula, such arguments appear meaningless. It is suggested that everyone choose, if not freely at least willingly, to devote their energies to other pursuits.

The author has psychologists particularly in mind, but the principle applies as well to sociologists. Good science entails holding to the conventional wisdom of Durkheim's advice (1964: 141): "sociology does not need to choose between the great hypotheses which divide metaphysicians."

In a society where science carries so much authority, however, such a conclusion needs to be carefully assessed. There is a deep psycho-logical connection between the image of humanity dominant in the sciences and the image informing our fundamental value orientations, and we must guard against the reification of epistemological assumptions which have proved useful. Whatever the status claimed for our images of humanity, it must be recognized that at root such images are ethical fictions which entail normative prescriptions about human capacity and potential (Dawe, 1978: 369).

My concern here, however, will not be with the social and political implications of adopting a free or determined conception of humanity. Rather, as stated by Paul Tibbetts in a similar context, "what I am looking for is an argument why anyone is bound or obliged to consider [these implications] (Tibbetts, 1984: 99). What is of interest are sound epistemological reasons for the adoption of basic units and frameworks of analysis in the study of social and religious action which allow for human freedom.

To this end it should be noted, I think, that the notion of free agency is central to a whole network of ideas that define the human condition: ethics, education, law, politics, and religion. It is irresponsible and unrealistic to think that there neither are, nor should be, any referential connections on this issue between the world of science and that of ordinary life. This is not said by way of abandoning science's hard won principles of empiricism and value-neutrality, but in agreement with Alan Dawe when he says (1978: 409):

> We live in the world we also watch, and our living informs our watching. A science which divorces the two 'always obliges us to forget what we know' of the social world whose story it is our job to tell. If we cannot converse with ordinary men–with ourselves as ordinary men–we cannot begin to speak of 'life as it is lived.'

Concepts are intrinsically reductionistic and goal and value relevant. But this does not mean they are arbitrary: unconnected with or uncorrected by reality. Precisely how concepts relate to reality is a matter to be given some consideration in Part Two. The point here is that it is counter-intuitive to think that human freedom is not a social "reality." In the face of this reality the social scientist must strive to overcome the tactical blindness of his or her method. On the issue of human freedom, as Hollis stipulates (1977: 3), "there is no shirking questions of quasi-fact, of normative analysis and praxis." In a fundamental sense humans either are or are not free. If they are deemed free, then the methodologically self-conscious theorist must address the question. Is it possible for sociological theory to incorporate the idea of human freedom into its scientific mode of explanation?[4]

Sociologists of religion in particular should recognize the need to address this question. In the conclusion to *Religion and Society in Tension* (1965), the American sociologists of religion, Charles Glock and Rodney Stark, propose that the deterministic ideology of the social sciences throws into question the social scientists' contention that their investigations pose no threat to religion *per se*. The centrality of a free will understanding of humanity to religion belies, they argue, the illusory nature of all claims to a "rapproachment" between religion and science (1965: 296-97).

> Theological images of man differ, of course, in different religions and, over time, may differ in the same religion. In the midst of differences in detail, two central ideas about the functioning of man are curiously combined in virtually all religions. The one idea sees man as created by God and subject to God's will. The other accepts God as creator but conceives of man as essentially in control of his own destiny.... In combination they form the basis of religious commitment. The one warrants commitment by establishing the ultimacy of divine authority. The other makes reasonable the reward and punishment system through which that authority is exercised.

For the religious, humanity is free within the bounds of God's providence, and that freedom is held to be "relatively unrestricted"

(1965: 298). But the empirical study of religious phenomena implicitly denies and explicitly narrows the scope of human freedom
in a manner that religious perspectives cannot readily accommodate. The social sciences, "by making ambiguous just what it is
for which man can justifiably be held to be freely accountable,...
make ambiguous as well what it is that religion can justifiably ask
man to be" (1965: 303). Consequently, the conflict of religion
and science is still very much with us. The tension between these
worldviews can only be reduced, Glock and Stark conclude, with
"the innovation of a wholly new perspective which would resolve
the determinacy issue" (1965: 293).

   The reasoning seeems sound, yet the challenge has not been
taken up. In part, because the question of human freedom is rarely
approached as a subject in itself. Rather it is usually broached
as a sub-issue of two related but distinct controversies: the conflict between a sociology of social system and a sociology of social
action, and the conflict between positivistic and humanistic conceptions of sociology. In the field of religious studies, as noted,
the issue comes to the fore in augmented form in the parallel conflict between what broadly can be called phenomenological and
social scientific approaches to the study of religion. At the heart
of each of these debates, however, lies a common problem: the
old question of the unity of the sciences. The resolution of these
conflicts, that is, depends on the answers given to two epistemological questions: Do social phenomena require a method of study
distinct from natural phenomena? Do religious phenomena further
require a method of study distinct from ordinary social phenomena? Here, in line with Hollis, I will be arguing that the first
question should be answered with a qualified 'yes', and the second
question, in line with the argument to be advanced in Chapter
X, with a qualified 'no'. Natural, social, and religious phenomena
require different and distinct disciplinary approaches, but not to
the point of fostering conflicting methods of science.

The Axes of Debate

   The dichotomies used in sociology to identify the conflict of
the two sociologies and the positivism-humanism debate are too
simplistic. But the terms specified are cited commonly by sociologists to mark-out their differences. Hence these dualities do
point to real tensions and ambiguities in the history of the discipline. Nevertheless, neither framework really comes to grips with

the problem of human freedom. When pressed the substantive issues raised in the conflict of the two sociologies resolve themselves (if they are to become manageable) into the methodological concerns of the positivism-humanism debate. But this debate has itself collapsed under the weight of the criticism leveled at both the positivistic and humanistic accounts of social science. At the metatheoretical level, close study has brought about a convergence of the traditionally framed alternatives.

In practise, a positivist method of science has dominated the social sciences. It is this method that accounts for the orthodox passive model of humanity. Yet the criticism of positivism has been so intense that, as Hollis comments, one must be wary of tirades launched against positivists as "nowadays the verb 'to be a positivist' appears to lack a first person singular for its present tense" (1977: 42). To all appearances, at the metatheoretical level at least, the humanistic perspective (i.e., the claim for the autonomy of the *Geisteswissenschaften* from the natural sciences) seems to have triumphed. Certainly with the breaching of the verificationist and falsificationist barriers erected by the Vienna Circle and Karl Popper, there no longer seem to be convincing epistemological grounds for placing so-called metaphysical questions like that of human freedom beyond the pale of scientific consideration.

In the mind of even the most robust humanist, however, the positivist tradition has established the suspect character of all self-validating explanations (the insight was instrumental in the demise of positivism itself). And the success of the humanist critique of scientism has not been matched by the provision of incisive criteria for making inter-subjectively accessible and convincing choices between competing theories and concepts. Thus while the demise of the old empiricism has brought the traditional dilemmas of the human sciences, like the question of human freedom, into a new prominence in debates over the nature of science and the nature of knowledge, it has not brought us much closer to resolving these dilemmas. As embodied in the conventionalist or nonrationalist theories of knowledge and science of such figures as Thomas Kuhn (1970), Paul Feyerabend (1975), and Richard Rorty (1979), the humanistic perspective threatens to resolve the problem of freedom by subsuming all knowledge to the endless contingencies and relativities of the hermeneutical circle. In other words, it threatens to permit sociologists to speak meaningfully of human freedom at the price of severely debilitating their capacity to be scientific in any traditional sense. Consequently, most sociologists, including sociologists of religion, have continued to base their research, at least implicitly, on a 'soft positivism.'[5] And it is because of this state of affairs that the issue of scientifically conceptualizing human freedom has not been given serious consideration. In raising these points, however, we are moving beyond our immediate task and into the concerns of Part Two. Here the objective is simply to set the methodological stage for the drama to follow by outlining the two traditional sociological contexts in which the question of human freedom is raised and setting them against the backdrop of the established dilemmas of the free will-determinism debate.[6]

II.
The Conflict of the Two Sociologies

Dawe's Thesis

In a much acclaimed article, "The Two Sociologies" (1970), Alan Dawe proposes that the entire history of sociology has turned on a basic dualism of thought and analysis which amounts to a conflict between two distinct types of sociology: a sociology of social system versus a sociology of social action. Throughout the discipline's history, he writes (1978: 366),

> there has been a manifest conflict between two types of social analysis, variously labeled as being between the organismic and mechanistic approaches, methodological collectivism and individualism, holism and atomism, the conservative and emancipatory perspectives, and so on. The debates about these issues are central and perennial in sociological discourse and, at root they are all different versions of the fundamental debate about the abiding conflict between the domination of the system and the exertion of human agency.

In a sociology of social system, the behaviour and relationships of the individual, his or her very sense of personal identity, is determined by society. Social actors are socialized into society's central values and into the norms of their roles in the division of labour; these roles define them and their social place in terms of the purpose they serve in meeting the functional needs of the system. In Dawe's words, "social actors are pictured as being very much at the receiving end of the social system," and social action is seen as "the product and derivative of social system" (1978: 367).

In stark contrast to this, in a sociology of social action the social system is viewed as being derivative of social action and interaction. The system is a social world which is produced by its members, "who are thus pictured as active, purposeful, self and socially creative beings" (1978: 367). The social system is conceptualized as the emergent product of the interaction of social actors who define their purposes and situations in terms of 'subjective meanings.' Society is not a being *sui generis*, a self-generating and

self-maintaining 'organism' which is ontologically and methodologically prior to its participants. It is a central schema of meaning,
negotiated in accordance with the meaning-projects of individuals, as conditioned by their differential capacities to control other
participants.

The two sociologies represent two sides of the same coin; and
as their implications radically differ, no theorist has discovered the
trick of showing both sides of the coin at the same time. In the
history of sociology, the social system perspective is clearly more
orthodox and dominant. Sociologists of diverse backgrounds and
orientations commonly explain this dominance as stemming from
the historical links of the discipline with the problem of social
order.[1] As Dawe succinctly summarizes (1970: 207):

> Essentially, the argument is that sociology was shaped by the nineteenth
> century conservative reaction to the Enlightenment, the French Revo-
> lution and the Industrial Revolution. In opposition to what was seen
> as the subversive rationalism of the first, the traumatic disorder of the
> second and the destructive egoism of the third, the conservative reaction
> sought the restoration of a supra-individual hegemony. In doing so, it
> created a language which, at once, defined the solution of the problem
> of order and the sociological perspective; hence the centrality of such
> concepts as authority, the group, the sacred and, above all, the organic
> community.

The very persistence of the classic conflicts within sociology
clearly suggests, however, that despite the claims of its proponents, a sociology of social system does not address all the concerns of sociologists. Much of the sociological tradition, Dawe
proposes, has actually focused on a second central, though less
systematically developed, problem: the problem of control. This
problem is rooted in sociology's inheritance of the Enlightenment
commitment to human liberation. For as much as sociologists fear
the excesses and unintended consequences of the Enlightenment
legacy, they are also the heirs to the desire of the *philosophes* to
reveal "how human beings could regain 'control' over essentially
man-made institutions and historical situations" through the "application of reason and the scientific method to social analysis"
(Dawe, 1970: 211).

It is this second focus of attention that gave rise to the sociology of social action–a sociology which deviates from the almost
paradigmatic treatment of social action in synthetical sociological
schemas (like that of Talcott Parsons) by refusing to relinquish

the power of human initiative at any level of analysis. In the synthetical schemas the formal acknowledgement of human agency becomes subsumed within an overriding analytical orientation to the social system.

> As it has been developed in sociology, the language of social action begins with the subjective dimension of action; conceptualizes it as the definition of the situation; spells this out in terms of the actors defining the situation on the basis of ends, means and conditions; and posits action as a process over time, i.e. as history. It is at this point, however, that the language of social action is absorbed by that of social system. By a combination of the principle of emergence and the postulate of consensus, unit acts are systematized in terms of central values. In the consequent synthesis, actors derive their definitions of situations from the central value system, through their internalization of the social roles ultimately defined by that system (Dawe, 1970: 210).

Sociologists unhappy with the loss of human subjectivity and historicity, with the loss of individual initiative in such schemas, have rejected the postulate of consensus as an unwarranted a priori. In its place they favour a consistent stress, through all levels of analysis, on the interactive character of the construction of social reality.

In a broad sense there is an evident truth to the two sociologies thesis. But few scholars can be identified exclusively with one or the other of these perspectives. Formally, the methodological and substantive tendencies of most sociologists reflect a clear bias in one of the two directions. The Durkheimian tradition tends to be identified with a sociology of social system, while the Weberian tradition is linked with a sociology of social action. But historical insight militates against the absolutization of either alternative. In accounting for social change the theorist cannot isolate on the contribution of the individual or the social system alone. The tension between the two sociologies is most significantly manifested then, as an internal disharmony within comprehensive systems of sociological theory. Hence, as Dawe points out, the classic tradition is rife with inconsistencies (1970: 214):

> ... for example, the obvious conflict in Durkheim's ideal of 'a sociology justifying rationalist individualism but also preaching respect for collectivist norms' [(Aron, 1968, 2: 97)], and the consequent ambiguities in his view of the relationship between the social and the individual and of moral consensus. There is a similar conflict in the Marxian dialectic between the notion of socially creative man and the essentially Hobbesian view of nineteenth-century capitalist man. And in Weber,

too: the pessimistic chronicler of the 'supreme mastery of the bureaucratic way of life' is clearly concerned with the problem of control and
begins with a sociology based upon the subjective dimension of action.
But, partly because of his pessimism and partly because the sociologist
of the *machstaat* and of religion is also concerned with the problem of
order, he finishes with a sociology in which the bureaucratic system is
totally compulsive from the point of view of its participants.

Despite a number of "intellectual sleights-of-hand," in Dawe's
opinion, contemporary approaches fair little better. Berger and
Luckmann (1966), for example, are equally culpable of presenting
but a passive understanding of humanity dressed up in actionist
attire (1970: 217):

> They reconcile the perspectives in terms of a dialectic which, in
> fact, seems to be a simple juxtaposition. Institutions are, by definition,
> objectified, and once objectification occurs, the analysis depends on the
> concepts of socialization and internalization; it is thus essentially a social
> system analysis. What seems to happen is that the concepts of meaning
> and action are divorced, for the latter only appears in terms of an a-
> historical, dyadic situation. Once the dyad becomes both historical
> and more than dyadic, meaning is objectified and action becomes a
> derivative of system.

The integrity of the actor, Dawe implies, should be more consistently maintained.

Hollis' Response

In basic accord with Dawe,[2] Hollis has passed a similar judgement on the efforts of Berger and Luckmann (1977: 13). But the
investigation of such inconsistencies has led him to conclude that
the conflict between the two sociologies is more complicated than
it appears. Consequently, such a formulation of matters does not
provide an adequate focus for the discussion of the problem of
human freedom (1977: 18):

> Orthodox sociology has been marked by a long argument between
> structuralism and actionism, with much manoeuvre on the middle
> ground. It is easy to take this for a dispute between passive and active.
> Certainly the bald thesis that social structure determines social action
> favours the passive side. But it is not often put so baldly as to make
> men the mere puppets of external structures. Usually the thesis is a
> limited one, asserting the importance of trends and rates, for exam-
> ple, but allegedly saying nothing about the individual, or else making
> a restricted claim about what sociology can and cannot tackle and pre-
> scribing its proper method of enquiry. Also it is much debated whether

or not the crucial structures are normative and those who think they are have commonly kept some place for voluntarism.

Building on Dawe's insights, Hollis proposes that the conflict in question actually stems from the heritage of the Enlightenment itself. The mark of an Enlightenment thinker, Hollis suggests, was the belief that "man is perfectible through science." Yet this faith in the perfectibility of humanity was founded upon an ambiguous constellation of presumptions (1977: 6):

> Firstly, there are held to be, in Hume's phrase, 'constant and universal principles of human nature' (*Enquiries* VIII); secondly, social engineers are deemed to have a power of initiative and innovation, which somehow transcends these constant and universal principles; thirdly, human nature is taken to be fixed enough to have given needs and wants, yet mutable enough for those needs and wants to be satisfiable.

Humankind must be subject to laws of nature to be open to science and a criterion of progress. But to progress, and undertake scientific inquiry, someone must transcend those laws to innovate actions which are not readily explained as instances of a natural law. To serve the cause of human liberty, humanity must be open to manipulation (i.e., not wholly unpredictable), yet if mankind is manipulated too easily (i.e., wholly pliable) then the cause can have no significant meaning. Such is the predicament at the root of the modern western image of human nature.

In developing his thesis, Dawe's thinking shifts in a similar direction. In the article "Theories of Social Action" (1978), he too proposes that the two sociologies are best seen as conflicting responses to one problem, namely, the ambiguous experience of human agency in the post-medieval world. Sociology, he stipulates, came into being with the very predication of the need to develop and establish a view of human nature to replace the faded understanding of man as "merely an icon of divine nature" (1978: 378). Within sociology the articulation of a new comprehension of human nature took the form of the central problematic of the relationship of the individual and society. More specifically, the discipline concerned itself with "the search for the appropriate communal foundation for a genuinely moral individuality." In other words, all sociology was fundamentally conditioned by the recognition of the rise of human agency as the pivotal expression of the modern *Weltanschuuang*.

In response to the problematic of human agency it only appears that sociology bifurcated into two traditions based on either the affirmation or the denial of autonomous human agency. In point of fact, Dawe argues, "both not only entail but rest on views of man as autonomous human agent, and thus upon concepts of social action." Human agency is not fundamentally at issue. Rather the differences between the two sociologies are generated by what might guardedly be called their respectively pessimistic and optimistic assessments of human nature. In terms of ideal extremes, a sociology of social system views humans as self and socially destructive, while a sociology of social action views humans as self and socially constructive. The social system image "is less one of an infinitely manipulable creature than one of a being who 'if left to his own unconstrained devices,' will create chaos and anarchy; which, of course, is as much a view of man as autonomous human agent as that to be found in the social action perspective." The central problems of order and control, therefore, "constitute opposed formulations of human agency and its consequences," and the two sociologies' "doctrinal answers to these problems [constitute] opposed versions of the appropriate communal foundations for a genuinely moral individuality. At root... both sociologies are sociologies of social action" (1978: 379-80).

In other words, sociology does contain within itself a tension between an essentially deterministic tradition and one dedicated to the principle of human freedom. But this contrast is not founded on the simple denial or affirmation of freedom. It is founded on differing judgements about the degree of order necessary to bring human freedom into harmony with the needs of human communities, and the conditioning of these judgements by opinions on the inherent virtues and vices of humanity. The conflict of types of sociology rests then, on a clash of value preferences–individualistic and communalistic sentiments.

This acceptable, because impossible to resolve (definitively) tension of values does not, however, stand on its own. In the history of sociology it has become linked with a duality of methodological options which does entail, implicitly, the denial or affirmation of freedom, which is open to effective practical assessment. Accordingly, the bulk of the argument to follow will focus squarely on the methodological level. But at all times it must be remembered that the relatively resolvable methodological disputes under discussion stand against a background of more metaphysical conflicts in value preferences. In fact, as will become apparent with the development of the extended line of argument advanced in

Part Two, in the social sciences all questions of methodology depend on certain judgements about human nature. For, as Hollis stipulates, "both the identification of a social scientist's data and the proper criteria of scientific explanation hang on it" (1977: 19). More immediately, in Chapter VI, it will be shown that the tension of positivists and humanists over the question of human agency is also more a matter of appearances than reality. Through the detailed analysis of the positivist method as applied to economics, Hollis and Edward Nell (1975) provide further support for Dawe's thesis that at root all sociologies are sociologies of social action. But this state of affairs is indeed less than apparent, so for the present we will have to rest content with this hint of things to come and view the methodological tensions at hand in a more conventional and straightforward manner.

Methodologically, as Dawe notes, because a sociology of social system treats subjective meanings as, in the last analysis, external conditions of the actor's environment, it views human behaviour as amenable to the methods of the natural sciences. Thus a positivistic logic of inquiry is adopted by such a sociology, and social systems are "conceptualized in terms of convenient analogies with natural scientific constructs" (1970: 210). For a sociology of social action, on the other hand, the base unit of analysis is the social actor, and social life is delineated in terms of the human construction of a realm of meaning. Thus it is inadequate to conceptualize social phenomena on the basis of a logic of inquiry suited to the nonconceptualizing subject matter of natural science. In line with the humanities, such a sociology is concerned first and foremostly with interpretative understanding of human meanings, hence it advocates the *Verstehen* view of the nature of sociology.[3] In the next chapter, this second mode of sociological discourse on the question of human freedom (i.e., the positivism-humanism debate) will be delineated and probed for its conceptual limitations.

III.
The Positivism-Humanism Debate in Sociology

The Parameters of the Debate

Positivism and humanism are seen as the two mutually exclusive alternative methods for the study of society. As indicated above, the former is identified with a deterministic conception of social action, while the latter is identified with a voluntaristic view of human activity. Such an identification is essentially true but by no means straightforward. Positivism does not deny the existence of human freedom, it merely excludes it from scientific consideration. But from a positivist perspective on the nature of knowledge and the role of science in our society, this exclusion amounts to the same thing as its outright denial. In what follows I will develop a picture of positivism, so to have (as Clifford Geertz says) a stick to beat it with. But this does not mean that I will be content with a naive notion of the principles underlying positivism, or for that matter those of the humanistic point of view. In the last analysis, much that has gone under the rubric of humanistic sociology has proved to be equally deleterious to the project of sociologically conceptualizing human freedom.

Positivism is not readily defined as it represents an extremely complex movement with many internal variables and diverse manifestations. Historically, there are two main sources of methodological prescriptions: the social theory of Auguste Comte in the early nineteenth century, and the epistemological studies of the Vienna Circle in the early twentieth century. Positivist sociology combines elements from both traditions. But the spirit of the positivistic philosophy which really conditioned sociology was established in the interim, during the dominance of what Wilhelm Dilthey disapprovingly called a "coarse naturalistic metaphysics" (Ermarth, 1978: 70). This naturalistic metaphysics consisted of a loose amalgam of Comtian positivism, naturalism, and empiricism; an amalgam which, in the face of the triumphs of the natural sciences, became the programmatic framework for social scientific

research from the 1850s onward. Overthrowing the idealist modes
of thought which had dominated the first half of the nineteenth
century, this framework instilled the belief that knowledge stems
from the explanation of phenomena along the lines laid down by
the physical sciences. It is the spirit of this orientation which still
marks the positivist perspective, as commonly understood, more
than the letter of the various proclaimed canons of the positivist
philosophy.

In the realm of sociology, the ideas of Comte's *Cours de
Philosophie Positive* (1830-1842) have been passed on, for the
most part, through the mediation of Durkheim and the modern
functionalists. Similarly, the arguments of the Logical Positivists
have had an influence on the work of sociologists only secondar-
ily through the writings of such later philosophers of science as
Ernest Nagel and Carl Hempel. Few contemporary sociologists
strictly adhere to the rules of a specific positivist method. Yet as
both Anthony Giddens (1977) and Percy Cohen (1980) surmise,
most sociologists actually do operate on the basis of a methodology
that is largely informed by a positivistic philosophy.

The basic tenets of this positivistic method of science are: (1)
phenomenalism (empiricism)–the thesis that all claims to knowledge must ultimately be grounded in sense impressions and sensory
observations; (2) nominalism (instrumentalism)–the doctrine that
universals (abstract concepts) exist only as names and without a
basis in reality (i.e., anti-essentialism); (3) the rejection of metaphysics as sophistry or nonsense; (4) the fact-value distinction–
the proposition that science in principle is incapable of resolving
moral issues and hence its activities should be restricted to questions of fact (i.e., the value-neutrality of scientific language and
judgements); (5) the formal unity of science–the logical, perhaps
even methodological, unity of the natural and the social sciences;
(6) the principle of verification–the most distinctive doctrine of
the Logical Positivists, which stipulated that for a proposition to
have "cognitive" or "factual" meaning it must supply the empirical conditions under which it could, at least in principle, be shown
to be true or false, or to some degree probable. These six factors constitute the core ideas of the positivist perspective in its
most straightforward 'inductivist' mode. With an increased appreciation of the logical and practical problems facing a purely
inductive logic of scientific inquiry, however, the positivist tradition has shifted its emphasis. Within its iconoclastic empiricist

framework, at a later date another mode of explanation emerged: (7) the deductive-nomological model. This approach argues that a legitimate scientific explanation of a phenomenon involves demonstrating the logical derivability of the phenomenon from a theory which in turn is a deductive system of empirically true laws, supported by a set of empirical observations about the relevant boundary conditions of independent variables affecting the phenomenon in question. This series of seven connected tenets is representative of the positivism manifested in sociology (where both inductivist and deductivist versions are invoked by different sociologists, and sometimes by the same sociologists in different contexts, as it suits him or her). Not all seven features need be present, however, to judge a scholar positivistic.

A positivistic sociology cannot be identified with any one specific model of humanity. The models used by positivists have varied with the purposes of their inquiries and their points of view. But the methodological strictures of positivist science are such that these diverse models have a common core in a behaviouristic image of individuals as programmed feedback systems. Emphasizing a naturalistic conception of a unitary law-governed world, positivistic sociology has tended to identify satisfactory knowledge of humankind with the empirical correlation of stimuli and responses. Inputs are matched to outputs and the human link between the two is left a mystery of minimal scientific importance. What counts is precisely the extent to which human behaviour is determined, for only such behaviour is knowable. Hence, in many respects, the positivist model of humanity represents no model at all (with the qualification of what has already been said in Chapter I).

Humanistic sociology does not represent a systematic doctrine of methodology, but an aggregate of reactions to positivism, derived from sometimes very different sources. Nevertheless, this reaction coalesces around certain consistent principles: (1) a presupposition of human agency and voluntarism; a view which integrally depends on (2) the 'reflexive' character of social life–the human capacity to orient activity to goals based on self-reflection, the rational monitoring of one's own conduct. This means that: (3) the intentional, subjective and interpretative elements in human action cannot be ignored or conceived as mere epiphenomena; and (4) social scientific analysis entails a double hermeneutic–social science deals with the already derivative ordinary language interpretations of reality which 'constitute' the social world and cannot be simply replaced by wholly technical metalanguages. Overall then humanistic sociologists are opposed to (5) scientism—the tendency to treat the experience of science as regulative for human experience and suggest that only by its method can the problems of life be solved. Humanists see science rather as (6) but one value perspective among others, and therefore they argue that the scientist has a responsibility to relate his researches to their potential effects on the quality of human life.

Humanistic sociologies do not share a model of humanity so much as a common orientation to the interruption of the naturalism of positivism through the assertion of the uniqueness of human nature. To comprehend human behaviour one must move beyond the isolation of natural laws. Between the input and the output, and the feedback from the output to the input, there is a substantive self which is important to understanding the full relations of inputs and outputs. The linkage between social phenomena is ideational and not just causal. Therefore, a full explanation of social action necessitates grasping the subjective meaning of an action for the actors involved.

Proponents of the humanistic approach are not out to deny the value and the viability of materialist and behaviourist accounts of human activities. Rather they are just asking if a science of that kind is capable of telling us what we want to know about people and society. These accounts overlook that which distinguishes humans from other animate and inanimate things—the capacity to reason and communicate. Pursuing the intellectual respectability of the natural sciences, positivists have selected to study (for reasons of methodological convenience) the visible and the measurable, whether or not they have human significance.

Hollis and the Redefinition of the Parameters

The question is: Which is more fundamental, charting the laws of behaviour or understanding the meaning of actions? Which is more important to the explanatory task of the social sciences, verifiability or intelligibility? No easy answer is provided by the practice of the social sciences. Either emphasis has its well-known empirical and methodological advantages and disadvantages. As a rule serious consideration is no longer given to the claim that all phenomena, natural or social, can be reduced to physical attributes or primary sense data.[1] (In other words, there is not a substantial unity or identity between the subject matters of the natural and the social sciences.) It remains a very active matter of debate, though, whether there is a formal unity to the two sciences. Are there any significant differences in the methods appropriate to studying social and natural objects? The humanists, on the whole, say there are differences. The positivists deny it. But if there are differences, then the important question is, are these differences simply indicative of the pre-scientific character of contemporary social studies? Or alternatively, are they indicative of the essential incompatibility of social realities and the scientific method?

Most positivists, as supporters of the formal unity of the sciences, have clearly been of the mind that existing differences can be discounted in anticipation of the eventual success of scientific procedures on the model of the natural sciences. The humanist response has been more variable and discontinuous. On the one hand, social scientists like Weber and Alfred Schutz have argued for a sociology which is geared to interpretative understanding (i.e., *Verstehen*), yet which maintains a claim to the rubric 'science' through a system of empirical tests. On the other hand, post-Wittgensteinian philosophers of social science, like Peter Winch (*The Idea of a Social Science*, 1958), A.R. Louch (*Explanation and Human Action*, 1966), and Michael Simon (*Understanding Human Action*, 1982), have sought to protect social reality from the reductionistic touch of the positivists by refuting the very possibility of explaining social facts scientifically.

Those who have sought to devise an interpretative social 'science,' have been unable to silence either the positivist or Wittgensteinian critics of their efforts. This is primarily because they have fallen short of fashioning a sufficiently rigorous and intersubjective mode of "understanding." The lessons of Theodore Abel's classic study remain convincing: *Verstehen* acts as "a source of 'hunches,' which help us in the formulation of hypotheses;" but it does not "add to our store of knowledge" or "serve as a means of verification" (1948: 218). This failure does not mean, however, that humanistic sociologists have no recourse but to capitulate to the extreme position of Winch, Louch, and Simon. The central question remains, it will be argued, not whether humanity is a subject for science, but what sort of science it requires.

In contrast to the position advanced by Michael Simon, for instance, here it will be argued that recognition of the free nature of some human actions does not entail rejecting the principle of the essential formal unity of the sciences. Simon correctly observes (1982: 173):

> It is a defining or conceptual fact of human social life, and not just an empirical condition, that the sphere of human action is dominated by events that cannot be controlled or determined in any completely effective way. .... A completely deterministic science of human action... could not be a science of human beings as we conceive of them.

But this does not mean that the ways of making sense of human social life have to be in principle radically opposed to the methods of the natural sciences. Support for the formal unity principle need not be equated with the subsumption of the subject matter of the social sciences under a positivist conception of the natural sciences. As Roy Bhaskar proposes, "the great error that unites [the naturalist and anti-naturalist traditions] is their acceptance of an essentially positivist account of natural science, and more generally of an empiricist ontology" (1978: 1). A compromise can be struck between the demands and advantages of verifiability and intelligibility. And this compromise need not consist simply of a replication of the ill-defined amalgam of disparate methods of analysis encountered in Weber's discussion of explanatory adequacy at the levels of meaning and causality.[2] In line with Hollis, it will be proposed that it is possible to give an account of science which rejects the positivist version of naturalism[3] and does justice to the hermeneutical character of the human sciences, without losing or abusing the principle of an essential formal unity to the sciences. The realization of this possibility hinges on the results of an integrated study of the epistemological underpinnings and methodological functions of the three concepts which are fundamental to social analysis: causality, rationality, and the subject self.

The strength of the positivist position lies, Hollis suggests, with its single robust mode of explanation–the method of science based on the principle of causality. Its immediate weakness lies with its discounting of the sense of self which is the natural point of departure for all thought about social reality. Contrarily, the strength of the humanist outlook is its recognition of the centrality of the subject self to the explanation of social action. Its weakness is the lack of a concept of explanation (an account of autonomy) that amounts to a method of science. In a sense, positivists have a method of science and no model of humanity, while humanists have a model of humanity and no adequate method of science. The weakness of the humanist approach means in effect, however, that "the active self [of social action theory] is the merest we-know-not-what" (1977: 15). Therefore, it is not surprising that the positivist perspective has tended to carry the day in sociological circles.

To rectify this situation, Hollis proposes that it is necessary to develop and capitalize on the latent ingredient of actionist accounts of the self: the paradigm of rationality at the base of our judgements of each other–at the base of our conceptualization of *humanitas* itself. Hence he cites as his objective the "constructive attempt... to find a metaphysic for the rational social self" (1977: 19). In the process of doing this he establishes that even a positivist social science cannot dispense with a model of humanity, and a rationalist one at that.

The impact of this insight, however, hinges on an epistemological decision, namely a decision about the nature of the relationship holding between the concepts of causality and rationality. Positivists see human beings as natural creatures in "a rational world of cause and effect." The antiphonal theme in Enlightenment thought, Hollis points out, is that we are "rational creators in a natural world of cause and effect" (1977: 11). It is this antiphonal theme which must be brought to the fore. It is rationality, as manifested in human creativity, that should take precedence over faith in causal order. Decades of hard-headed empiricist theorizing has only gone to show that an ontology of causality is not enough to produce an intellectually satisfying account of explanation (especially for the actions of humanity). The rationality of human being must be taken into account before science can begin to deal accurately with its creation, a rational world of cause and effect.

But these words cast our attention to matters far ahead. Therefore, let us modestly conclude with a look at how Hollis modestly frames his task (1977: 19):

> [My] conclusions are strictly to do with making the actions of Autonomous Man a subject for science and are not proposed as a nostrum for all areas. There is still a need for causal laws, even though they do not wholly explain social action; hermeneutics offer much but not all. We shall be working modestly to exploit the gap where partial determinism falls short of complete explanation.

To gain a sense of the nature of this gap, we will turn next to a brief consideration of the traditional free will-determinism debate and its relevance to sociology.

IV.
Causality, Rationality and Freedom

The Endless Argument

In terms of locating the question of human freedom within the social sciences, the positivism-humanism debate points us in the right direction, but it still proves to be misleading. Recast into the conflict of behaviour and meaning, the classical schools of sociological theory and their heirs can be roughly aligned against one another in terms of the Durkheimian stress on behaviour versus the Weberian stress on meaning. But Hollis asserts, when it comes to what counts, Durkheim and Weber are at one, and in harmony with the likes of J. S. Mill, Freud, and even B. F. Skinner. The great disputes between nature and nuture, psychologism and sociologism, can be added to Dawe's list of secondary and reducible conflicts within social analysis. and by-passed. It may well be, as George Homans claims in his classic article "Bringing Men Back In" (1964), that these disputes represent the most general intellectual issue in sociology. But a decision between the two or about their proportionate role in social analysis makes little difference to the question of human freedom. Both psychologism and sociologism are deterministic in their developed forms, and the debate over their relative virtues misses the heart of the matter as much as the two sociologies conflict itself.

What matters is that ultimately Durkheim, Weber, and Freud, all look to David Hume for their method of science. They "bid us generalize from experience in order to explain" (Hollis, 1977: 24); to explain a world of atomic, contingent phenomena, whose order is to be found in the patterns shaped by the concomitant variations of observables. The tenor of the approach is practical, and the object is to establish the truths of science by applying an empiricism founded on a presumption of causal regularity based on the observation of constant conjunctions. With the right observations and the postulate of a causal order in the world, everything, even humanity, is potentially open to the unerring inference of its

future condition through the isolation of the appropriate invari-
ant laws of nature. Under these conditions, it does not matter
if the humankind imagined is the empty one of Skinner, the in-
stinctive one of Freud, the socialized one of Durkheim, or even the
meaning-oriented one of Weber.[1] In each case the determinants of
action, in the last analysis, are placed outside of the control of the
agent. And it is this fact which, despite their various disclaimers,
has made these figures the bedfellows of determinism. In the discussion to follow it will be seen that freedom may be marked by
many subtle and complicated distinctions. But Hollis' stipulation
isolates the essential first principle of a genuine freedom: freedom
from causality. With this in mind, Hollis asserts, it is clear that
both Durkheim and Weber are determinists.

The veracity of this claim for Durkheim is manifest. In the
Conclusion to *The Rules of Sociological Method* (1964: 141), he
declares:

> Sociology does not need to choose between the great hypotheses
> which divide metaphysicians. It needs to embrace free will no more
> than determinism. All that it asks is that the principle of causality be
> applied to social phenomena. Again, this principle is enunciated for
> sociology not as a rational necessity but only as an empirical postulate,
> produced by legitimate induction. Since the law of causality has been
> verified in the other realms of nature, and since it has progressively
> extended its authority from the physio-chemical world to the biological,
> and from the latter to the psychological, we are justified in claiming
> that it is equally true of the social world.

In Weber's case, things are more complex. It is common practice, Hollis observes, to oppose the Weberian interest in subjective
meanings, "the rich currency of inner consciousness crucial to all
forms of actionism," to the Durkheimian focus on external and
constraining social facts. "And indeed Weber's ideas are at odds
with [such a view] and are justly included in the Old Testament
of Autonomous Man." But the common practice is too superficial
(Hollis, 1977: 31):

> 'subjective meanings' are not automatically the currency of a rival model
> of man. Weber himself seems to have seen them as an explanatory
> stock, imposed and ordered by some kind of central value system which
> is also the ground of Durkheimian social facts. For each actor they
> are external and constraining, or, if they are not, then they are the
> effect of something which is. Such an account differs importantly from
> Durkheim, Mill, Freud and Skinner but not by denying that men are
> [passive]. Weberian meanings, like Freudian interpretations, seem in

the end to be treated as ways of filling in causal connections. There is a many-handed dispute about where explanation rests but not about the kind of connections involved.[2]

In passing this judgement, Hollis has three things in mind. First, he is simply pointing out that logically the interpretative discovery of the subjective meaning of an action does not 'in and of itself' explain why an action occurred. Meaningful actions can still be unfree. Second, this is especially the case when the meanings under consideration can only be identified because they are conventional or, at any rate, socially given. And third, at the heart of Weber's method of social science, positivism persists in the guise of his assumption that interpretative understandings had to be validated through empirical "tests" which supposedly demonstrated their adequacy at the level of causality. Weber may have held to an active conception of humanity, but this counts for little when he failed to equip sociologists with a complementary method of science.

Causal thinking has become deeply ingrained in our interpretations of practical experience. We have become conditioned to assume, almost automatically, that every 'x because y' must find explanation in a chain of connections which necessitates that event x follow the occurrence of event y. Sometimes it is true, but not always. This is the most rudimentary claim of the exponents of free will in the face of the spectre of determinism.

When confronted with the common-sense arguments advanced in favour of assuming a causal regularity to the world, the humanist advocates of our freedom (the so-called libertarians), point to the equally strong intuition that people have the ability to act, or even think, differently than they presently do or have in the past. In accordance with this intuition, deliberation over different possible actions, different possible beliefs, is an elemental part of human life. And even in instances devoid of conscious deliberation, people sometimes have a clear sense of their actions as the product of their initiative alone. This sense of freedom might well be an illusion, but as the American philosopher Richard Taylor says, so might any philosophical theory, including causality, be false. In the end, Taylor states (1963: 37):

> The point remains that it is far more difficult for me to doubt that I sometimes deliberate, and that it is sometimes up to me what I do, than to doubt any philosophical theory whatever, including the theory of determinism. We must, accordingly, if we ever hope to be wiser,

adjust our theories to our data and not try to adjust our data to our theories.

Unimpressed, determinists point out that intuitions are notoriously unreliable. People may believe that their deliberations have force, but this does not mean that their experience of deliberation is not determined by unconscious drives or other material and biological factors. The libertarian notes in turn, however, that the evidence of the senses, upon which causal suppositions depend, is frequently just as unreliable. Yet the determinist does not on that account relinquish his confidence in empiricism. Moreover, the notion of causal regularity is itself empirically insupportable. It is neither possible to investigate all events to see if they have causes, nor is it possible to investigate all of the possible causes of any one event. In principle then, determinism is not an empirical theory. It can neither be conclusively verified, nor does it allow (any more that the doctrine of free will) for the possibility of its own refutation through some observable circumstance. Nevertheless, the determinist can turn with persuasive force to the constant progress of science as sufficient grounds for assuming that all events can be found to have a cause. But then the advocate of free will too can ask, Does this progress necessarily testify to the veracity of the positivist idea of the world?

With regard to social theory in particular, libertarians charge that determinism cannot be reconciled with the institutionalization of the principle of moral responsibility. It makes sense to reward or punish someone for their actions only if it is judged that they could have done otherwise. In rebuttal, the determinist states, it makes sense to hold people accountable for their actions only if something like a causal connection can be isolated. People cannot be subject to praise or blame for chance occurrences, which is technically what uncaused actions appear to be.

In the face of the impasse created by these conflicting views, there are five theoretical options open to social scientists: they can adopt either a radical or a compatibilist variant of determinism (i.e., in the terminology of William James, be a "hard" or a "soft" determinist), they can favour a simple indeterminism, or they can advance something like a radical or a compatibilist version of, what I will call, an actionist orientation (i.e., be a proponent of agent causation or the argument from rationality). Of the five, it is the compatibilist positions that have exerted the greatest influence, therefore they will be the primary focus of attention.

The hard determinist simply dissolves the problematic nature of moral responsibility, with or without causality, by arguing that the idea of moral responsibility is an illusion. Punishment represents but a form of behaviour modification, and incarceration but an expedient measure for the protection of society from deviant behaviour. Each is imposed simply on the basis of a system of rules that reflects a consensus of likes and dislikes, and not objective values. Utility and contract are the sole foundations of society. But if this is the case, the libertarian wonders, why is it that languages so universally distinguish between what is liked and what is good? It is too counter-intuitive to dismiss such distinctions without providing explanations for their existence in the first place—explanations which go beyond, for example, the utilitarian theory of forgotten functions so roundly criticized by Nietzsche or Nietzsche's own fantastic conspiracy of *ressentiment*. What of the unshakeable conviction of most people that at least some actions are reprehensible or virtuous in the eyes of every rational being?

Too many aspects of our social life must be reinterpreted or explained away at too great an effort and expense to rest content with the hard determinist resolution. Therefore, a much more common response to the impasse is some version of soft determinism. In William James' distinction between hard and soft determinism, soft determinism meant any theory that maintained a place for freedom in a causally determined world by reverting to sophistical and contorted definitions of freedom. Many eminent and influential figures in the history of western philosophy, however, have argued that if freedom were only seen in the right light then it would become apparent that in fact it is and must be compatible with determinism (i.e., a world totally regulated by causal connections).

Proponents of this form of compatibilism claim that there is no conflict between our intuitions of freedom and the fact that we live in a causally regulated world. When we intuit that we are acting freely we are not intuiting all that is going on inside of us—in our brains and our subconscious minds. An intuition of free choice involves only an awareness that there are no external forces compelling or prohibiting us from acting or deciding in certain ways. But this, of course, does not mean that our behaviour might not be the result of some cause within us. Freedom from this perspective, then, merely represents the absence of any external constraint which might prevent us from doing as we want.

For any true exponent of human freedom, the freedom granted
by such a compatibilist thesis is bogus. In the first place, a robot
might experience a freedom of this kind. Second, if causes of
any sort, external or internal, account for an action, then there
is no avoiding the linkage of that action with a transitive chain
of causal connections going back to before the birth of the agent
of the action. There can be no true freedom to choose differently
under such circumstances.

Continuing the debate, the soft determinist can point out, however, that his restricted definition of freedom conforms to the ordinary usage of the word "free." In Hollis' words, "the line catches
our habits of thought well enough, as we divide shoplifters from
kleptomaniacs, pianists from pianola players, sane men from psy-
chotics" (1977: 33). Our everyday practice of morality and our legal system ignore the possibility that ultimately we are all robots,
or that all of our actions might be caused by a chain of events
stretching back to before our birth. The meaning of "being able
to act differently" presupposed by ordinary conceptions of moral
responsibility is simply "not being forced to act as one does or not
being prevented from acting differently." The thief who is culpable
is one who was not forced to commit a theft. He or she was free
to do otherwise, though this does not mean that his or her action
was without causal determinants. Rather it was caused by his or
her beliefs and desires, which reflect the conditioning effect of his
or her whole life history. But in committing the criminal act he
or she was uncompelled by any person or circumstance, and hence
with rare exceptions, in our society he or she is guilty as charged.

It is this soft determinist perspective that holds sway practically in the courts of science as well. And under such an orientation, as Hollis concludes, humans are free in a most peculiar way
(1977: 35):

> ... man does not so much choose freely, as act freely. For choice is the
> emergence of effective preference out of a conflict of preferences and
> effective preference is action. So a man acts freely when he gets what
> he wants because he wanted it; and freedom is the power to satisfy
> emerging desires. A man acts under compulsion when he does what he
> does not want to do, either because there are constraints external to
> him or because his desires conflict.

Faced with this state of affairs, libertarians must turn their
backs on the detials of the common usage of "free," while nevertheless relying on the prevalence of the use of the idea of freedom

in ordinary life to justify their concern to refute determinism in the first place. It is an ontological freedom, however, that they seek to defend–the ability to act differently, even if all of the immediately prior conditions are the same. At least some events, namely human choices, are not caused. If a choice is caused in any sense, externally or internally, then the determinants of action are beyond the control of the actor. But if this is the case, then we are driven back again to the question, In what sense is an uncaused action (i.e., a chance occurrence?) within the control of the actor?[3]

It is the dilemma posed by this question which led Hobbes, Spinoza, Locke, Hume, Mill, and Ayer to conclude that it remains preferable to distinguish within the class of caused actions between the compelled and the free.[4] The reasoning behind this conclusion Hollis explains as follows (1977: 32):

> Once free action has been equated with chance action, there is little left to say. Some romantics have been content, in the belief that free action is spontaneous and so unpredictable and so in the realm of chance. But the price is to make free action inexplicable and, conversely, to make explicable action unfree. By this account every advance in social science further destroys our illusions of freedom and so further confirms an atavistic distrust of the scientific enterprise.

The argument makes much sense and is persuasive. Nevertheless, Hollis does not think that the compatibilist thesis is preferable. Scrutinizing the argument, as advanced by Mill in Book VI of *A System of Logic* (1843) (1977: 33-35), he finds the freedom secured by Mill to be (in a Jamesian manner) too sophistical and contorted. In the last analysis, he concludes, Mill continues to situate the determinants of action outside of the control of the individual, hence the freedom granted is a pseudo-freedom at best. But the real problem with the soft determinist version of compatibilism lies with the mistaken assumption that the options available are limited to two possibilities: either actions are subject to traditional causal analysis and hence explicable, at the price of determinism (ontologically), or they are free because they are chance occurrences (i.e., uncaused), at the price of being inexplicable.

It is the romantics who equate free acts with spontaneous events who are the particular objects of Hollis' scorn, since their position entails conceding the viability of the positivist worldview. This is the error of the simple indeterminists. They are willing to sacrifice the possibility of explaining our actions to secure what must then amount to a meaningless freedom. By failing to question the legitimacy of the positivist context of explanation, the simple indeterminists imply that science can only progress at the expense of our sense of freedom, and such a view does an injustice to science as well as human freedom. To equate free acts with chance events, does not even satisfy Richard Taylor's reasonable supposition that our conception of free action should accord with our data about the human experience of freedom.

The theory of agent causation comes closer to satisfaction on this score, but it still poses some serious problems. This theory simply posits that "in the case of an action that is free, it must be such that it is caused by the agent who performs it, but such that no antecedent conditions were sufficient for his performing just that action" (Taylor, 1963: 50). This view surely does fit our common-sense conception of human nature. "When I believe that I have done something, I do believe that it was I who caused it to be done, I who made something happen, and not merely something within me, such as one of my own subjective states, which is not identical with myself" (Taylor, 1963: 50-51). Agent causation is the one perspective that is consistent with our intuition, with the data of deliberation. Moreover, as Taylor concludes (1963: 52):

> The theory of agency avoids the absurdities of simple indeterminism by conceding that human behaviour is caused, while at the same time avoiding the difficulties of determinism by denying that every chain of causes and effects is infinite. Some such causal chains begin with agents themselves.

Taylor admits, however, that "this conception of activity... involves two rather strange metaphysical notions that are never applied elsewhere in nature" (1963: 51). The first is the very notion of a 'self' or 'person' which is the *primum mobile*. What are the defining attributes of this personhood? What are the parameters that mark off the agent from "an assemblage of physical things and processes, which act in accordance with those laws that describe the behaviour of all other physical things and processes[?]" As indicated, for the soft determinist the individual simply is his or her actions, and the latter are simply instances of intersecting causal laws. The second strange notion is the philosophically unorthodox idea of causality, whereby a substance (i.e., the person) and not an event, is the cause of an event. "This means that an agent is sometimes a cause, without being an antecedent sufficient condition; for if I affirm that I am the cause of some act of mine.

then I am plainly not saying that my very existence is sufficient for its occurrence, which would be absurd" (1963: 51). In general, it is far from clear how a volition is the cause, or the origin, of an action-event.

In the light of these difficulties it appears that the agent causation thesis still purchases freedom for humanity at the expense of explicability. This approach also fails to escape, truly, the deterministic identification of explanation itself with some form of causal analysis. And by continuing the radical humanist tendency to conceive of freedom as an attribute of humanity's very nature, the need for developing a criterion for differentiating between free actions and caused actions is overlooked. Human actions are not just free, anymore than they are simply caused. They are one or the other according to the circumstances. But what, at the ontological level, are these circumstances?

In action theory, the argument from rationality is offered in answer to this question. The impasse created by identifying freedom with chance and explicability with causal necessity, can be surmounted by realizing that "regularity in conduct could be the result either of causal factors or of rational choice" (Campbell, 1981: 235). An act may be done for a reason, it is suggested, and whatever the results of reasoning are, they are neither inevitable and binding, nor are they random. The appeal to reasoning, it must be stressed, does not conclusively prove that we are free, hence we will have more to say on this below. But as Tom Campbell says, by providing "an alternative account of regularity in human behaviour [it does] undercut one of the determinist's main points" (1981: 236). In his words:

> ... rational behaviour is also predictable. Rational people follow rules; and they consider that a good reason in a particular situation remains a good reason in all similar situations. This leads them to make the same type of response to similar situations. Further, most people would be most surprised to learn that such regularities are causally determined if this carries the implication that rational consistency amounts to causal necessity. Most of us take it for granted that we could stay in bed in the morning even when we choose, with good reason, not to do so (1981: 236).

But the question immediately arises, what does the concept of rational action involve? In what sense, and to what degree does it represent an adequate alternative mode of explanation to that of causal analysis? The answer to this question is complicated and controversial. For as Campbell comments, in behind this question lies the second intractable philosophical issue confronted by social theory: the very nature of explanation. A proper answer can only come at the conclusion of this study, but here a few initial comments can be made to establish the place of the concept of rationality in the explanation of social action.

As we have seen, the only rival to the causal mode of explanation normally cited by social theorists is the appeal to the priority of the intelligibility of social action. Pointing out that humans have conscious motives for their actions, however, does not in itself provide the footing for a sharp contrast between the nature of explanation in the natural and the social sciences. The introspection of the motive forces, the desires, leading to human action provides the social scientists with a special way to account for these actions which is not available to the natural scientists in their study of the world of things. But in principle there is nothing about the capacity to introspect that marks the explanatory linkages made between phenomena by such a means as different from the causal explanations of non-human events. Accordingly, the humanist must invoke the further postulate of purpose. People do things for purposes. They choose between objectives, that is, "on criteria other than the relative strength of their existing desires" (Campbell, 1981: 237). They use their knowledge of the world, including their knowledge of causal connections and their perception of their immediate situation, to choose the best means to obtain their freely selected ends.

> The basic insight here is that it is always intelligible and explanatory to say that a person acted as he did because he thought that this would have the results he wished to see realized. The 'because' here is not a causal one. It is not implied that when men act rationally they have to do what they do. We therefore have a form of explanation which is intellectually satisfying but non-causal (Campbell, 1981: 237).

But is this intellectually satisfying? [5] To have an explanation of someone's actions that is comparable to a causal account we must know why that person had the particular ends that they did. Much behaviour can be commonly explained in terms of most familiar reasons for certain ends. An act may be done to obtain food, affection, or prestige. In practice, however, there is much that humans do which is not readily gauged in terms of an imaginative extension of one's own motivations (a murder, for example). And for the social scientist, interpretative explanations based on familiarity are of little help in explaining the actions of members of a culture quite alien to that of the inquirer. In principle, as Campbell does acknowledge, the reversion to familiarity "removes only the psychological not the intellectual need for further explanation" (1981: 237). The familiar motive might well be caused, thus the citation of a reason for the action would be superfluous. To circumvent this possibility, to halt the regress to causes, it must be shown that the action has not just been done for a reason but for a 'good reason.' In other words, the axiom that a rational action is its own explanation must be invoked and successfully applied to the action under consideration. Then and only then, have the libertarians found a foundation for their claims.

The Moral of the Story So Far

The moral so far, then, is that social analysis does tangle with metaphysics. The metaphysical question of free will underlies both substantive and methodological disputes in sociology. In the case of the conflict of the two sociologies, the debate between social system and social action perspectives appears to be straightforwardly about the question of human freedom. Instead, what is at issue is a normative judgement about the essentially social or anti-social character of human beings. But this judgement does not stand alone. Rather it has been aligned, negatively or positively, with the methodological decision to found the social sciences on a positivist method of science. This alignment draws the two sociologies debate back into the framework of the free will-determinism debate. For the positivist method, with which the social system perspective identifies itself, places the the requirements of verification before the need for intelligibility. Therefore, it discounts the role of a subject self (and hence any essentialist view of human nature) in the explanation of social phenomena and places explanatory emphasis instead on disclosures of causal regularity. The resultant mode of explanation is straightforwardly deterministic because it places the determinants of action beyond the control of the subject self or agent. Yet the strength of this characterization of the nature of explanation is such that, when compared with our intuitions of freedom, most philosophers have elected to restrict human freedom to the legalistic notion of "absence of external force," and not the absence of causality per se.

There is, however, another mode of regularity, and hence potentially another mode of explanation: the order provided by reason.

But for this order to challenge the hegemony claimed for causal explanation, the social actor (i.e., subject self) who exercises reason must be defined in such a manner that he or she is rendered autonomous from the web of intersecting causal laws. The humanistic focus on subjective meanings fails to penetrate to the element of human self-definition which truly interrupts the positivist ontology of causality. It is in choosing to do what is rationally best that humans assert their autonomy from causal explanation. But then how are we to assess what is best (i.e., most rational), and hence have the capacity to determine if our own actions or those of others are free? What is to count as our standard of rationality? To answer this question much more must be said about the nature of scientific explanations, most specifically causal explanations. Is the faith of most social scientists in a 'soft positivist' method of science, resting on the equation of explicability and causal regularity, warranted? This is the next issue to be explored.

Part Two
Explanation in
the Study of Human Action

We think we actually understand things only when we have traced them back to what we do not understand and cannot understand–to causality, to axioms, to God, to character.

Georg Simmel,
Diary Excerpts in
Fragmente und Aufsätze, 4.

Part Two
Explanation in ...
the Study of Human Action

V.
Soft Positivism: The Bogus Barrier

The General Thesis of the Argument from Rationality

Hardcore positivist or humanist sociologies are rare. In the history of sociology the two extremes have tended to converge, producing a base methodology in much sociology which is an awkward hybrid. A watered-down positivism is brought to the rescue of a stalled *Verstehen* sociology, or vice versa, and a difficulty like the free nature of some human actions is covered over with a veneer of pragmatism.

It is this 'soft positivist' model of convergence (to be detailed below) which accounts for the dominance of a passive conception of humanity in the social sciences. Human action is viewed as a natural and determined phenomenon, for it is assumed that human actions must be correlated with natural laws to be properly explained. To overthrow this view it is necessary to establish alternative grounds for the convergence of the positivist and humanist traditions—ones which allow for the actions of humanity to be viewed as wholly explicable, but only partly determined. This entails calling these presumed natural laws into question by demonstrating that the explanatory power of scientific theories does not reside solely with the assimilation of the principles of lawfulness and causal regularity. The social world undoubtedly has its regularities. But, as Hollis argues, in the first place there is not sufficient reason to assume that all such regularities are causal. And even if there were, there is insufficient reason to think that the idea of natural laws can be derived from what we logically know about the character of detected causal regularities. "It is all too easy to assert in ontology," he notes, "what, as epistemologists, we could not possibly know to be true" (1977: 42).

The epistemologically unsound dependence of soft positivists on presumed laws of causal regularity derived from empirical observations and experiments should be abandoned, Hollis proposes, in the face of the more fundamental epistemological realization that all sciences depend on necessary truths knowable a priori. It is this general philosophical thesis that accurately points to the source of the quality of lawfulness which must be present in scientific explanations. In the social sciences, the necessary truth knowable a priori upon which these sciences depend is the idea of rational human agency. Before this idealist core to the social sciences can be exposed, however, the bankruptcy of the positivist method must be conclusively demonstrated in order to disenfranchise the soft positivists once and for all.

The Deductive-Nomological Variant of Soft Positivism

Soft positivism can be differentiated from positivism proper by its declared support for something like the deductive-nomological (cf. Carl Hempel, 1965; Ernest Nagel, 1961) or hypothetico-deductive (cf. Karl Popper, 1959, 1963) models of scientific explanation. These models are the products of a complicated evolution within the positivist tradition itself. Most specifically, in referring to soft positivist sociologists I have in mind those non-Marxist sociologists who accept one or the other of these models as definitive of science and logically viable as the basis of social science, without being very explicit in stating the grounds or degree of their commitment to the model. Soft positivist sociologists are like the sociologists Percy Cohen characterizes with the following more charitable words (1980: 153):

> sociologists of this type are somewhat wary (and weary) of excessive scientism but, tacitly, or even explicitly, acknowledge the need for explanatory hypotheses and for some rules for testing them; and they are somewhat weary of those never-ending denunciations of positivism which seem to function as an excuse for arbitrariness, dogmatism or sloppiness....

Soft positivists, in other words, are sociologists who have sought to use one of these derived forms of positivism to maintain the supposedly hard empiricist orientation of their discipline. Implicitly, then, soft positivists have perpetuated the positivist identification of talk of human freedom with meaningless metaphysics. Therefore, though I sympathize with the wariness and weariness of the soft positivists, these positivist paradigms must be criticized in order to give force to the claim that there are no sound methodological reasons for categorically blocking the scientific treatment of human freedom.

Modern science came into being with the assertion that the limits of empirical science are the limits of possible knowledge of the world. It is this theme that the positivist tradition has taken up with a passion. Most fundamentally, the positivist tradition gets its character from an insistence on the epistemic primacy of direct observation. Following David Hume, positivists argue that experience is the key to knowledge, and that inference to the absent [in space or time] or the general is justified only if it can, in principle, be checked by the senses. Science, however, requires an assumption of order, and this poses a problem for the positivist, since this order is not simply given to the senses. Rather, as Hume realized, it is blocked by the problem of induction. Simply put, the problem is that no number of observation statements can of themselves logically give rise to an unrestricted general statement about the true nature of things. If one observes that an event A is attended by an event B on one occasion, it does not logically follow that it will be attended by it on any other occasion. Nor would it follow from two such observation, nor from twenty, nor from two thousand. Generalizing from previous observations goes beyond the evidence of the senses. Nevertheless, for positivists, as Hollis states (1977: 44):

> it is thought defence enough against the sceptic, if the order assumed consists only in the sort of particulars and relations we can be acquainted with. Hence Hume analyses the crucial relation of cause and effect as holding between events a and b when (i) a is contiguous with b, (ii) a is prior to b, (iii) whenever A (events like a) then B (events like b) and, on another note, (iv) we are accustomed to associating A and B. The upshot is to make the statement of a causal law a legitimate conclusion of an inductive inference, and so supposing a solution to the dire riddle of induction, within the scope of empirical knowledge. It is done by stripping the concept of law of all ideas like production, force, purpose or necessity, which would take us beyond possible experience. That leaves the idea of correlation to do the work... of wresting the empirical world from the Cartesian demon of doubt.

It is this Humean view of causality that provides the meagre epistemological infrastructure for a dizzying complexity of alternative renderings of the positivist method of science. This fact is overlooked, however, in the face of the stress laid by positivists on a simpler operational criterion: any legitimate claim to knowledge must be testable. Accordingly debates between the alternative renderings of positivism have focused on the structure of 'scientific' theories and tests. But the more fundamental issue, Hollis asserts, is the inability of any positivist method to satisfy our need "to be able to tell a law-like generalization from an accidental one" (1977: 48).

While retaining the experiential emphasis of earlier forms of positivism, the deductive-nomological (hereafter cited as D-N) approach was designed to compensate for the inadequacy of two of the central tenets of earlier forms of positivism. The first tenet was the assumption that the truth of this world is manifest and can be inductively derived from simple observations. The second tenet was the assumption that all that is cognitively meaningful in this world can be described, in principle, with a language the descriptive predicates of which denote purely physical and observable properties. In contrast to the sensibility of these assumptions, the D-N model argues that scientific explanations should be conceived as a form of logical argument. The conclusion of this form of argument is a statement describing the event to be explained. The premises of this form of argument are of two kinds: statements of empirical laws and statements of antecedent conditions. Things or events have been explained when they have been subsumed under, or accounted for, by a law. The link is deductive, but the epistemological commitment remains experiential. It is the 'empirical' law that does the explanatory work.

But there is a difficulty, the grounds for stipulating a general law are problematic in the light of the meagre epistemological basis of the positivist understanding of causal laws. Empirical generalizations do not constitute empirical laws. No finite amount of observational evidence can establish the potentially infinite validity (i.e., the universal lawfulness) of a detected empirical correlation. As stated by J. S. Mill, "we can know that a generalization is truly an empirical law, only when we have a causal law to explain it" (Hollis, 1977: 48). Yet the positivist conception of causal laws does not, for the same reason, imply any necessity to the correlations noted.

To circumvent this problem, an exclusive and exhaustive dichotomy was constructed between two types of languages: observational and theoretical. Knowledge resides with an ontologically and epistemologically privileged language of observables. It is this language which provides the bedrock for testing the validity of competing theories. These theories, however, make use of theoretical terms to introduce, conjecturally, the order which is not immediately given to the senses. In themselves these theoretical terms are merely heuristic devices. They are "analytic truths," devoid of intrinsic meaning. That is, they are not strictly to be thought of in terms of their truth or falsity. Observation statements alone, "synthetic truths," are true or false. Theoretical ideas are tested precisely by seeing if it is possible to draw "correspondences" between theoretical terms and observational truths. The value (i.e., synthetical content) of a theoretical hypothesis is determined by running experiments with the intent of gathering empirical evidence which confirms "predictions" made using this hypothesis. If the predictions are deemed to be confirmed well enough, then the theoretical hypothesis behind them constitutes an empirical law. With the deductive application of this law, mere descriptions of things and events are elevated to the status of explanations.

Distilling the essence of this approach, Hollis summarizes it in terms of the central concept of natural laws (1977: 47):

> A natural law is a regularity in nature holding in specifiable conditions; we know we have found one, when we have a well-enough confirmed theory; a theory is a set of logically-linked, high-order generalizations; the only test of a theory is the success of its predictions; prediction and explanation are two sides of the same and only coin, in that explaining a phenomenon is finding a theory from which it could have been predicted.

The logical assimilation of prediction and explanation, in other words, is now doing the work previously done by shear correlation. This assimilation is, however, problematic.

In spite of the *prima facie* sense of the putative differences between observation terms and theoretical terms (e.g., "... is blue" and "... is a neutrino"), scepticism prevails about the possibility of specifying the qualities of an observation statement free of all theoretical content, and in reverse, advancing analytic truths free of all empirical content. Therefore, it can be wondered whether it is possible to determine the parameters of a decisive test of any theoretical statement without in some measure pre-determining the results of its test. In their critique of positivist micro-economics, Hollis and Edward Nell (1975), deftly expose this deficiency by examining three steps involved in the testing of any hypothesis: (1) supplying the criteria of application for theoretical terms, (2) specifying *ceteris paribus* clauses, and (3) advancing rules for adjusting observed variables to remove distortions.

In the first place, problems arise for the D-N model from the fact that there are two relations involved in the definition and use of a theoretical term.

> Firstly. the term must be related to others.... Secondly, if economics
> is to be proudly distinct from magic and demonology, we must be able
> to know when some empirical statements containing the term are true,
> which requires knowing which actual phenomena the term applies to....
> Otherwise the explanation will be wholly formal, internal or semantic.
> Terms defined wholly by interrelating them cannot yet be used and
> criteria of application are needed for at least one of them. Theoretical
> terms must be attached to the world as well as to one another (1975:
> 98).

It is the criteria of application that are all important. Yet if the
criterial statements are analytic, then how can they anchor the
term to the world? If they are synthetic, does this not mean that
we have already decided the 'real' meaning of the theoretical term
(i.e.. that it possesses a factual truth)? The positivist cannot
escape the dilemma by pragmatic appeal to habitual criteria of
decision and usefulness. Habits too are based on criteria of some
sort.

Sciences in general need sets of statements that can be treated
as primitively true. Such statements are used as evidence for
judgements of a more general and complex nature. But to function
so, these statements must ideally be free of all references to the
interpretative principles of the sciences in question. The prospects
of this being the case are not bright.

> Problems of classification, of identification and of detecting errors in
> specification arise only on the assumption that there are functional re-
> lations between variables. These relations must be known to be lawlike,
> if they are to license what philosophers term 'counter-factual condition-
> als' (Hollis and Nell. 1975: 85).

But the ability to know lawlike relations is blocked by the hoary
old riddle of induction.

To the problem of circularity can be added that of infinite
regress, for the restricted application of any science means that all
tests must be framed with *ceteris paribus* clauses. These clauses
state the conditions under which the test of a theory is to count
as decisive. For them as well, it must be possible "to decide independently of the theory whether they hold in a given case or
not. Otherwise... there will be no way of knowing whether a dis-
crepancy between theory and facts refutes the theory or merely
shows that *ceteris* were *imparibus*" (1975: 27). In other words, an
interdisciplinary theory, more sophisticated than the theory being tested, is needed to support the application of *ceteris paribus*
clauses. This theory will also have to pass tests involving *ceteris*

paribus clauses and so on. The regress can only be halted, once again, with a solution to the problem of induction.

Both of these dilemmas are compounded by the need to adjust the observed values of variables to create the true values of a test situation. This need stems in part from the fact that statistical measures are invariably contaminated by influences which must be taken into account to assure that a test provides information about a specific theory and not just about the situation from which the data was drawn.

In the end, Hollis and Nell conclude, the positivist economist is led to assume the correctness of some specific understanding of a situation and to base adjustments on it. But this transforms supposedly synthetic predictive statements into covert analytic statements (1975: 33):

> 'The test of a theory is the success of its predictions' originally seemed to say that a theory predicted an actual order of events and that a hypothesis was to be discarded when the predicted sequence failed to occur. But it now turns out that the theory is to predict not what will be observed to happen, but what would be observed, if the values of the variables were the true ones and if 'other things' were 'equal.'... Consequently no theory can be refuted merely by showing its assumptions to be unrealistic or its predictions not to fit the facts. For predictions are standardly tested against observed values of variables in conditions where 'other things' are not 'equal.' If it further turns out that what the true values are and by how much other things are unequal depend on the theory being tested, then predictions will be standardly irrefutable.

The problems of induction and the discovery of natural laws are not effectively circumvented then through recourse to the D-N account of scientific explanation. If positivists wish to insist that we live in a world deterministically ruled by a network of causal laws they can do so only through faith in the Hume's principle of correlation.[1]

With a twist of the basic premises, the hypothetico-deductive method (hereafter H-D) claims to have logically avoided this fate. Therefore, before turning to draw some larger conclusions from Hollis and Nell's insights, let us tie up all the loose ends by subjecting the hypothetico-deductive model to a similar scrutiny.

The Hypothetico-Deductive Variant of Soft Positivism

In response to the dilemmas faced by conventional soft positivism, some social theorists have sought to have recourse to the

philosophy of science of Sir Karl Popper. Popper's philosophy
represents a critical revision of the views of the Vienna Circle.
Popper claims to have avoided the problems of circularity and
infinite regress which block the confirmation of theories through
induction. For the sociologist Percy Cohen, the H-D method of
science entails recognizing the following (Cohen, 1980: 154-55):

> that if one's task is to explain, then one must start with a question or
> problem to be explained, which must be stated as clearly as possible...
> ; that any such question can be put as an indicative statement; that
> the question can be particular or general... and can, therefore, be put
> in the form either of... 'this did occur,' or 'this tends to occur.'..; that
> the explanation of such statements consists in deriving them logically
> from other statements; that the movement from the statement to be ex-
> plained to that or those which explain it is carried out without benefit
> of any logical procedure, such as induction, and is, therefore, a hunch
> or hypothesis; that the hypothesis can be tested by 'deducing from it
> other statements ... which, if true, confirm it and which, if false, dis-
> confirm it; that, if such new deductions–or predictions–do not confirm
> the hypothesis, then the latter must be either rejected or modified.

Stated in such a manner, the H-D model appears to differ little
from the D-N one, and in highly general discussions the two are
often found lumped together under one or the other rubric. There
are, however, two important distinctions. First, as Cohen stresses,
Popper's perspective is more "uncompromising" in its acceptance
of the truly hypothetical or conjectural character of scientific theorizing. Second, his position actually rests on a doctrine of falsification and not verification. The key to the testing of theories,
Popper asserted, is a logical asymmetry between verification and
falsification.

Observation as such cannot be prior to theory, Popper realized,
since theory is presupposed by any observation, if only at the level
of unconscious and/or inborn expectations. Hence so-called facts,
like theories, are to be treated as provisional and always subject to
revision, for they may be based on poor theories. When combined
with Hume's problem of induction this means that explanatory hypotheses are most definitely just hunches. But these hunches can
be tested by attempting to falsify them, for logically, falsification
obviates the doubts about induction. The reasoning is as follows:
although no number of observation statements reporting observations of white swans allows us logically to derive the universal
statement "All swans are white," a single observation statement
reporting the observation of a black swan, allows us to derive the

statement "Not all swans are white." Empirical generalizations, hypotheses, then, are testable in spite of being unprovable: they can be tested by systematically attempting to refute them. Good hypotheses resist refutation.

Now as Cohen notes, this method's uncompromising affirmation of the hypothetical status of both theories and observations has led to the charge that it permits a vicious circularity into science by making theories dependent upon facts which are, in turn, dependent upon theories. The force of this objection is checked, however, by two qualifactory rules. First, the facts used to falsify an hypothesis should not be dependent on the theory being tested. Second, every effort should be made, rather, to use factual statements which are dependent on theories which are at that time not considered problematic. The solution is not fail-safe. But one must inevitably rely, Popper points out, on a certain amount of apparently well established "background knowledge" (Popper, 1963: 238). This background knowledge can, at best, only be criticized in a piece-meal manner through a slow process of feedback.

More importantly, theories can be tested for their verisimilitude (i.e., nearness to the truth) through comparative analyses. Without knowing the truth of a situation, various hypotheses about it can be contrasted nevertheless, and one can be selected as potentially more satisfactory. Simplifying Popper's precise argument, the preferable theory should (1963: 232): (1) provide a solution to the problem and explain facts explained by earlier and/or alternative theories; (2) be compatible with all known observations; (3) explain where other theories are inadequate or false and itself account for the falsifying evidence; and (4) give rise to new and essentially unexpected knowledge and problems or theoretical difficulties. The preferable theories in other words, must have greater content than their rivals.

This comparative orientation probably accurately reflects what most scientists do. But when pressed, Popper's model falls prey to much the same logical and practical difficulties as the D-N model. When forced to choose between two equally reasonable, competing theories, the bottom line for Popper is that one should select the theory with higher content or which provides more testable propositions. But neither of these considerations guarantees that the theory is more true. They only suggest that it is potentially more productive (though quite possibly false). And the productivity itself can be called into question if the theory cannot be subjected to conclusive tests. Conclusive testing of high content theories is blocked, however, by at least five arguments.

The first four of these arguments are variations on the theme of demarcating the finite in the infinite. In the first place, the necessary leap from apparent verisimilitude to actual verisimilitude is blocked by the simple fact that "we can never be sure that [a predicted] observation is false–for there may be technical fault in making it, or fault in the theory used to establish it... "(Cohen, 1980: 163). Second, the H-D model glosses over two crucial indeterminancies. As pointed out by Pierre Duhem, any theory is a conjunction of many hypotheses, the refutation of any one predicted observation points the finger at no hypothesis in particular. The refutation may be of one of the ancillary premises of the theory and not of the hypothesis being tested. Further, as already noted, "a commonplace of '-metrics' (econometrics, for instance) is that observed data have to be adjusted to get their true values and there is always room for dispute and reinterpretation" (Hollis, 1977: 52). Third, in line with Popper's suggestion that the proper aim of science is verisimilitude rather than truth per se, it is necessary to postulate that there are a finite number of possible conjectures about nature, so that by progressively refuting them we get nearer and nearer to the truth. But such an assumption is unwarranted, especially in the light of Popper's vision of knowledge as the product of the comparative analysis of theories born of the endless revision of background knowledge (Giddens, 1977: 61). Fourth, if we look at what William Newton-Smith calls the "deductive closure" of theories to detect which has greater content, "we shall find that any interesting scientific theory has the same amount of content. For any such theory will entail an infinite number of empirical assertions" (Newton-Smith, 1981: 56). Formal measures have been derived for comparing intervals of a Euclidean straight line. Nothing analogous exists for non-trivial comparisons of "infinite sets of sentences."

Fifth and lastly, the principle of decision employed in the theory of verisimilitude is actually the idea of corroboration. The greater the number of attempted falsifications a theory survives the more corroborated or truthful it is. Yet as Newton-Smith observes, "there is no way within the confines of the Popperian system to ground rationally the claim that corroboration is linked to verisimilitude." The assumption that the two are correlated really involves abandoning "what was unique and interesting in

Popper: namely, the jettisoning of induction." And "if we concede a role to induction [at this high level] there is no reason not to admit inductive arguments right from the start" (1981: 70).

In the last analysis, then, there is little reason to have any more confidence in the H-D model of science than in the D-N model. Rather, as Cohen comments, the peculiar lesson learned from a careful examination of these soft positivist models of science is: "If the positivists are wrong about factual bedrocks they are most certainly not wrong in pointing to the consequences of abandoning the belief in their existence" (1980: 158). The failure of the positivist programme has simply generated an epistemological rebound in the direction of complete cognitive relativism and anarchism.[2] Of course, the ground was prepared for this development, ironically, through the positivist tendency to assimilate predictive and explanatory knowledge, since it is difficult to distinguish the account of scientific explanation resting on this assimilation from a straightforwardly instrumentalist or pragmatist view of science. Formally, the positivist regards the laws of a D-N explanation to be either true or false. The instrumentalist, on the other hand, considers such laws only to be devices for the generation of predictions which are valuable to the extent that they practically contribute to our ability to manipulate and relate to our environment. But in the light of the unreliability of positivist test procedures and the consequent weight placed by the positivist programme on the tenuous notion of correlation, "it is easy to conflate these two attitudes, or slide from one to the other" (Keat and Urry, 1975: 64).[3]

This slippage from positivism into instrumentalism or pragmatism has considerable impact on the question of human freedom. Passive conceptions of humanity view human action as a natural and determined phenomenon. They attempt to explain human behaviour as the necessary consequence of the conjunction of constant natural laws. In the moral world as much as the natural one, it is argued that x because y is to be read as x is caused by y. But as we have seen, it is "all too easy to assert in ontology what, as epistemologists, we could not possibly know to be true" (Hollis, 1977: 42). The tests undergirding the positivist faith in causal order are all too circular and inconclusive. This being the case, Hollis proposes that a natural or causal law simply takes on the form "In conditions C, A is a sufficient condition for B" (1977: 45).[4] In like manner, Percy Cohen remarks (1980: 167):

A cause, in our view, is a logical concept which implies that one set of
events is necessary, sufficient or contributory to the occurrence of another; what particular kind of process is involved characterises different
forms of causal connexion; the core is the logical requirement of asserting that a particular type of connexion does or does not exist between
events.

If this understanding of causality holds true, then the claims of
a humanistic sociology no longer interfer with the doctrine of the
formal unity of the sciences. The door has been opened to at least
the possibility of scientifically conceptualizing human freedom. To
this end, though, many more epistemological and methodological
hurdles must be surmounted. Other equally antagonistic theories
of knowledge have risen from the ashes of positivism, and the
exponents of a humanistic sociology which is "scientific" must fight
to stake its epistemological claim amongst them.

VI.
The Strategic Choice:
Idealism, Pragmatism or Empiricism

The Qualified Idealist Counter to Soft Positivism

Humanistic sociologists have held all along that human activities, and the patterns which they form, cannot be explained in the sense that natural events can be explained. They can, however, be interpreted: and the logic of the interpretation is not the logic of science, but that of hermeneutics. Under the collective impact of the differing yet convergent writings of such philosophers as Willard V. O. Quine (1961), Thomas Kuhn (1970), Paul Feyerabend (1975), Hans-Georg Gadamer (1975), Jürgen Habermas (1971, 1979), and Richard Rorty (1979), it has recently become suspect, however, whether there is a logic of science distinct from that of hermeneutics. Soft positivism and humanism seem to have converged, giving a hermeneutical twist to the social sciences.

Between the natural and the social sciences there undoubtedly are important differences in concrete method, analysis and procedure. Yet as another scholar, Karin D. Knorr-Cetina, has recently argued, philosophical investigations and empirical observations "suggest that natural science investigation is grounded in the same kind of situational logic and marked by the same kind of indexical reasoning we are used to associate (sic) with the symbolic and interactional character of the social world" (1981: 336). By this she does not mean just that science as a 'social system' portrays the same properties as other social realities. Rather she means that scientific reasoning and the technical production of research are interpretive processes no different in kind from those of the social sciences. In her own words (1981: 399):

> In sum, we seem to be confronted with a situation in which interpretations (observational 'facts') can only be explained and justified by reference to other interpretations on which they partly depend (theories) and by reference to their relation to the whole, our overall 'home theory' [to use Quine's expression]–an exact definition of an interpretative cycle called hermeneutic... in the cultural sciences.

Sociological studies of laboratory conditions and procedures are showing that in the hardest of sciences the products of experimentation comprehensively reflect the effects of the indexical logic which characterizes their production. In ethnomethodology where the concept of indexicality gained currency, indexicality refers to the situational location of utterances in a context of time, space, and tacit social and communicative rules. Through her participant observation at a large American institute, Knorr-Cetina came to the conclusion that processes of interpretation, negotiation, and mobilization of contextual considerations (e.g., ever so briefly: machinery, materials, procedures, and personnel available; institutional and administrative restrictions and habits; personal idiosyncracies, etc.) are required in at least three areas of scientific choice (1981: 355):

> 1. Questions of 'composition,' or questions which relate to the selection of specific substances, ingredients or to specific means of instrumentation. 2. Questions of 'quantification,' or questions which bear on the selection of how much of a substance is to be used, of how long a process should be maintained, of when a measurement or a sample should be taken, etc. 3. Questions of 'control,' or questions which refer to such methodological options as simplicity of composition versus complexity, strict versus indirect comparability, etc.

Consequently, she concludes:

> Given these choices, research in the natural and technological sciences cannot be partitioned into a part which is open to situationally contingent selections and to contextual influences such as the part in which a research problem is defined, and into a part which consists of the internal, objective and standardized execution of the necessary inquiry. Since the choices exist throughout the process of experimentation, there is no core of the production of research which is in principle left unaffected by the circumstances of production.[1]

Given this state of affairs, it seems reasonable to assume that the customary distinctions drawn between the natural and the social sciences, and hence also the almost congruent distinctions drawn between positivist and humanist sociologies, should be forfeited.[2] As suggested by Dilthey long ago, "different regions of facts cannot be conceived of ontologically but only epistemologically. They do not 'exist'; rather they are constituted. The difference between the natural and the cultural sciences must therefore be reduced to the orientation of the knowing subject, to its attitude with regard to objects" (Habermas, 1971: 141). Each discipline fashions its subject matter out of the criteria of application that inform its perceptual understanding of nature or some aspect of nature (including the human world). Hence the world is apprehended on a variety of analytical levels, each level undergoing continuous transformation under the influence of their own internal logic, the pressures generated by interdisciplinary rivalries, and extraneous social forces. "Whatever is at a given moment considered to be a 'fact' of nature," Eric Jacobs observes, "will endure only so long as it is not contradicted, transformed, or altered by new perceptual understandings, which having drawn upon previous work or more sophisticated theories, techniques, observations, etc., are able to provide a more compelling and intellectually satisfying interpretative knowledge of the world than had been previously available" (1978: 74). In this vein Quine goes so far, Hollis notes, as to suggest that physical objects represent but convenient cultural posits conceptually imported into situations to help us predict and cope with future experience in the light of past experience. Epistemologically, Quine states, physical objects are comparable to the gods of Homer, and "the myth of physical objects is epistemologically superior to most [only] in that it has proved more efficacious than other myths as a device for working a manageable structure into the flux of experience" (Hollis, 1977: 54).

Ultimately, Hollis agrees, logic does force us to precisely this extremity: to a kind of conceptual pragmatism. But then the important question becomes, "if empiricism must abandon belief in given, independent, objective facts as a crucial constraint on what it is rational to accept, what becomes of natural laws and causal explanation?" (Hollis, 1977: 53). It seems that a causal law is nothing more than an observed regularity, and this regularity is in fact nothing more than a statement "well-enough entrenched in our conceptual scheme to be above at least ready suspicion, when experience proves recalcitrant" (Hollis, 1977: 54).

This being the case, Hollis concludes, we are led to a crucial decision (1977: 55):

> So far a bare notion of observable particulars has yielded too bare a notion of a natural law. We need Mill's distinction between the 'empirical laws' and the 'causal laws which explain them' but, epistemologically, cannot yet have it. Pragmatism, which lets us say what we want, does not stop us saying what we please. There is now a choice. We either enrich our ontology beyond what Positivism allows or strengthen the claim of theoretical connections to do what Pragmatism asks. There

needs to be more to a natural law than regularity, if we are to tell the
lawlike from the accidental, and the choice is whether to put the 'more'
in the world or in the theory.

In making this statement Hollis is advancing two propositions.
First, in spite of the limitations recognized in the Humean notion
of causality and the failure of positivist attempts to circumvent
these limits, claims to knowledge still essentially entail the invocation of some implicit form of natural necessity.[3] Second, once
such claims are seen to entail something more than mere regularity, the issue becomes what sort of necessity is best invoked. Hollis
notes that three forms of necessity have been advanced: logical,
ontological, and epistemological.

In the *Ethics* of Spinoza one can encounter a comprehensive
account of a world ruled by logical necessity. But, Hollis comments, "a world where nothing is contingent is too high a price
to pay for a clear notion of a natural law" (1977: 57). Therefore,
he argues that in fact "the strategic choice is whether to locate
the necessity in the world and then pick out the sort of theoretical
statements which reflect it or whether to discern it in theoretical
truths and argue from what is theoretically true of experience to
what is therefore true in it" (1977: 57).

Under the first or ontological approach Hollis lumps, in effect,
two modes of argument: arguments for a "physical necessity" and
arguments for an "experiential necessity." The former type of
argument undergirds Realist philosophies of science like that of
Rom Haré (though Hollis does not explicitly point this out). As
summarized by Russell Keat and John Urry (1975: 27-45), the
Realist view entails rejecting the deductive-nomological identification of scientific explanation with a form of logical argument and
the Humean view of the nature of causality. In their place, the
Realist argues that on the basis of scientific experience the discovery of regular relationships between events constitutes sufficiently
strong evidence for the postulation of real causal connections and
the presence of some intervening mechanism whereby a cause actually produces an effect. In other words, the Realist position entails
making ontological commitments to models of causal mechanisms
which have held up under repeated tests of their descriptive adequacy. Only this approach, the Realist asserts, provides a satisfactorily complete explanation of phenomena. But as Realists like
Keat and Urry admit, in the last analysis, nothing more than an
essentially psychological argument has been provided for assuming

the existence of a natural necessity beyond Humean regularities. "The realist has provided no adequate analysis of causal, or natural, necessity" (Keat and Urry, 1975: 42).

The latter type of ontological arguments, (i.e., those referring to an "experiential necessity") Hollis associates with attempts to account for the apparent necessities found in theoretical statements by appealing to very general facts of experience. Hollis illustrates the position by citing the second edition of Lionel Robbin's celebrated *Essay on the Nature and Significance of Economic Science*. In this book Robbin attempts to explain the sense in which economic laws are "necessities to which human action is subject" (1977: 57). He treats economic theory as a set of linked statements which consist of deductions from postulates based on "almost universal facts of experience" known through introspection (1977: 59-60). Hollis takes a dim view of such arguments (1977: 60):

> the snag is to find an account of introspection which would allow knowledge of general truths. Perhaps some Cartesian would care to extend the clear and distinct perception of 'cogito' to 'almost universal facts' but I cannot think an empiricist would tolerate general laws known by immediate acquaintance. Short of such heroics, we shall have to treat necessities in experience as problematic.

The second of Hollis' two overall approaches to necessity, the epistemological option, involves the promotion of what he calls "definitional necessity." This approach strikes him as more promising than is usually thought. The idea is to trace "the necessities to which human action is subject back to axiomatic or definitional statements introducing... key concepts" (1977: 59). That is, social theory is to be treated as a sort of social geometry or mechanics. Resolving a social problem simply involves, then, "applying a model which yields values for some variables, given the values of others." The model in this view constitutes "a convenient device for assembling all the predictive, explanatory, programming and productive roles of theory in mechanics, economics or any other science." The model, that is, can provide several services, "depending on which values are given and what questions are asked" (61-62). But if the statements in the model are only convenient and not true, how does this approach differ from conventionalist and pragmatist approaches?

Granted, Hollis observes, what we know about the underdetermination of theories by experience, the statements in the model are either mere empirical generalizations or empty tautologies. And given the rampant circularity of such models, as the harshest of critics might assert, they are more likely the latter. Therefore, Hollis boldly concludes, "the most promising line is, in effect, to deny that tautologies need be empty" and to look upon these statements as 'real' and not just 'nominal' definitions. They are telling us about the essence of things and processes in this world and not just the human usage and intention behind concepts and assertions.

By referring to real definitions, Hollis is by no means implying a return to the perspective of the Realists. As indicated in the following passage, he has something much more subtle in mind (1977: 62):

> The statements of [the model] are not tautologies, if a tautology is defined as a statement whose truth is guaranteed by logic alone. Although there is dispute about the exact scope of logic it is safe to say that concepts like 'force,' 'utility,' 'scarcity,' 'integration' are not concepts of logic. Any formal system with a domain (for instance neo-Classical micro-economics) includes concepts which mark its domain (for instance 'utility'). The concepts are essential both to the axioms and to the implications of the system.

If this is the case, then, he concludes (1977: 63):

> What makes a formal system an economic theory is the essential presence of economic concepts throughout. What makes an economic theory true is that some of its axiomatic statements are unconditionally true.

Such a view of matters is contentious, to say the least. It obviously involves a clean break with positivism over the status of a priori knowledge, and in this vein Hollis recognizes that the whole perspective runs afoul of one problem (1977: 64):

> The root question is whether necessary truths can be shown importantly distinct from contingent truths (contrary to Pragmatism) without making them empirically vacuous (as Logical Positivists would suspect).

It is this difficulty that has led Hollis (as noted in the Introduction) to record the important proviso that the special thesis of the argument from rationality is independent of the general thesis. And it is this problem to which we will have cause to return in Chapters IX and XI.

While suggesting the possibility of equating natural necessity with conceptual necessity, Hollis declines to demonstrate how conceptual truths and relations could be used to actually account for the necessities to which human action is subject. But he is drawn to this orientation, relative to the other equally indefinite conceptions of necessity, because of its promising implications for the crucial task of distinguishing between the lawlike and the accidental.

> If there were a theory of a priori knowledge which makes conceptual truth as objective a part of our knowledge as are truths of fact, then we could account for the missing difference between empirical laws and the causal laws which explain them. If there were, in Kantian spirit, unique ways of conceptualizing domains of experience and it made sense to speak of getting it right, then theory would have an honest task of showing why what is must be.

For Hollis all of this only lies in the realm of the possible (perhaps probable). But with an eye to accounting for the missing difference between empirical laws and the causal laws which explain them, he might have had recourse to the intriguing arguments of Nicholas Rescher (and perhaps Alfred Tarski as well).[4] It is his second point, however, which plays a more important role in the justification of the argument from rationality (in spite of the problematic nature of the idea of definitional necessity). And on the topic of unique ways of conceptualizing domains of experience Hollis does have something of significance to say with regard to the social sciences and the notion of rational human agency. Prior to engaging this topic, however, a few more words need to be said in support of Hollis' epistemological approach to the question of natural necessity (i.e., about his new idealism).

It could be argued that between the ontological and epistemological options to the location of necessity there is very little to choose "since the only way to justify ontology is through epistemology and... every epistemology involves commitment to an ontology." But, Hollis insists, the choice does make a difference "in the sense attaching to 'natural necessity'" (1977: 57). At first sight, Hollis surmises, the epistemological approach seems actually to involve a stronger ontological commitment to some natural necessity than does an explicitly ontological approach. Does not theorizing in terms of certain structures commit one (as the Realists suppose) "to believing there are corresponding structures in reality[?]" No, Hollis replies (1977: 65),

> ... nothing said here has required this relation of correspondence. To borrow a later point, the rational agent does the rational thing and theory explains why; but there is no ontological sense in which he has to. Similarly, although the snooker ball has to move as it does, the

necessity arises only because it features in the solution to a theoretical problem in mechanics.

In truth, then, the epistemological perspective involves a weaker sense of natural necessity because it "can rest content with wholly contingent connections among the referents of concepts, among which there are necessary connections. Empirical notions of natural necessity are forced into bolder claims" (1977: 65).

This attitude to the question of distinguishing the lawlike from the accidental is methodologically analogous to the testing of conjectures in mathematics (Hollis, 1977: 64):

> In the end, no doubt, we shall be able to prove or disprove Fermat's last theorem but, until then, we seek negative instances, offer partial proofs and find ways of showing it more or less likely that the propositions at issue are indeed necessarily true. It is in principle no more a threat to empirical science than to mathematics that the aim would be to arrive at necessities.

In other words, Hollis is arguing that the principle of the formal unity of the sciences is to be accepted, but stood on its head, so to speak. The distinction between analytic and synthetic truths is to be collapsed, but in precisely the reverse manner to pragmatist philosophies of science. Both the pragmatist response to the demise of positivism and Hollis' new idealism, point to the existence of a single notion of "causal-cum-theoretical explanation" underlying all the sciences—a mode of explanation which appears to be open to the full explanation of human action, including free action. With the scrutiny of the special thesis of the argument from rationality, however, it will become clear that only the epistemological or idealist approach really permits the identification and assessment of free actions. It alone is open, in principle, to the discovery of the truth of a situation in such a way that the constitutive role of human intelligence is neither made the be-all-end-all nor pushed into the background. It is these limitations on the constitutive function of human thought which detract from the alternative compromises struck between the lessons of pragmatism and positivism by a "second generation" of soft positivists who balk at Hollis' revamped idealism.

In the remaining sections of this chapter we will undertake a brief examination of two representative examples of these other types of compromises. First, we will look at the attempt made by the American philosopher and social theorist Paul Tibbetts to recast the positivism-humanism debate in sociology into a conflict

of "linguistic grids." Second, we will look at the attempt made by
the British philosopher and anthropologist Ernest Gellner to find
a new epistemological foundation for empiricism. Taken together,
the two perspectives frame the immediate context of the debate
over the feasibility of scientifically treating human freedom. The
first approach attempts to render the issue inconsequential. The
second approach provides a new justification for limiting social
scientific thought to the language of determinism. Here it will be
argued that it is the weakness of the first position and the apparent
strength of the second which recommends the fuller development of
the argument from rationality. Further, through the examination
of these proposals, more specific insights will be gained into the
precise epistemological choices that must be made in selecting a
method of science for the academic study of social and religious
action.

Soft Positivism with a Pragmatist Slant

In "The Positivism-Humanism Debate in Sociology: A Reconsideration" (1982), Paul Tibbetts argues that there are no longer
grounds for "the claim that positivism and humanism are mutually exclusive alternatives to the study and amelioration of human
society" (1982: 184). To this end he demonstrates that care has
been taken by contemporary positivists to address humanistic concerns about "scientism, the value-laden character of all scientific
inquiry, and the relation between science and human emancipa-
tion" (1982: 184). In the process he typically implies that an
intellectually satisfying social science is emerging from a kind of
enlightened co-optation of humanistic insights into the hermeneutical character of scientific inquiry. This co-optation is possible,
he suggests, because the claims associated with a humanistic sociology are not "inherently incompatible with the outlook labeled
as 'positivistic'" (1982: 196).

Tibbetts falls short of proving this thesis, however, because he
fails to come to grips with what he stipulates as the first claim of
a humanistic sociology (1982: 188):

> The presupposition of voluntarism: Human beings are autonomous
> agents capable of rational reflection and purposive action toward freely
> posited goals.

Misconstruing the meaning and significance of this claim, he attempts to explain the problem of human freedom away as an unnecessary linguistic confusion brought on by the failure to realize

that the fundamental methodological differences between the positivists and the humanists can be boiled down to a choice between linguistic grids suited to different purposes. The positivists were right. in his opinion. to have perceived no obligation to employ a method of science which recognizes human freedom. But then by the same token they were wrong to believe that the scientific view is strictly aligned with an essentially deterministic account of phenomena. It is but a question of semantics whether human freedom is acknowledged in a scientific study or not.

In a commentary on his article. James Lemke. David Shevach, and Richard Wells take Tibbetts to task. They charge that "Tibbetts' mischaracterization of semantic issues... keeps him from appreciating fully the powerful impact of metaphysical positions (or 'linguistic grids.' as Tibbetts calls them) on social relationships" (1984: 90). But by limiting their criticisms to Tibbetts' insensitivity to the social and political implications of semantic choices these critics permit Tibbetts to pose a telling rejoinder (1984: 99):

> Granted that there are such social and political implications. what I am looking for is an argument why anyone is bound or obliged to consider them. I would claim that evaluating the humanistic sociology-positivism debate with such social and political implications already in mind could very well distort one's analysis of the epistemological dimensions of this debate–and it was this dimension that particularly interests this writer! To claim that epistemological and conceptual matters cannot be analytically isolated from social and political implications is to resituate the... debate into the sociology-of-knowledge arena.

On this point Tibbetts is essentially correct (though it is he who has opened the doors to the sociology of knowledge with his talk of alternative "linguistic grids"). His preoccupation with salvaging positivism through the introduction of a linguistic twist, however, leads him to overlook the most pivotal epistemological issue of this debate. The humanistic presupposition of voluntarism involves a conceptual commitment to a model of rational human agency, and this commitment constitutes a necessary presupposition of all sciences of human action. Therefore, contrary to Tibbetts (1982: 192-93 and 1984: 98-99). there are sound epistemological reasons for why sociologists are neither free to choose their linguistic grids nor. consequently. their basic units and frameworks of analysis.

Positivists. Tibbetts notes. recognize that humanity has a mental life which can be grasped introspectively. But "as to the matter of whether such cognitive states are causally efficacious," he declares, they have "rightly avoided metaphysical questions concerning the freedom-determinism issue" (1982: 193). Instead, following Carnap, they postulate the "unified language thesis" (Tibbetts' favoured rendering of the doctrine of the formal unity of the sciences.) In its original physicalist guise, this thesis claimed that all phenomena can be described with a language focused strictly on physical and observable properties. In this reductionist form, Tibbetts acknowledges, the thesis has been abandoned as unfeasible. Nevertheless, the virtue he sees in the linguistic twist given to the unity of science tenet leads him to rather surprisingly conclude that the conflict within sociology over positivism's reductionistic orientation concerns but "a preference for one 'linguistic grid' over another." "I fail to see," he states, "where a humanistic sociology would be threatened by a mere semantic preference" (1982: 193).

> On this point I am personally sympathetic with the position that 'free-will talk' versus 'causal-deterministic talk' reduces to an essentially arbitrary preference for one preferred mode of speech over another.

These comments miss the point of the humanists' protest against the application of causal-deterministic language to human affairs. At the same time they do an injustice to the intent of the positivist turn to language. As demonstrated by ordinary language philosophers like Wittgenstein (1958) and Austin (1962), and anthropologists like Whorf (1956) and Lévi-Strauss (1966), by shaping human perceptions, languages have the power to shape (though not determine) human reality. The choice of a language, therefore, is hardly "arbitrary." It is charged with explicit and implicit epistemological and practical consequences. Accordingly, the unified language thesis was not advanced as a mere preference, but as a normative prescription for science, and it is hard to see what merit there is in reducing it to an ability to arbitrarily identify one and the same action as both caused and free. It is neither necessary to decree that all actions have causes (i.e., determinism), nor that all human actions are ultimately free (i.e., libertarianism). It is necessary, however, to be able to say (recognizing the implicitly evaluative character of all judgements) with some degree of regularity, when an action is in the last analysis one or the other.

Qualifying his own argument, Tibbetts admits (1982: 193):

> To say it is a matter of semantic preference is not to ignore the important ramifications for sociological theories and, on a more concrete level, for social policies that adoption of one mode of speech may entail

over the other; there could be political and ideological considerations at
work here in one's semantic choice.

But this statement continues to miss the mark. It appears that
Tibbetts is operating under the peculiar notion that the use of
a language only has serious consequences if it is not purified of
"political and ideological considerations." This assumption, I suspect, displays the latent influence of the positivist quest for a pure
observation language. Yet, as Tibbetts acknowledges, "no cognitively adequate version of either the elimination of metaphysics or
the verification principle has thus far appeared" (1982: 194).

Tibbetts' semantic preference proposal is supposed to carry
us beyond the limitations of the old positivist programme. Yet no
humanist could really rest content with Tibbetts' simple disclaimer
that

> ... the last thing the sophisticated positivist wants to do is to dogmatize
> about unresolvable metaphysical issues such as "Is human behaviour,
> in the last analysis, free or determined? .... Is human reason and ratio-
> nality an illusion, a mere epiphenomenon?" (1982: 193)

Such a statement merely reiterates the quite unsophisticated
positivist condemnation of humanistic claims to human freedom
and rationality as "metaphysical." But in light of the fate of the
positivist programme, what does it mean to label the very raising
of these questions (so central to the humanist perspective) metaphysical, in some pejorative sense? How is it that this means that
these questions are unresolvable and hence only open to dogma-
tism and not reasoned argument? As Tibbetts goes on to note
(1982: 195), ambivalently:

> ... it should in all honesty be recognized that this bias against
> metaphysics... remains only a bias and without adequate cognitive war-
> rant until the logical and conceptual problems associated with the ver-
> ification doctrine... are satisfactorily resolved...

If this is the case, then what justification is there for avoiding the
judgement that while human rationality and freedom are certainly
mysterious, they are not simply illusory?[5]

Tibbetts points out that "unless a humanist is prepared to be
so open-minded (or indifferent) as to allow 'any' set of claims to
be cognitively meaningful, then he or she will be as suspicious as
the positivist of quasi- or even pseudo-scientific assertions" (1982:
195). I agree, and accept further that humanistic sociologies exclude as nonsense that which they cannot identify with reliable

empirical knowledge. But in the light of the fate of verification-ism (and falsificationism), the question is, What counts as reliable empirical knowledge? Positivists and humanists agree on a broad range of practical knowledge and low-level facts. As Tibbetts says, humanists like positivists are unlikely to have faith in the power of witchcraft to cure leukemia (1982: 195). But unlike positivists, and apparently Tibbetts, a number of scholars think it is possi-ble to advance our understanding of the theoretical and empirical conditions of rational human action, and hence for some, the con-ditions of free human action as well (e.g., Jürgen Habermas, 1971, 1979, 1984; Martin Hollis, 1977; Robin Horton, 1979; Max Black, 1982; Avrum Stroll, 1982; and Donald Davidson, 1982).

For lack of references it is not clear what Tibbetts intends by his semantic preference proposal. At face value it makes the free-will and causal-deterministic linguistic grids incommensurable, and the relationship of either to the independent reality of the world purely idiosyncratic. But such a stance is neither in accord with the pos-itivism which Tibbetts seems so intent on giving a better press (see 184, 190-93, and 195-96), nor is it credible–if only from the perspective of his own practical empiricism. The mere drawing of a distinction suggests that there are important implications to our choice of descriptive languages. This in turn implies that there must be significant inferential connections between the two modes of explanation. The languages of freedom and causation are not wholly incommensurable. Positivists did not see them as incom-mensurable; they did not want to be free to use one language or the other according to their theoretical interests. They saw the languages as commensurable but incompatible; they thought one could replace the other at the level that counts. The same holds true for the humanists.

The failure of the positivist formulation of the nature of the inferential connection, moreover, does not mean that there is no connection. Nor does it mean that the only way still available for rendering "free-will talk" and "causal-deterministic talk" non-competitive is to see them as incommensurable linguistic options. Only an inquirer whose thinking remained paradoxically too at-tached to the positivist programme would be inclined, I think, to interpret the demise of this programme as logically meaning that matters had simply reverted to "arbitrary preference." In general, this claim attempts to purchase peace between the positivists and humanists at a price that is too great, in terms of cognitive rela-tivism, for the principled exponents of either tradition.[6]

The positivist tradition has itself established the suspect character of all self-validating forms of explanation. Yet, when the test procedure at the heart of the positivist mode of inquiry is pressed it becomes clear that some untouched central hypothesis actually determines when an inquirer will reject a prediction or, alternatively, decide that the test conditions are faulty. This does not mean, however, that these central hypotheses cannot be rationally called into question. Objections can be raised on the basis of a direct clash of presuppositions. And though Tibbetts seems to misunderstand its significance, this is precisely the kind of objection raised by the exponents of a humanistic sociology. Logically, prior to demanding the use of "free-will talk" per se, the humanistic presupposition of voluntarism demands the recognition of two fundamental conceptual necessities in analysing human activities: people as agents constitute the basic units of sociological explanation, and rationality constitutes a basic principle of order alongside chains of causes and effects. Neither "necessity" is overtly recognized by the method of science tied to "causal-deterministic talk." Thus, more than "preference" comes into play in the substitution of one language for the other.

In discussing the physicalist version of the unified language thesis, Tibbetts correctly suggests that a humanistic sociology has nothing to fear from positivism, since it "never said that the 'subject matter' of sociology is reducible to... individual psychology... animal biology, neurophysiology and organic chemistry." This, he says, "would have been too metaphysical a claim for any logical positivist to assert." Erroneously, however, he goes on to conclude: "If there is an elimination here it is not of humans per se (whatever that would mean) but of one type of descriptive predicates in favour of another" (1982: 192-93). But in weeding out certain descriptive predicates, positivists do eliminate humans (as that term is commonly understood) from their investigations. As pointed out in the Introduction, Chapter III and the first part of this chapter, positivists do make metaphysical claims. On the basis of a priori and epistemological grounds they assert informative propositions about the stuff of human behaviour. They reduce the individual to the intersection of determined systems of behaviour.

Humanists, as noted, do not deny the existence or importance of such determined systems. They simply assert that the full explanation of human action requires the use of a more substantive notion of the self.[7] No doubt the attempt to differentiate this self definitively from systems of biological, psychic, and social variables, leads into an interminable philosophical analysis (see Chapter VII for some discussion of this point). But such a feat of definition is no more imperative for the humanistic outlook than the conclusive formulation of the nature of empirical "facts" is for the positivist position. Selves may not be fully knowable, but this does not mean their reality can be discounted in entirety, at any point, in the explanation of human actions.

In point of fact, in *Rational Economic Man*, Hollis and Nell demonstrate that an assumption of rational human agency underlies the most rudimentary predictions of a positivist social science like neo-Classical ecomonics. Yet no direct portrait of this agent is given by such a science: no attempt is made to justify this most operationally imperative of all *ceteris paribus* clauses. None can be given. For the necessary presumption that there are rational economic agents cannot be formulated within the positivist framework (i.e., linguistic grid). It is, Hollis speculates, in all probability, a synthetic a priori truth. Nevertheless, Hollis and Nell argue, the rational agent assumption is the ingredient in the positivist formulation of general social scientific laws that does the real work of "buckling theory to facts."

A social science must be able to claim that its theories embody certain general truths about the functioning of institutions, typical consumers, or whatever. It must be possible to deduce which observed processes or tendencies can be projected into the future, can be hypothesized as lawlike. In the last analysis, this calls for a solution to the problem of induction. But overlooking this hurdle, the positivist notion of a general law presents us with a more immediate difficulty. Hollis and Nell pinpoint the problem as follows (1975: 86):

> The positivist notion of 'general law' strikes us as unsatisfactory, since it conflates two distinct problems. One is that of determining the form of the functional relations between variables; the other is that of deciding the scope of their application. *Prima facie...* there is a distinction between the properties which a scientist finds to be interrelated and the objects or agents which bear those properties. ... The question is whether this distinction is genuine or relevant. The positivist holds, and must hold, that it is not. He takes all laws to assert only correlations between variables. ... The formulation conjures bearers of variables out of existence....

The positivist model of a lawlike operation, expressed either in symbols or words, is a model of the action of a rational agent. But

it is formulated in abstraction from the agent (e.g., in economic
theory, the rational consumer does not appear in the formulation
of utility functions, describing his or her relative preferences). The
agent appears only when questions of application are raised. "In
other words, the formulation is doing no work whatever and the
burden is wholly carried by its interpretation. The formulation is
in no sense an analysis of the statement of law" (1975: 88). For in
the positivist scheme, statements of law are statements of regular
but contingent connections (i.e., synthetic statements).

Further, the positivist conception of lawlike hypotheses dis-
guises the effects which the range of application of a theory can
have on its formulation. By assimilating "the ascription of properties of bearers of variables to the specification of relations between
variables... [the positivist] presupposes implausibly that all differences between theories in range and type of subjects they apply to
can be fully expressed in the choice of variables and their range of
value" (1975: 96).

Positivists do not recognize the necessity of developing an independent and explicit formulation of the rational agency model
undergirding social sciences, since an agentless formulation of general laws "accords well with the idea that causal relations are reducible to concomitant variations between atomic states of the
world" (1975: 86). Essential economic concepts like production,
consumption or exchange, however, are not atomic states of the
world. Few social phenomena are brute facts. The reason "is
that [these] terms range over the activities of economic agents-
producers, consumers and traders."

> These activities are interconnected both in the practical sense that their
> performance depends upon expectations about and reactions to other
> related activities and in the conceptual sense that description presup-
> poses a certain allocation of social roles. ... Basic economic terms apply
> to agents who would not be agents unless they had dispositions and,
> furthermore, dispositions which can be described only by reference to
> the surrounding system (1975: 108).

In other words, in the language of a humanistic sociology: social scientific analysis entails a double hermeneutic—social phenomena are preinterpreted relations which cannot be properly compre-
hended without the infusion of some ordinary language meanings
into the technical metalanguages of the various disciplines. Therefore, the paradigmatic assumptions of the causal-deterministic language grid are insufficient for any true 'social' science.

Responding to Lemke, Shevach, and Wells' criticism of his argument. Tibbetts reasserts that the choice of "frames for conceptualizing human actions" is "dictated to a large extent by *extrascientific* considerations and is arbitrarily stipulated. In other words, the choice is logically independent of, rather than necessitated by, the explanatory frame in question" (1984: 98-99). But now it can be seen that this conclusion poses a number of problems.

Tibbetts, for instance, concludes his discussion of the positivism-humanism debate with a call to recognize the "significant parallels and even convergences between these two complementary frameworks of analysis" (1982: 196). But if all is arbitrary (incommensurable?), can there be any real convergence? Also, if decisionism is the order of the day, is not all talk of science (and epistemology) out of place? If not, then how are the considerations affecting the choice of semantic grids to be deemed "extrascientific" when the criteria in question constitute, pragmatically, the defining features of scientifically acceptable method? And in light of our heightened appreciation of the essentially circular and infinitely regressive character of the assumptions undergirding our models of science, what can it mean to claim that the criteria determining grid choice are logically independent of the explanatory frame in question? Tibbetts' ambivalent pragmatism does not allow for such a possibility, while his ambivalent positivism cannot support it.

Hollis would suggest that *the* condition determining grid choice is the a priori necessity of conceptualizing human action with a model of rational agency. Conforming to Tibbetts' epistemological desires, this condition is not necessitated by the explanatory frame in question, if by this Tibbetts means the linguistic grid in question. Rather it is the condition that necessitates the use of the free-will talk grid. If by the explanatory frame in question, however, Tibbetts means the field of human action, then contrary to his desires this condition is necessitated by the explanatory frame in question. The principle of rational human agency, in other words, is perhaps one of those "unique ways of conceptualizing domains of experience" to which Hollis refers in speaking of the attractions of adopting a qualified idealist approach to the question of necessity. Whether one wishes to dress such an insight in its full Kantian garb or not, it does seem clear that it is hardly adequate to characterize our choice of linguistic grids for the analysis of human action as "largely arbitrary."

Soft positivism with a pragmatist slant, then does not pose a serious threat to Hollis' project. The metaphysics of human rationality and freedom are an essential part, whether one chooses to recognize it or not, of the conceptual infrastructure of the social sciences. Or at least such is the case for conceptions of the social scientific process which still rest, like Tibbetts', on what amounts to a Humean philosophic base.

Soft Positivism with an Empiricist Slant

The theory of knowledge sketched in Ernest Gellner's *Legitimation of Belief* presents a more formidable challenge to Hollis' reading of the methodological options open to the student of social action. Gellner, like Hollis, looks more to Kant than to Hume. Yet with a twist not considered by Hollis, he uses an epistemological approach to the question of necessity to, in effect, radicalize the positivist mode of explanation. Tracing the origins of the present standards of knowledge, in a highly innovative manner, he argues that we have no recourse but to accept the deterministic and dehumanizing implications of a new style empiricism.

The modern confrontation with the problems of the infinite regress of premises and circularity should lead one, Gellner reasons, to the fact that epistemologies are not so much descriptions of the nature of cognition as prescriptions for the habits of cognition. The operationalization of the dominant epistemological principle of our day, empiricism–in the form of Skinnerian behaviourism–has demonstrated strikingly how feeble theories of knowledge are if taken literally as descriptions. And this state of affairs, Gellner dryly observes, cannot simply be read as evidence for the unique vulnerability of behaviourism, since "no one has [even attempted to do] for Hegel what Skinner endeavored to do for Hume...." What is important to remember is that "the failure... of such models as explanations, does not exclude their usefulness or validity as 'Norms,' as charters of cognitive practices" (Gellner, 1974: 35).

Gellner suggests that over the last three hundred years philosophy has attempted to come to grips with the bind of circularity in two ways. These ways he calls "re-endorsement theories" and "selector theories." By way of definition he offers the following comments:

> Re-endorsement theories are those which, after profound reflection, reach the conclusion that all is well with the existing bank of beliefs.

or at least with a substantial part of it, simply in virtue of it "being" the existing bank of beliefs....but above all, they endorse ⌊existing beliefs⌋ *qua* correct beliefs, not in virtue of satisfying some unique criterion imposed from outside....

By contrast, selector theories set up some criterion, some touchstone or sifter, which is to sort out the cognitive sheep from the goats. It is of the essence of this approach that the principle of selection claims to be independent of the current and local set of beliefs, to stand outside them and to be endowed with an authority external to that set.... (Gellner, 1974: 47).

As Gellner emphasizes, "the really important difference between the two species is not the nature of the conclusion, but the manner in which it is reached" (Gellner, 1974: 47).

Under re-endorsement theories Gellner groups all species of relativism, evolutionism, and what he calls negative re-endorsements (views which argue that our existing beliefs would be essentially correct with the removal of some "big error," e.g., the influence of class interests or the bewitchment of language). Under selector theories he lists three approaches: empiricism, materialism, and philosophies of logical form. Or as he more commonly refers to them in his text: the Ghost, the Machine, and the Skeleton.

After scrutinizing each of these positions, Gellner gives his vote of confidence to the selectors. He makes one exception, however, the skeletonism of Russell and the early Wittgenstein, which is dismissed as a misguided pursuit of the right approach through the wrong means.

By the Ghost Gellner means empiricism. Empiricism asserts that "a claim to knowledge is legitimate only if it can be justified in terms of experience." By the Machine Gellner has in mind materialism "(alias mechanism, or structuralism, with other possible variant names)." Materialism asserts that "a claim to knowledge is legitimate only if it is a specification of a publicly reproducible structure" (Gellner, 1974: 56). It is these two epistemological principles that have shaped the world of science in particular and hence the modern world in general. In *Legitimation of Belief*, Gellner demonstrates that these two principles have been both ideological and historical "allies" and "enemies." Despite their historical antipathy, however, their systematic convergence and application in Western society has proved quite disastrous to the inherited traditional worldview.

To simplify a complicated situation, it might be said that these two criteria have come into conflict over the question of determinism. The conflict stems from the fact that the Ghost lends itself to a radical idealism and subjectivism, whereas the Machine entails an equally radical realism and objectivism. Ultimately the Ghost humanizes life by granting a certain root autonomy to human experience and action, whereas machine-like explanations of phenomena dehumanize the world by their very nature. Adherence to the Machine leads to a full recognition of the problem of the "incompatibility of cognition and identity" (Gellner, 1974: 101). But in the last analysis, Gellner argues, this is a tension that we must and are learning to live with (1974: 106):

> There is no escape: it is not the content, the *kind* of explanation which dehumanizes us: it is "any" genuine explanation, as such, that does it. The sooner we realize this, the sooner we shall seek no further spurious escapes.

Only views of the world holding to this insight, exercising the inhuman "selector" capacity of the Machine, can escape the circular self-validation by which Gellner pejoratively identifies "ideologies" (Gellner 1974: 204).

Now Gellner's structuralism is not completely free of circularity, as he freely acknowledges. Formally, he asserts, the problem of infinite regress of premises and circularity is insoluble. Practically, however, with the loss of the authority of traditional norms, we must make do with the best solution available; and re-endorsement theories will not do. In the words of Gellner, they are "all-too-benign judges" of our beliefs. They are flagrantly circular and "covertly" normative. But most of all, by evading the specification of a positive criterion of truth they foster a normative and cognitive relativism that is detrimental to the advancement of our understanding of the world. Ultimately, Gellner asserts, "it simply will not do to say that because the attempts at 'reducing' the 3-D [(dimensional)] world to a 2-D one has failed, therefore the 3-D world, the *Lebenswelt*, must be taken as given" (Gellner, 1974: 53).

Moreover, the Machine orientation to 'form' of explanation has dovetailed with the Ghost orientation to the 'content' of knowledge. And in his opinion, "the empiricist identification of 'experience' as the ultimate, crucial, and in the end perhaps unique judge," cuts the Gordian knot of circularity and renders epistemology "overtly" normative in the best possible way. Flatly stated, the norm of 'experience' prevents a vicious circularity because "this judge is less corruptible than the others, less liable to

be secretly in the pay of this vision or that, even if we do not accept the myth of his total purity" (Gellner, 1974: 109). Thus the
Ghost comes to the rescue of the Machine. Gellner is careful to
point out, however, that the convergence of the Machine and the
Ghost is in large measure the product of a certain pervasive utilitarian bent in the West. This not altogether explicable bent has
served to free the Ghost of its most solipsistic and quietistic implications (unlike the East where it was precisely these implications
that were philosophically developed) (Gellner, 1974: 113-18).

The triumph of the Ghost and the Machine has habituated
us to apply certain rigorous standards to theories, concepts, and
assertions which have markedly altered the character of our patterns of thought. One may be less enthusiastic than Gellner about
the merits of the world which has resulted from the dominance of
these principles. But there is no doubting the depth and breadth
of the changes the Ghost and the Machine have introduced and
the uniqueness of the *Weltanschauung* they undergird. Stressing
this Gellner warns:

> The world of regular, morally neutral, magically un-manipulable
> fact, which some of us are now in danger of taking too much for granted,
> and which is presupposed by science, is in fact not at all self-evident.
> Far from representing some kind of normality, a natural starting-point,
> historically it is a great oddity. It is separated from most or all other
> worlds in which men have lived by a profound chasm (Gellner, 1974:
> 180).

In Gellner's eyes, Kant defined "rationality" for the modern
world by perfecting the epistemic and ethical convergence of the
Ghost and the Machine. Yet ironically, Kant accomplished this
great task because he was "simultaneously inspired by two fears
(1974: 185):

> The first fear is that the mechanical vision does 'not' hold; the second
> fear is that it 'does.' ... If the machine hypothesis does not hold, then
> science is impossible—for science is based on the assumption that genuine
> explanations are available and are there to be found. ... if the machine
> hypothesis does hold, then... human freedom, responsibility 'and' the
> attribution of validity to our own thought, all fly out the window. Either
> way, disaster.

The great virtue of the Kantian opus, however, is that "Kant
never stooped to the silly supposition that accepting either one of
the two disasters would evade the other. He attempted to prevent
both" (1974:185). It is Kant who foremostly showed that the world

is necessarily an ordered thing for humanity. Things must be "rule-bound in their behaviour" in order that we might distinguish the most essential contrast in sequences: objective sequences which happen to the world and subjective sequences which happen to the perceiver of the world. The telling insight of Kant, though, is that the basically mechanistic order used to draw this distinction is not in the world to be seen but rather is imposed on the world by the act of seeing. The restrictions which exist in the structure of reality are the a priori restrictions present in our powers of conceptualization. " 'We' are constrained. not nature" (Gellner, 1974: 187). There is room for freedom in this world, then, Kant reasons, as we the imposers of order may grant ourselves a partial exemption from the cold regularity of reality. Experience in its broadest sense supersedes all else.

This is "a desperate remedy." Gellner concedes, justified only by the great need to preserve the absolute minimum of that "which gives meaning to our lives." and made possible only by "the previous discovery that causal necessity was man-made." It is a remedy made palpable to Gellner, it seems. by Kant's "scrupulous fastidiousness" (1974: 187).

> Valuation, obligation, validity of thought, freedom – these were the kinds of minimal equipment, for Kant, which needed to be saved from the encroachment of the mechanical world if we were to remain human. What is remarkable about him as a thinker is not that he tried to save them, but that he tried to save so little. His severe restraint stands in contrast with the greed or self-indulgence of later thinkers who faced the same predicament.

But Kant, Gellner concludes. was ultimately mistaken "in supposing that he was dealing with a universal human predicament rather than a historically specific one" (1974: 188). Max Weber corrected this state of affairs by arguing that the "rational vision" was but a necessary condition and consequence of Western civilization (particularly modern industrial capitalism). And as a sociologist and historian of vast erudition he recognized. perhaps more fully than Kant, that "we are doomed to the rational vision" at the heart of the civilization to which we are wed. To which Gellner adds, if we wish our "explanations" to bear power then we must accept the iron cage of this imperfect rationality. We must acknowledge that "the price of real knowledge is that our identities, freedom, norms. are no longer underwritten by our vision and comprehension of things. On the contrary we are doomed to suffer from a tension between cognition and identity" (1974: 207).

Hollis is in full agreement with this diagnosis of our present epistemological lot. But of course he rejects the kind of resignation or. to put a better face on it, stoicism which Gellner appears to be advocating in the face of the disjunction of modern modes of self-understanding and understanding of the world. There is a ring of historical and personal accuracy to Gellner's argument for the overriding influence of the epistemic principles of empiricism and materialism-structuralism on our theoretical and daily conceptions of "rational" thought and action. Yet we cannot help but be nagged by our strong intuitions of human freedom and the threatening sense of constriction which surrounds the use of the Ghost and the Machine alone to sift the truth from the welter of human experience. Therefore. even though neither Gellner's empiricism nor Hollis' idealism can be recommended with certainty. for they are after all but prescriptions for the habits of cognition. I think that for practical reasons Hollis' prescription provides a more enlightened foundation for the study of human social and particularly religious action.

In the closing pages of *Legitimation of Belief* Gellner effectively summarizes his position with the colourful imagery of a raft adrift at sea (1974: 206-08).

> If we adopt the simile of shipwreck, we might say that Descartes made the mistake of supposing that, when the old ship sank, a really reliable and seaworthy new one could be found. In truth, there is flotsam floating about. and it does not seem that any one piece of it will carry our weight. But some bits are better than others, and some jointly, when lashed together. will make a passable raft.

His own raft. Gellner goes on to say. consists of four planks: (1) the Ghost and (2) the Machine. (3) a recognition of the limited truth of cultural relativism. and (4) a "truncated evolutionism" which is concerned "not with the 'development of all things.' but with the specific development of the industrial civilization to which we are ineluctably wedded." Hollis could join Gellner on this raft. but he would bring along a fifth plank which both changes the overall configuration of the raft and the relative importance of each of its planks. This fifth plank. which would cushion the impact of the first two. would consist of the proposition that not all tautologies are empty (see Hollis. 1977: 61-65: outlined earlier in this chapter). In other words. while the selectors have proved to be very useful devices for sorting out the wheat from the chaff in the pursuit of reliable knowledge. there are certain root ideas. (e.g..

rational human agency), definitive of specific realms of discourse
(e.g., the analysis of social action), which cannot be dispensed with
simply because they fail to conform to the dictates of the Ghost
and the Machine.

Displaying the wisdom of the post-positivist age, both Gellner and Hollis refrain from raising the old metaphysical issues,
of freedom and determinism or whatever, in the sense that they
circumvent making ontological claims. Ever conscious of the problems of circularity and infinite regress of premises, both hold to an
epistemological approach and identify their theories of knowledge
(i.e., methods of science) as "prescriptive." Nevertheless, there is
a descriptivist, or perhaps better a neo-descriptivist, component
and/or quality to both of their arguments. In Gellner's case the
sense of a descriptivist component is admittedly indirect. It is
created by his almost fatalistic attitude to the tension of cognition
and identity and the stridency of his advocacy of the Ghost and
the Machine over all other possible epistemic principles when he
knows full well that there is no sure argument for his case. In the
case of Hollis matters are more straightforward, since he actually
entertains the idea that at the base of every analytical framework
there are sets of assumptions which are probably best treated, if
their apparent necessity holds up under a thorough scrutiny, as
"real definitions." In a sense then, the difference in the two positions can be characterized as a difference in the relative weight
given to the prescriptivist and descriptivist components in theories
of knowledge. This distinction becomes muddled however, when
one considers that Hollis thinks he is isolating a priori synthetic
truths when he uncovers a discipline's base assumptions. But as
will eventually be argued. I think it is possible to accept the gist
of Hollis' perspective without dressing it in its full Kantian garb.
The bottom line is to believe that some premises, like rational
human agency, while ultimately perhaps prescriptivist in nature,
deservedly enjoy at present and for the forseeable future a certain almost objective status (i.e., they are pervasive and clearly
nonarbitrary).

The ideas being bandied about at this juncture could well be
drawn up, for example, into the vortex of debate surrounding
Kant's critiques of "pure" and "practical" reason. But such a
pursuit of the issues would neither suit my intended audience nor
my purpose. Thus like Hollis (and Gellner essentially). I will rest
content with a programmatic statement of theories of knowledge

which it is believed are best. Others may pursue the philosophical issues in greater depth. My attention will turn to the completion of the demonstration already begun of the relevance and feasibility of the argument from rationality as viewed from within the present problematic methodological frameworks of sociology and religious studies (i.e., developing the special thesis of the argument from rationality).

In closing I would simply note that Gellner's Kantian acknowledgement of human freedom remains too abstract. As Gellner's method of science operates with a strictly deterministic "linguistic grid," it seems to me that it must lead inevitably to the unwarranted neglect of human freedom as a significant and calculable factor in the affairs of humanity. It makes it too easy for less philosophically self-conscious social scientists to slip from a position of epistemological empiricism into one of *de facto* ontological determinism.

VII.
The Conditions of Autonomous Action: Social Species and Rational Self

The Special Thesis of the Argument From Rationality

In pointing to the reliance of micro-economics on an assumption of rational human agency the subject matter of the special thesis of the argument from rationality has already been raised. But to gain an accurate knowledge of the full nature, context, and significance of such assumptions in the social sciences, a more direct link must be established with the whole issue of incorporating human freedom into social analysis. First, though, the time has come to say a few more things about the meaning of the term freedom, in order to isolate a conceptual tension inherent to the notion which frames Hollis' examination of the place accorded to free agency in social analysis through role theory.

In *The Idea of Freedom* (1958), Mortimer Adler surveys the views of the great writers of the Western tradition and develops a typology of generic conceptions of freedom. His types are based on a "minimal topical agreement" amongst different groups of thinkers. Without subscribing to the details of his analysis (especially not his interpretation and grouping of specific authors), it is enlightening to cite his typology because it provides a quick insight into the parameters of the idea. According to Adler there are three main conceptions of freedom (1958: 606):

Circumstantial Freedom of Self-Realization: To be free is to be able under favourable circumstances, to act as one wishes for one's own individual good as one sees it.

Acquired Freedom of Self-Perfection: To be free is to be able, through acquired virtue or wisdom, to will or live as one ought in conformity to the moral law or an ideal befitting human nature.

Natural Freedom of Self-Determination: To be free is to be able, by a power inherent in human nature, to change one's own character creatively by deciding for oneself what one shall do or become.

In shorthand one might classify these views as the Liberal, Classical, and Existential. But as Adler cautions, none of these types is exclusive to any one author or period. Therefore no attempt will be made to align Hollis with one of the types. Yet the features of each type and the contrasts between them are productively noted for many of them have already been encountered and will be encountered further in the discussions undertaken here.

What is of more immediate value is Adler's further distillation of that which is general to all three understandings of freedom (1958: 614):

> A man is free who has in himself the ability or power whereby he can make what he does his own action and what he achieves his own property.

This definition conforms closely to Hollis' conception (see the introductory comments to Chapter IV). It also pinpoints two features of the idea of freedom which generate a great deal of conceptual ambiguity because of their apparent incompatibility: features which Hollis has tried to reconcile better with the argument from rationality.

First, the definition makes it clear that to be free is "to be the active source of what one does or becomes, and not a passive subject acted on by another" (1958: 615). Adler comments that this "explains the sense in which the words 'independence' and 'autonomy' are so frequently used as synonyms for 'liberty' or 'freedom' " (1958: 613). Second, and in apparent opposition to this theme of autonomy, the freedom under consideration is that of a finite being, and hence the independence in question is "relative" (or 'relational').[1] Only the freedom of an infinite being is complete or absolute. All finite conceptions involve a relationship of self and other (for the divine there is no true other), and the essential difference between authors writing about freedom lies with the question: How limited by, or dependent upon, the other can the self be and still be called free? (This question, note, is simply the obverse of the one underlying the two sociologies conflict.[2])

In sociology this conceptual ambiguity is expressed in terms of the tension between the autonomy of the individual and the process of socialization. "At least from the time of Descartes," Bernard Dauenhauer points out, "there has been a growing tendency to understand freedom in terms of autonomy" (1982: 77).[3] In line with the political philosophy of the liberal-democratic age, the idea of freedom has been identified with a view of humans as discrete individuals. Advances in sociology, however, have led to a growing appreciation of the highly social nature of human existence, and this view has undercut the social contract theories with their "pacts among fully-fledged pre-social individuals already blessed with conscious goals and a language for planning how to achieve them" (Hollis, 1977: 69). Humans are not the radically independent creatures presupposed by the doctrine of freedom underlying the contract theories of Hobbes, Locke, Rousseau, and today Rawls. Yet some measure of autonomy is clearly essential both to the idea of freedom and that of human efficacy.

Hollis struggles to break free of this dilemma by arguing four points. First, by means of an examination of sociological role theory he pinpoints a space for a free self in a picture of social reality that takes proper account of social facts. Second, he posits an identity for a free self which can be inserted into this space. The identity in question is not prior to the stock of characters provided by society, yet it is nevertheless not identical with the characters assumed by an individual. Third, having set the social stage, as Hollis says, and distinguished the actors from the characters they play, he anchors the actions of the actors (i.e., the free selves) in a non-causal mode of explanation based on reasons for actions. Fourth, he provides a justification for this mode of explanation by establishing our cognitive dependency on an assumption of the epistemological unity of humankind. This assumption constitutes an ideal limit to the infinite regress of causes and hence a sufficient foundation for at least starting all social analyses from the perspective of the humanistic presupposition of voluntarism.

The first two of these points will be delineated in this chapter, and the last two in the next. The points of Hollis' arguments are interdependent, however, and hence the two chapters overlap each other at points. Further, in order to situate Hollis' ideas in a wider context, the discussion presented departs at points from the steps of Hollis' argument and calls upon the views of others.

Role Theory as Explanation

Hollis turns to the dramaturgical analogy employed by sociological role theory to draw out the problem of the tension between
autonomy and socialization in all its suggestiveness. The influential notion that society is a stage on which actors play diverse
roles in the scenario of actions that is life appears to lend itself,
he notes, to both passive and active conceptions of humanity. It is
rarely recognized, however, that for the theory to provide complete
explanations it is necessary to make a consistent choice between
these readings of the human condition. Nevertheless, a consistent
choice is rare, perhaps because it is perceived that either option
poses serious methodological problems for role theory.

For the purpose at hand it will suffice to state that roles are sets
of normative expectations attached to social positions. In Hollis'
words, "positions are the static and roles the dynamic aspect of
a normative classification of social actors" (1977: 71). Roles are
the point of intersection between the individual and society. hence
to the role theorist they are the mechanism by which human in-
teractions are orchestrated. Human acts are given their meaning
and configuration by the roles they are associated with. But role
theory is not explicitly deterministic.

Depending on where the stress is laid the dramaturgical analogy can be used to foster the image of either "Autonomous Man"
or "Plastic Man". Autonomy is suggested if the stress falls on the
notion of the actor "who dons and doffs the mask. is wholly distinct from the *dramatis persona* and owes no part of his identity to
the stage." Social plasticity and passivity is suggested if the stress
falls on the notion of characters. with the actors presumed to be
but characters in the larger play of their own lives. their identities
and behaviour programmed by a script they did not write (1977:
72). Of course neither stress in itself is faithful to the intentions of
role theory. The value of making roles central to explaining social
life lies with taking advantage of the descriptive properties of both
notions. thereby overcoming (at least superficially) the dichotomy
of sociologies of social systems and social agents. When pressed,
however. the opaqueness of the imagery must give way to a choice
between whether actors create roles or roles create actors.

It might be thought that the dramaturgical analogy clearly
indicates the former. If the analogy is taken seriously. though. the
matter remains ambiguous. for as Hollis observes: "The mark of

great acting is that the character lives in the actor and becomes part of his self-image. The actor does not so much impersonate the character as personify him" (1977: 72). It is surely a poor actor who does not owe some important part of his or her personal identity to the characters played on one stage or another.

All the same, the thespian model does quite literally call attention to the fact that every performance, social or otherwise, is the product of the collaboration of two elements: a character and an actor. Even the most passive version of role theory must take this fact into account in the form of concepts like role-distance, if only to allow for innovation and to explain those emergent developments and qualities in a social drama for which there is no scripted reason. Active or agent oriented versions of role theory are obliged to do more: they must provide a positive sense of the self which is distinct from the social roles it portrays. But in either case, a normative explanation does not provide a complete explanation unless it is backed up with an assertion about the nature of the self.

As Hollis outlines (1977: 77):

> An action A has a normative explanation... in so far as
> (1) The agent occupied a position with a role R requiring A
> (2) The agent knew that R required A
> (3) The agent did A because of (1) and (2).

At each step of this argument there are objections that can be raised which require the inquirer to commit himself to either a passive or autonomous understanding of human nature. In the first place, "a single role rarely requires a unique course of action and, even when it does, there is often more than one way of discharging the duty." Therefore, the first premise must be reformulated as "the agent occupied positions with roles $R_1,... R_j$, requiring A." This indicates that an action is really the result of a kind of "role algebra" whereby the indeterminancy of individual roles is rendered determinant in combination (1977: 77-78). It can still be objected, however, that the first premise of the argument "holds usefully only if the agent has a consistent set of roles. Otherwise it holds vacuously, in the sense that an inconsistent $R_1,... R_j$ require A but also require not-A. ... Role conflict being endemic, we can be charged with backing a sure loser." In reality people cope with role conflict through recourse to "sorting devices like immediacy, hierarchy and severity of sanctions." But, Hollis concludes (1977: 80):

[the] rebuttal is not wholly convincing and an implied view of human nature which had men always behaving consistently within consistently ordered role-sets would strike us as most fanciful. It seems wiser to recognize some limit to the scope of normative explanation, while also some internal ordering. The limit can either be descriptive or, so to speak, prescriptive. In other words we can grant that not all socially significant action does have a normative explanation and then treat the fact either as an invitation to add to the list of elementary forms or as a clue to the art of increasing human autonomy.

Along similar lines it can be objected that the second premise of the argument is also too restrictive or idealistic. It requires that an agent 'know' just what it is that his roles oblige him to do. "This makes the schema apply only to agents who are wholly socialized or wholly rational. That seems to exclude most of mankind" (1977: 80). Methodologically, Hollis suggests, the objection can be parried by arguing that "the idea is to set up two ideal types of agent whose conduct has a normative explanation and then to explain departures in part by their degree of approximation" (1977: 80). It must be crucially realized, however, that highly socialized and highly rational agents stand in a different relation to the norms which guide their actions.

The difference in question comes to the fore in Hollis' comments on the concluding statement of a normative explanation (1977: 77):

It will be seen that the third clause is obscure and is doing too much work. The 'because' in it is ambiguous between reason and motive and fails to make clear the step from (1) and (2) to the doing of A. We can read it as asserting that (1) and (2) caused him to do A in that he was so well socialized that he always acted on a normative syllogism with true premises. This makes (3) into a statement of motive, where motive is so defined as to suit a passive conception of man. But, alternatively, we can treat (1) and (2) as reasons for doing A which apply to this particular agent and (3) as asserting that these reasons were his reasons. This reading leaves his motives enigmatic, the subject of a further and different enquiry.

In the end, then, we have the rather paradoxical state where if a normative explanation is to be a complete explanation it must assume a passive *homo sociologicus*, and this is what most of the advocates of role theory have, implicitly at least, done. Yet such a passive account undercuts one of the most appealing features of role theory, relative to other sociological approaches–the dramaturgical analogy. Moreover, the passive solution does not in the last analysis render matters more certain. It too represents but a metaphysical postulate necessitated only because it figures in the resolution of a theoretical problem. Also, as indicated, it resolves the one problem only to pose another: how is social innovation and change to be accounted for?

But on the other hand, if one attempts to hold true to the distinction between actor and characters, normative explanations become incomplete. "Autonomous Man" takes the social stage as a character and assumes the norms associated with the character. But the autonomous social actor is distinct from the role he or she is playing, and the "legitimating reasons" supplied for the actions of the character "are not automatically his reasons. To be precise, they are his reasons for the choice of means, granted that he has reason or motive to achieve the character's proper ends." In the social world, however, we cannot even be sure that the reasons supplied to the character count as reasons for the choice of means to an end if we do not know something about the agent's "real reasons." It is possible, Hollis observes, for the actor to wish on the character the legitimate means which best suit the actor. But we cannot know unless we have access to the actor's "real reasons." As Hollis surmises, "Autonomous Man needs distance and hence a gap between accounting for himself and accounting to himself." But, if the gap between professed reasons and real reasons is "impassable," from the perspective of the outside inquirer, it is not possible to draw any clear conclusions from an agent's mere fulfillment of a role (1977: 81-85).

Role theory, Hollis states metaphorically, can fashion a cap which fits the actor in a social drama but it cannot answer the question, "Was he wearing it?" (1977: 81). To answer this question Hollis takes a most unexpected tack. He tries to close the gap between professed reasons and real reasons "by arguing that there are no criteria for the agent's identity, if all roles are played without commitment" (1977: 85).

Autonomy and Socialization

To understand this statement and to perceive precisely how it provides a foundation for identifying certain actions as essentially free, it is necessary to grasp a very complicated and really rather round-about line of argument advanced by Hollis. The central principles of his ingenious response to what he calls "the strange lacuna in role theory" (1977: 88) can be presented, however, in a more streamlined manner. Hollis' own account veers-off at several junctures into philosophical debates which do much to illuminate the philosophical context of his discussion. But these debates can be circumvented since the conclusive resolution of the issues raised (if possible at all) requires a plunge "deep into epistemology" which Hollis himself declines in favour of a more modest, indirect, and practical approach (1977: 97-98). Hollis' search for the actors to undergird an actionist reading of the social drama will be approached through a two step analysis. First, an effort will be made to sketch the broad outline and rationale for the special thesis of the argument from rationality. Hollis' presentation will be simplified by demonstrating how his ideas fit with, and in fact represent a logical advance on, a recent reiteration of the autonomy and socialization debate in the pages of *Mind*. This much will be done in the present chapter. In the next chapter, a thorough examination will be undertaken of the logic behind Hollis' conception of rationality and its place in the study of human action.

Hollis opens the fifth chapter of *Models of Man* with the following observation (1977: 88):

> Admirers of Goffman... are well served with nuanced, cooly sardonic tales of how actors in the life-world play their parts with varying styles and skill, at varying degrees of distance and for varying ends. Interactions are far from mechanical and the actor can keep control of them by means of secondary adjustments, distancing rituals and elusive negotiations. If he succeeds, he has an identity not merely defined for him or thrust upon him; and this identity is crucial in understanding and explaining his conduct. Although 'identity' here is in part a set of attributes, it refers also to a subject or substance who manipulates his attributes and his *Umwelt*. Hence Goffman owes us a theory of self as subject, something more robust than a notional we-know-not-what, to sustain the active base for its social transactions. Notoriously the debt goes unpaid.

A similar state of affairs is encountered with regard to the pure individualism of classical utilitarian and liberal theory. Traditional social and political theorists, however, did recognize the need to found their conceptions of rational human agency in suppositions about our ultimate interests as derived from our essential human nature. "They held," Hollis states, "that whatever constitutes us human beings is *pro tanto* something we have good reason to preserve and foster by our actions" (1977: 100). The speculative mode of their claims, though, are no longer acceptable. From a contemporary scientific perspective the traditional theorists have also left a debt unpaid.

Even so, taking his cue from traditional political theory, Hollis proposes an ambitious thesis about autonomy (1977: 101):

> An autonomous man acts freely by definition. He acts freely, only if he has good reasons for what he does (and no better reasons for doing something else). He has good reasons, only if he acts in his ultimate interests. His ultimate interests derive from what he essentially is. What he essentially is depends partly on what is essential to his being any person and partly on what is essential to his being that particular person. The thesis will be defended [later] but its ambitions are vain unless the concept of 'what he essentially is' is, so to speak, load-bearing. I shall try to show... that the load requires strict criteria of identity for persons, criteria which let the self stand outside the [social] construction.

By strict criteria of identity Hollis means criteria which cannot be satisfied by more than one candidate (1977: 90). Role theory, for example, does not employ strict criteria for it defines people in terms of sets of roles, without going so far as to entail the assumption that a person ceases to be him or herself if removed from his or her roles or, conversely, that any other person put into the same roles would become that person. Practically we do identify and differentiate people by the combinations of roles they occupy, but in principle this leaves what they are essentially a mystery.

Adopting a somewhat different procedure to that taken by Hollis,[4] the necessity of working with strict criteria of identity can be effectively drawn out through a summary of an exchange between Robert Young and Mark Bernstein. In an article entitled "Autonomy and Socialization" (1980). Young sets out a positive account of autonomy and argues that the processes of socialization do not represent "an insurmountable obstacle to our achievement of autonomy" (1980) 565). In a rebuttal entitled "Socialization and Autonomy" (1983). Bernstein acknowledges the value of Young's analysis but denies the viability of his conclusion.

Autonomy, Young proposes, depends upon the idea of a person's choices and actions being self-directed. "An individual's life is self-directed," he reasons, "insofar as he (or she) exercises his freedom so as to order his life according to a plan or conception which unifies and expresses his choices" (1980: 567). The key notion is that of authenticity. A person's decisions and actions must be expressive of his or her 'own' preferences. Yet clearly, Young recognizes, "the socialization and education we all undergo as children, adolescents and as adults develop in us the desires, tastes, opinions, ideals, goals, principles, values, preferences and so on which in turn determine how we feel, choose, act." Thus apparently, "our options are marked out for us well before it is meaningful to talk about our choosing to order our lives in accordance with a conception that expresses our will" (1980: 571). It is this state of affairs which leads Bernstein to conclude flatly that socialization "makes authenticity, and therefore autonomy, impossible" (1983: 120). This restriction, Young suggests however, can be circumvented.

A human life, Young argues, should be seen as a series of stages through which an ever-increasing sense of self is shaped by the actions of a present and partial self on a past and even more incomplete self. Between the two selves there is continuity and accidental change, but there is also the occasion for the kind of conscious change which is the foundation of autonomy. As studies have shown, in the United States, political orientations (party loyalties and so on) are established at a very early age. When in late adolescence or adulthood, however, a person is confronted by events (like the Vietnam war) which call into question the political values ingrained during primary socialization a critical and quite radical reorientation of convictions can take place. From this fact Young draws the conclusion that the power of socialization processes is relative to "the strategic significance of [our] awareness of our particular socialization."

Expanding on this insight, Young formulates the following thesis (1980: 573):

> The force of our socialization is apt to be clearest on those occasions when we recognize that, for example to satisfy certain important desires we entertain would involve risk or great sacrifice... or necessitate doing things to which we are averse.... In such cases we may accept that our socialization precludes our adopting our motivations *de novo*, but believe as well that we have the choice of making them our own by

identifying with them in our reflective judgings or rejecting them. Once privy to such awareness it does not matter so much how one came to have one's particular first-order desires, but whether or not on reflection one desires to have such desires.

Such a thesis is interesting, but as Bernstein surmises, it does not stymie the objections of any thorough-going socializationist. He simply argues that the only people who can engage in a self-scrutiny whereby hidden motivations are raised to consciousness and accepted or rejected are those whose socialization has conditioned them to the activity. What is more, the stances chosen by such individuals with regard to their newly appreciated motivations are also the direct consequent of socialization.

But an understanding of socialization along these lines, Young responds, entails a theory which is unrealistic because it too strongly assimilates socialization with a coercive process. Young only backs this reasonable qualification of the nature of socialization, though, with the weak observation that "there just do seem to be people who undergo processes (therapeutic or otherwise) of whom it would not be accurate to say that these processes were only made possible by their having been manipulated or coerced. Rather these processes depend on the agent's reflective powers" (1980: 576).

This rebuttal gives Bernstein no pause. No matter how enlightened an agent may be, he suggests, given the global nature of socialization, there is no way to be assured that the agent can make the motivational structure they have their own. All new knowledge, Bernstein asserts, is "just more grist for the socializationist mill. ... The socializationist can always continue his regress argument showing that higher vantage points add nothing to sheild" notions of autonomy, like Young's, against his attack (1983: 123).

Recognizing this state of affairs Hollis states that the attempt to work with "degrees of identity and individuality" plays too readily into the hands of the proponents of "Plastic Man". "Autonomous Man" still needs a strict principle of personal unity to halt the infinite regress of socializationist determinism. No philosopher has been able, however, to specify satisfactorily a set of strict criteria of identity. Therefore, Hollis proposes, a more audacious tack must be taken in support of the authenticity of some of the actions performed by an actor while in a role.

In examining role theory it was discovered that a full explanation is possible "only if the reasons for action which the agent has, because he was set a problem as the occupant of a set of social positions, are also his own reasons." For *homo sociologicus* this poses no problem as the identity of professed reasons and real reasons is assured. From this perspective even distance from one role simply means greater subjection to another. Where autonomy is assumed, however, it is anybody's guess whether the cap supplied by the normative structural theory is actually being worn by the actor, since it is impossible for us to be ever very certain about what is going on in the minds of others. Consequently, Hollis contends, if we wish to proceed at all we must assume that sometimes it is true that "what the character has good reason to do, the actor *eo ipso* also has good reason to do. Necessarily the autonomous actor must be himself in some of his characters" (1977: 103-104). Personal identity is inevitably encompassed by social identity, yet it is distinct because, Hollis stipulates, it consists of those roles which an actor has "rationally" consented to identify with. As Young's reference to the "reflective" judgements through which personal identity is constructed indicates but does not specifically pinpoint, the key to the objective foundation of authenticity is the *rationality* of an act.

> Physical actions individuate the agent by netting him into the space-time grid. But this [gives] us only a strict identity of bodies. ... when the individuating actions are essentially those of a character the agent has rationally become, we get a strict identity of particular persons. There are many kings of Ruritania but each does and is responsible for doing a unique set of kingly actions. When the actions are essentially kingly and autonomously those of a particular king, we have the missing relation. He is not just playing king nor is he passively following a script. His different actions are rationally his and also those of numerically the same king. On these terms he achieves a strict identity. No doubt it is always precarious but, while it lasts, it belongs to an active social self standing outside the [social] construction.

This strict, because rational, identity puts an end to the infinite regress of socialization just as the assumption of rational human agency in general terminates the regress of *ceteris paribus* clauses in most social scientific explanations.

But in what sense can a decision to conform to the given obligations of a role be considered rational? As Hollis admits, there is a formidable snag (1977: 104).

> Either the individuals [in the social contract situation] had real interests all along or they acquire them with their positions. The former option takes us back to pre-social atoms with, presumably, identical interests or presupposes a hidden prior contract to play the game which

results in the visible contract. The latter option makes us wonder how it could have been rational to agree to the visible contract. Since we want rational paths to self-realization, neither option is enticing.

Hollis, however, immediately offers a curious, though in light of Young's analysis, not totally unusual solution to this problem (1977: 105):

> My own view is that, despite the snag, real interests are acquired within a social contract. The initial choice of position, non-rational in prospect, can be rational in retrospect or, if irrational in retrospect, can be rationally corrected. A man can, I think, have good reason to be glad today that he got married yesterday without thereby having to have had good reason yesterday to be glad at his impending change of state.

Like Young, then, Hollis is also actually working with "degrees of identity and individuality," in the sense that he has tied human freedom to a dynamic understanding of the progressive attainment of individual self-definition (though, of course, Hollis did so prior to Young). Unlike Young, though, he has escaped the socializationist circle by anchoring this dynamic perspective in an alternative non-causal mode of explanation; one based on the principle that actions done for good reasons are self-explanatory. It is to the character of this alternative mode of explanation that our attention must now turn, taking up the issues that were left dangling in the first part of this study.

VIII.
Asymmetry in Modes of Explanation

Three Points to Be Clarified

The central and almost deceptively simple idea of the argument from rationality is the contention that true and rational beliefs and actions need one sort of explanation, false and irrational beliefs and actions another. With a touch of wit, Hollis illustrates the nature of this distinction in the following manner (1982: 75-76):

> In one of James Thurber's *Fables of Our Time* a man finds a unicorn browsing among the tulips in his garden. He informs his wife, who remarking with scorn that the unicorn is a mythical beast, summons the police and a psychiatrist, to have him certified. She tells them what he said, and they ask him to confirm it. 'Of course not,' he replies, 'the unicorn is a mythical beast.' So they shut her up in an institution and the man lives happily ever after. It seems patent that the truth of the various beliefs makes all the difference. If there actually was a unicorn in the garden, his belief is not certifiable. If he actually said that there was, her belief that he did needs no psychiatrist to explain it. The psychiatrist intervenes only where beliefs are false or irrational.

In relation to beliefs which refer to the contents of commonsense reality, we frequently trade upon an apparent asymmetry between the explanation of reasonable and unreasonable beliefs and actions. But can we generalize from this situation to instances where the objects of belief and action are not so obvious? Can religious beliefs and actions, for example, be discriminated on such a basis? Hollis' work suggests that, while things get complicated, we do inevitably draw distinctions along these lines [1]; and in slightly different ways, Alasdair MacIntyre (1971), Quentin Gibson (1976), and Michael Simon (1982) agree.

There was a time, MacIntyre notes (1971: 244), when it was in fashion to attempt to understand the history of human endeavor, and most especially the evolution of religious beliefs, in terms of an opposition between the rational and the irrational. Anthropologists such as Frazer and Tylor and intellectual historians such as W. E. H. Lecky and Dickson White, all assumed the validity of such a procedure. Of course the parochialism of these scholars, exemplified by their naive confidence in their own standards of rationality, led to the serious misdescription of other cultures. But in rightfully rejecting the work of these scholars, with its excessive reliance on the culture-bound concepts of the late Victorian age, contemporary critics have blinded themselves to the continued importance of ascriptions of rationality and irrationality in the human sciences.

To correct this situation, clarifying the continued viability of the principle of asymmetry in the study of human actions, three interrelated points must be established: (1) it is not possible to study actions in isolation from identifying beliefs; (2) explanations in terms of reasons cannot be satisfactorily translated into explanations in terms of causes; (3) in explaining an action in terms of reasons, if a full explanation is the objective, then there is no option to using an epistemic, as opposed to a merely practical or technically specific, standard of rationality.

Beliefs and Actions

In the essay "Rationality and the Explanation of Action" (1971). MacIntyre argues that social scientists must assess the rationality of beliefs since there are important differences in the modes of explanation logically appropriate for rational and irrational beliefs. Choosing a more conventional illustration than Hollis, he notes that Hugh Trevor-Roper may be able to explain the European witch-craze of the sixteenth and seventeenth centuries in terms of the venting of fears and anxieties brought on by social tensions stemming from religious conflicts. But a similar approach cannot be used to explain the contemporaneous acceptance, by most astronomers, of the existence of the moons of Jupiter. The latter belief is not "the outcome of antecedent events or states of affairs which are quite independent of any relevant process of appropriate deliberation." Rather, to explain belief in the moons of Jupiter, one must have recourse to the various canons of proof and discourse employed by scientists, and to the way in which Galileo's telescopic observations were judged, according to these canons, to provide rational grounds for belief.

Drawing a methodological conclusion from this comparison, MacIntyre states (1971: 247):

> ... the explanation of rational belief terminates with an account of the appropriate intellectual norms and procedures: the explanation of irrational belief must be in terms of causal generalizations which connect

antecedent conditions specified in terms of social structures or psychological states–or both–with the genesis of beliefs.

This statement is accurate as far as it goes. It falls short, however,
of adequately establishing the principle of asymmetry in modes of
explanation.

In the first place, as MacIntyre realized, a behaviourist could
acknowledge the distinction in question yet argue that ultimately
it is irrelevant. The social sciences concern themselves with the
study of actions and not beliefs and the former can be reductively
analysed in terms of overt behaviour and dispositions to behaviour.
Any reference to mental predicates can be eliminated and the difference between so-called rational and irrational phenomena can
be accounted for in terms of different causal sequences of prior behaviour and external events. Countering this reasoning, however,
MacIntyre points out that it is a central feature of actions, and
not just a contingent fact, that they are expressive of beliefs.[2]

> An action is identifiable as the action that it is only in terms of the
> agent's intention. An intention can only be specified in terms of a first-
> person statement. The expression used in formulating such a statement
> (even if the agent does not himself formulate it explicitly) will presup-
> pose certain beliefs on the agent's part. ... It is for this reason that it is
> possible to predicate of actions characteristics which it is in the province
> of logic to consider. An action may be consistent or inconsistent with
> another in terms of the beliefs presupposed. As Aristotle pointed out,
> an action may conclude a syllogistic argument in a way analogous to
> that in which the utterance of a statement may (1971: 253-54).

Human action cannot be understood merely as behaviour, especially when behaviour is conceived essentially in terms of bodily
movements. Most actions, it is true, are distinguished through
reference to some bodily movements. But not all movements are
actions (e.g., a sneeze) and any given action (e.g., playing a game)
may be associated with a diverse array of different types of bodily movements. In the words of Michael Simon, "there is more
than one way to skin a cat, but proper bodily movement description must pick out all the possible cat-skinning specifications if the
equivalence of action description and bodily movement description
is to be sustained" (1982: 8). Conversely, any one bodily movement may be indicative of a diverse array of actions. For example,
Simon observes, "removing one's eye-glasses in one situation may
be getting ready to fight, whereas in another it could be making
a bid in an auction." Therefore, it would seem that if actions are

to become the subject of a systematic account, they have to be
identified with descriptive predicates beyond those sufficient for
the delineation of bodily movements.

But this is not all. It also appears that "movements become
actions only when they are executed in appropriate contexts." Action descriptions, in other words, are relational. If we press matters, however, so are movement descriptions. What matters, then,
is not the relational nature of the two phenomena but the nature of the relations that shape the explanatory context of each
phenomenon. The impossibility of obtaining translations between
action descriptions and movement descriptions only negatively indicates that there is a difference between actions and behaviour.
A positive distinction is drawn between these two phenomena by
noting "the fact that an action involves somebody 'doing' something, whereas a bodily movement connotes merely a 'happening'
" (Simon, 1982: 10).

Accordingly, as MacIntyre states, what differentiates an action
is its intentional character. Indeed, in common speech it is precisely the intentional or unintentional nature of an activity which is
used to decide whether the activity is an instance of inaction (e.g.,
a deliberate silence) or mere inactivity. Extending the point, Hollis
points out, "how the phenomena of human life should be grouped,
what counts as doing the same or doing different, depends on the
intentions of the actor" (1977: 114). The classification of human
actions inevitably depends on consideration of the beliefs of actors.

Further, MacIntyre points out, the noncontingent connection
between beliefs and actions is demonstrated by the inability of the
behaviourist programme itself to account for the notion of 'belief'
(1971: 254):

> For all such accounts must, as their proponents allow, include reference
> to what they quaintly call "linguistic behaviour." More particularly, if
> they try to analyse the notion of belief in behavioural terms, then to
> say that someone believes that such and such is the case will have to be
> analysed not only in terms of dispositions to do and to expect certain
> things, but also in terms of dispositions to say certain things. What sort
> of disposition to say will be involved? The answer must be a disposition
> to make assertions. But what is an assertion? It is the utterance of a
> statement in such a way as to give a hearer or reader to understand
> that the statement is believed by the speaker or writer and is worthy
> of belief. Thus, the notion of belief has not been analysed away into
> behavioural terms, for the notion of assertion—which any analysis which
> sought to be convincing would have to employ—can itself be understood
> only in terms of the notion of belief.

This being the case, then the distinction between actions and behaviour holds, and actions can be differentiated, at least in principle, according to their rationality.

But we are by no means out of the woods. As Hollis reminds us,
there are still many problems. The relationship between intentions
and actions is itself problematic (1977: 114):

> The same action can take different forms, only if there is a way of
> identifying form independently of intention; the same form can express
> different intentions, only if intentions can be identified independently of
> form.

Understanding what a person is doing calls for the identification
of their intention. But how are we to arrive at their intention except by inference from activities that we have already identified
as intentional? The relationship between intentions and actions is
circular. Such circularity, as we have seen, is not unique to explanations calling upon intentions.[3] But it is no less troublesome, and
it leads Hollis to question whether referring to the intentionality of
an action provides a sufficient basis for its explanation. He doubts
that it does, since this circularity means that explanations from
intentions do not truly commit us to deciding between active and
passive renderings of a given action.

For the behaviourist, the usual ascription of an intention is not
explanatory since it does not conform to the pattern of a causal
law: it does not reflect a generalizable connection between distinct contingent events. The intention to do something is not a
logically distinct entity antecedent to the action it is associated
with; and the intention "causes" the action without the actor having to know that the connection is an instance of a general class.
But this does not mean, Hollis stresses, that we have encountered
a true alternative mode of explanation to that advanced by behaviourists and positivists. With a little more ingenuity, Hollis
suggests, even intentional actions can be subsumed by a causal
analysis.[4] But whatever the merits of such speculations, even if it
were possible to identify intentions independently of actions they
are associated with, the citing of intentions alone would not necessarily explain an action. For given their independence, there
could be cases of bodily movements preceded by intentions that
would not deserve to be counted as actions. The mere presence
of an intention would not unquestionably account for a movement
(i.e., render it an action). A connecting mechanism, distinct yet
comparable to causality, must be specified between intentions and

actions. To specify that the alternative mechanism is reason or rationality merely pushes things back another notch. Much more must be said with regard to how reasons generate actions.

Now it is at this juncture that Hollis parts company with MacIntyre—one of his closest intellectual allies. For reasons to be explored below and contrary to his earlier views (MacIntyre, 1957 and 1962), MacIntyre proposes that the link between reasons for doing something and actually doing it is causal. Hollis rejects any such conflation of reasons and causes, and it will be argued that his greater daring pays better explanatory dividends.

Reasons and Causes[5]

According to MacIntyre, there is an asymmetry in the modes of explanation appropriate for rational and irrational beliefs. There is also a noncontingent connection between beliefs and actions. Therefore the study of human actions is equally subject to the asymmetry in modes of explanation. Yet, in sharp contrast to Hollis, MacIntyre does not hold to the proposition that rational action is its own explanation. Instead he takes care to maintain the following somewhat peculiar position (1971: 255):

> ... to say that rational belief cannot be explained in causal terms is not to say or imply that actions, even the actions of a man who acts upon rational belief in a rational way, cannot be explained in causal terms. Indeed, as I have argued elsewhere, to treat an agent's actions as the outcome of the reasons which he possessed for acting in the way that he did is precisely to point to one kind of cause as operative and to exclude other possible causal explanations. The notion that an agent's having a reason to do something may be the cause of his doing it is necessary if we are to distinguish reasons which are genuinely effective from mere rationalizations which are not. But although actions can have causes (in the sense of sufficient and not merely of necessary conditions), the close link between actions and beliefs would suggest that the asymmetry between the explanation of rational belief (sic) for which I have argued ought to entail some asymmetry between the explanation of rational action and the explanation of irrational action.

It is important to understand the rationale behind this type of compromise position with regard to the argument from rationality, and why it is defective. The lure of causal modes of thinking remains strong even amongst those scholars who actually rely on some form of the argument from rationality. Yet any reversion to causes renders the asymmetry in modes of explanation superficial and undermines the true explanatory value of differentiating between rational and caused actions in the first place.

To understand MacIntyre's reasoning, consideration must be given to the arguments, which, as he says, he has presented elsewhere. He first raised the idea of treating reasons as causes in the essay "The Antecedents of Action" (1966). His position is better known, however, from the brief reiteration of his views given in his critique of Peter Winch's work, in his own essay "The Idea of a Social Science" (1967). It is the latter discussion which will be examined here. In this essay MacIntyre explains that what bothers him about the claim to an incompatibility between acting for a reason and behaving from a cause is the failure to "distinguish between the agent's having a reason for performing an action (not just in the sense of there being a reason for him to perform the action, but in the stronger sense of his being aware that he has such a reason) and the agent's being actually moved to action by his having such a reason" (1971: 215-16). Most analyses of what it is to act for a reason, he notes, "begin from the apparently simple and uncomplicated case where the action is actually performed, and where the agent had one and only one reason for performing it, and where no doubt could arise for the agent as to why he had done what he had done." If any of the conditions are made more complicated, then doubts arise as to the nature of the connection between reasons and actions. The problem of the circularity of intentions and actions, for example, raises just such doubts. More straightforwardly, MacIntyre asks us to suppose that we have two agents, both with the same reasons to perform an action, and neither with any good reason, that he is aware of, not to perform the action. In this instance how would one explain the relationship between reasons and actions if but one of the agents actually performs the action? What made the "reasons or some subset of them productive of action in one case, but not in the other?"

Answering his own query, MacIntyre turns reasons for actions into causes of a type by making the explanation of an action according to reasons subject to empirical tests of the truth of a presumed underlying causal generalization. His reasoning to this effect is sufficiently subtle and unusual to warrant being quoted at length. As his test case MacIntyre works with the frequently cited example of a post-hypnotic suggestion.

> Under the influence of post-hypnotic suggestion a subject will not only perform the action required by the hypnotist, but will offer apparently good reasons for performing it, while quite unaware of the true cause of the performance. So someone enjoined to walk out of the room

might, on being asked why he was doing this, reply with all sincerity that he had felt in need of fresh air or decided to catch a train. In this type of case we would certainly not accept the agent's testimony as to the connection between reason and action, unless we are convinced of the untruth of the counter-factual, "He would have walked out of the room, if no reason for doing so had occured to him" and the truth of the counter-factual, "He would not have walked out of the room, if he had not possessed some such reason for so doing." The question of the truth or otherwise of the first of these is a matter of the experimentally established facts about post-hypnotic suggestion, and these facts are certainly expressed as causal generalizations. To establish the truth of the relevant generalization would entail establishing the untruth of the second counter-factual. But since to establish the truth of such causal generalizations entails consequences concerning the truth or untruth of generalizations about reasons, the question inevitably arises as to whether 'the possession of a given reason' may not be the cause of an action in precisely the same sense in which hypnotic suggestion may be the cause of an action. The chief objection to this view has been that the relation of reason to action is internal and conceptual, not external and contingent, and cannot therefore be a causal relationship; but although nothing could count as a reason unless it stood in an internal relationship to an action, 'the agent's possessing a reason' may be a state of affairs identifiable independently of the event which is 'the agent's performance of the action.' Thus it does seem as if the possession of a reason by an agent is an item of a suitable type to figure as a cause, or an effect. But if this is so then to ask whether it was the agent's reason that roused him to act is to ask a causal question, the answer to which depends upon what causal generalizations we have been able to establish. This puts in a different light the question of the agent's authority as to what roused him to act [(Winch had proposed that the agent had essentially the first and last word on his own activities)]; for it follows from what has been said that this authority is at best prima facie (1971: 216).

The argument is ingenious, if a little oblique. Hollis' discussion of the inner logic of explaining actions according to reasons, however, provides a number of effective counter arguments.

In the first place, as pointed out, it is difficult to identify intentions independently of the actions they are associated with. Therefore, how feasible is it for MacIntyre to assume that the condition of "possessing a reason" can be identified independently of the event which is "the performance of the action"? I suspect that the assumption is not very well founded.[6]

Second, when MacIntyre speaks of the possession of a reason being the cause of an action "in precisely the same sense in which hypnotic suggestion may be the cause of an action," he seems to be suggesting that when a reason motivates an actor without his awareness, the reason is functioning "causally" or in a cause-like manner. Hollis questions any such association. Taking rationality, for the moment, to be *Zweckrationalität* (i.e., the selection of the best means to attain one's end), Hollis notes that "the mere fact that [an] actor hits on [the best means to his end] is not sufficient and perhaps not necessary for the action to be zweckrational" (1977: 125). It is necessary to know that the actor knows that he has found the best means, and that "he has arrived at it not by guess and by God but by calculation and evidence." Now "*sub species acternitatis*," this may appear a "tall order, requiring, for instance, that he solve all the unsettled questions in economic theory." In point of fact, however, there may be but one way for an actor to obtain his or her goal, if it is to be attained at all, and the actor's choice of this way is no less rational because of this fact. Similarly, and of significance in the immediate context, rational activity does not actually require that every action undertaken by an actor be the product of a deliberate choice.

> Like the rational motorist, the rational gymnast, poet, yogi and commissar all need an unthinking control of their vehicles. Otherwise there will always be yet another preliminary decision. It would be foolish so to define the rational man that he cannot get as far as his own front door.... Habit can be rational. There is no snag, provided the actor is also in the habit of monitoring his habits to check for changes in himself and his surroundings. He must respond with fresh habits to growing deaf or a rise in bus fares (1977: 125).

As both Young and Hollis recognize, what renders a post-hypnotic suggestion an instance of caused action is first and foremost the fact that hypnotized subjects are robbed of their capacity to monitor their actions. It is not simply the fact that at the time of action the agent was not aware of the true "reason" for his or her action.

Third, because the reason offered by the agent for his or her action may be affected or even falsified by the establishment of a relevant causal generalization, it does not follow, as MacIntyre implies, that the possession of the reason by the agent can be treated as a type of cause of the agent's action. Surely, Hollis observes, it can be rational for a man to take an umbrella to work on a day when it did not actually rain, because the barometer showed it was likely to rain. The reason for the man's action, his belief that it was going to rain, is rendered false by the facts. But we would not deem his action irrational. because there was good justification for his belief (i.e.. the barometer reading). If, however. the man had taken the umbrella to work on a perfectly sunny day because "he heard what he now knows to be distant lorries and took them for thunder." then in proportion to how weak we deem the justification to be, his action will appear irrational. The important point, though, is that in neither case does the 'because' exemplify the law-like, transitive relation of cause and effect. It is important because. as Hollis argues (1977: 127):

> Knowledge of a fact is not to be analysed as true belief caused by the fact. When my phone rings. I may truly believe it is George, but without reason to expect him or to justify claim to psychic powers, I do not know it is him. Equally I believe truly that there is no highest prime number but what causes this belief, if anything does. is the proof and not the fact. The predicates 'true' and 'justified' do not attach to beliefs as 'painted green' attaches to doors. Admittedly I know a fact, only if there is such a fact. But the fact is not the cause of a state of mind but the reason for judgement. Knowledge is a matter of how belief is justified.

In some respects this statement merely amounts to an expression of the chief objection foreseen by MacIntyre to his views, namely, "that the relation of reason to action is internal and conceptual, not external and contingent. and cannot therefore be a causal relationship." But Hollis does not rest content with this rebuttal; though clearly its force should not be underestimated, as testified to by MacIntyre's rather extreme evasive manoeuvre. Sometimes. Hollis notes, both belief and action can be caused, and hypnosis presents the classic case. The reasons offered by hypnotized subjects for their actions, however good or true. are but rationalizations. Yet conversely, and in direct opposition to MacIntyre's line of thought, Hollis immediately points out (1977: 128):

> where good reasons do explain action. they also explain any relevant general connection. For example, if it is rational for a chessplayer to play 30.Q-Kt3 ch for the sake of a smothered mate in five, then all rational players so placed would do the same. But it is not thereby true that 30.Q-Kt3 ch is played 'because' all rational players would also play it because it is the best move. It would put the cart before the horse to collect a bag of cases of 30.Q-Kt3 ch and then explain all before explaining any. ... The rationality of the single case is prior to and sufficient for whatever is to be said about the general.

Admittedly, the example of chess represents an ideal case which is rather distant from the messiness of social life. But this admission does not lessen, as will become clearer later, the force in principle of Hollis' objection to treatments, like MacIntyre's, of explanations based on reasons for action. Anyway, it should be noted that MacIntyre's focus on hypnosis is equally distant from our daily experience of human action.

In general Hollis is drawing our attention to the fact that the occurrence of the term 'rational' in the explanation of an action is not comparable, if properly used, to any other predicate. The inclusion of the term "is a compressed gesture to there being good reason for [an action]," and Hollis contends that "it is always a priori what is rational in given conditions" (1977: 129). This is a contention to which we will return, but from what has been said it does seem clear that, contrary to MacIntyre's implication, the determination of the relationship between a reason and an action is not always an empirical question. Hollis underwrites this insight with the following observation (1977: 130):

> Causal laws about... agents are of the form 'All X are Y' and claims to have found one are testable.... If, however, we say to a neo-Classical economist, 'Here are some rational businessmen: let us test your theory by seeing if they equate marginal cost with marginal revenue,' he can object that they are rational, only if they supply whatever quantity makes MC=MR. Since he can prove it, we can challenge only his assumption that profit is a rational goal and this would take us out of the realm of *Zweckrationalität*. Theories prescribing the rational thing to do are criticizable but not testable as causal theories are testable.

This claim carries us back to the lessons of Chapter VI: to the suggestion that the natural necessity presupposed by traditional science is really but a form of conceptual necessity. Nothing is definitively testable, and human action least of all, for by definition it is anchored in the presupposition of rational human agency. Therefore, MacIntyre's whole effort to account for the efficacy of certain reasons by reconceptualizing reasons for action as a species of cause is misconceived. Treating reasons as causes is a retrograde step and only obscures matters, unless a great deal more is offered with regard to the precise meaning of the assertion that there is a 'causal' relation between any two things.

Reiterating the point first made in Chapter VI, the passage cited above argues that the only way to escape the self-validating circles of a world ruled by conceptual necessity alone is to question the root assumptions, that is, the norms of rationality, informing whatever explanatory framework is found wanting. But MacIntyre has barred himself from this possibility by preemptorily concluding that "the explanation of rational belief terminates with an account of the appropriate intellectual norms and procedures." If by such a statement MacIntyre means the simple specification of the norms at work, and this is what he implies (in this article), then he has left himself with too ambiguous and limited a notion of rationality to be able to apply the principle of asymmetry fruitfully to the study of human action. As will be demonstrated below, MacIntyre is working with a 'practical' conception of rationality, and such a conception simply will not support his overall thesis. What is needed is an 'epistemic' standard of rationality.

Practical and Epistemic Rationality

Rather curiously, when MacIntyre turns to illustrating the presence of the principle of asymmetry in modes of explanation in the social sciences he chooses to focus on a contrast of situations in which the beliefs and actions of an individual or a community are either in accord or disaccord. He does not focus directly, as Hollis does, on whether actions are rational or irrational. Though implicitly his perspective relies just as straightforwardly on this balder and bolder contrast.

In parts of Latin America, MacIntyre notes, "belief in sacramental monogamous marriage is part of the Catholicism of the inhabitants, but the actual forms of their sexual unions rarely, if ever, conform to the Catholic pattern." By contrast, in some Greek highland villages the day-to-day social life of individuals appears to be informed in detail by their professed beliefs. The difference in these types of situations, he reasons, calls forth a difference in the modes of explanation appropriate to each case. "For actions which accord with the beliefs of an agent stand in need of no further explanation than do the beliefs themselves; actions which do not so accord clearly do stand in need of an independent explanation, and the gap between belief and action itself requires to be explained" (1971: 255). This distinction is a real one. But the asymmetry established is hardly profound. The conformity or nonconformity of different sets of beliefs and actions can be determined on a strictly empirical basis, and the beliefs held by a people, no matter what their relationship to the

actions of individuals, can be accounted for through a causal analysis. Therefore, this asymmetry in what needs to be explained
does not really provide grounds for a fundamental asymmetry in
modes of explanation.[7]

Sensing this inadequacy, MacIntyre reformulates his asymmetry thesis (1971: 256):

> Where actions do accord with beliefs, the form of explanation will be
> one in which the whole complex of belief and action is to be explained
> together; and when the beliefs are rational, explanation will terminate
> with the account of the norms involved. Where, on the other hand, the
> beliefs are irrational or actions do not accord with beliefs, explanation
> will have to go beyond the delineation of the relevant norms; for we shall
> need to know at least why discrepencies and incoherencies, contradic-
> tions and other irrationalities are tolerated by the agents concerned.

Now in this passage the semblance of a real asymmetry of
modes of explanation has been smuggled in through reference to
rationality and irrationality. But the claimed asymmetry still does
not ring true, for the reference to rationality remains dependent on
the previous formulation of the principle of asymmetry. Where actions and beliefs accord they can be explained as a whole. But the
explanation need not be different in nature from that applied to
actions not in accord with beliefs. All can be explained causally. It
is only when the beliefs in question are rational that this is not the
case and a true asymmetry of explanation exists. MacIntyre draws
our consent to this proposition because he is trading implicitly on
the notion that rational beliefs and actions are self-explanatory.
Conversely, irrational beliefs require some further explanation of
their persistence. But what, according to MacIntyre, renders a
belief irrational? An action requires further explanation if it does
not conform to professed beliefs. So apparently, for MacIntyre, the
grounds for saying that a belief is irrational is its failure to conform
to the existing "norms and rule-governed practices" of rationality (note: MacIntyre lumps discrepencies and so on with "other
irrationalities"). But these norms remain insubstantive in Mac-
Intyre's formulation of the asymmetry principle. Therefore, the
notion of rationality itself consists merely of conformity to these
norms. It is not some intrinsic quality of these norms and practices that is doing the work of differentiating between the types
of explanation appropriate to different circumstances. It is simply
the principle of conformity or nonconformity to some such norms
and practices. Is conformity to an existing set of norms, however,

a sufficient standard of rationality to warrant declaring a belief and its related actions self-explanatory? To make this kind of discrimination MacIntyre must pay his epistemological debts more thoroughly.

If this analysis is doubted, then consideration should be given to the following passages. Towards the end of "Rationality and the Explanation of Action," MacIntyre concludes (1971: 256):

> ... the problem of rationality is a problem of the relationship of the beliefs and norms which define the roles which structure action in a given social order and the beliefs and norms of the agents whose behaviour is characteristically governed or defined by these roles.

The orientation reflected in this passage is inconsistent with MacIntyre's overall objective. The statement suggests, once again, that any belief which conforms to a set of norms having to do with what is thought sensible to believe in some social order is self-explanatory. Yet this view of matters conflicts with MacIntyre's stated interest in distinguishing "reasons [for action] which are genuinely effective from mere rationalizations which are not." To do this, we have seen that he is driven to the extreme of interpreting reasons as a type of cause–but with very unsatisfactory results and at the expense of placing the principle of asymmetry fundamentally in doubt. Now it can be understood why MacIntyre has taken this unusual route. He does not have a sufficiently strong conception of rationality to be able to use it alone to differentiate true reasons for action from mere rationalizations. Of course, the same message is driven home by Hollis' rebuttal of the attempt to conflate reasons and causes in the first place.

Earlier in his essay MacIntyre declares that the error of the liberal historians of the late Victorian era lay in their tendency to "confuse the question of rationality with that of truth." Explaining, he states (1971: 248):

> ... I will simply point out that "true" and "false" are predicated of 'what is believed,' namely of statements, and the truth or falsity of a statement is a matter quite independent of whether that statement is believed by anyone at all. Rationality is predicated of the attitudes, dispositions, and procedures of those who believe; a man who uses the best canons available to him may behave rationally in believing what is false, and a man who pays no heed to the rules of evidence may behave irrationally in believing what is true.

This passage is reasonable, but is it true? What MacIntyre separates from the question of truth and labels rationality is more accurately called "reasonableness." People who believe things which are in conformity with the norms of proper belief in their society, whose actions are in conformity with their stated beliefs, and who nevertheless believe something which is false, are being reasonable and not rational. As Hollis says somewhere, the right target is better missed than hit for the wrong reasons. The target here is the principle of asymmetry, and at the heart of this principle lies the idea that rational belief and action is its own explanation. Why? Because it is true! This may be a difficult notion to retain and justify in the age of post-positivist philosophy, but its lack of conformity to existing "attitudes, dispositions, and procedures" does not make it any less true. It is the only claim that can ground the principle of asymmetry in modes of explanation.[8]

Rationality and truth must be identified, in the last analysis, in order to use the principle of asymmetry to ground the presumption of human freedom. In two earlier essays (1957, 1962), MacIntyre himself argues this point. But, by the reasoning of the specification of the "problem of rationality" cited above, to be rational is to be consumately unfree, since to be rational is to be normal—to live in accord with the norms of sensible behaviour in one's society. MacIntyre, it is true, at one point denies the possibility of finding causally sufficient conditions for the emergence and institutionalization of norms and procedures involved in the explanation of rational beliefs. "The notion of a causal explanation for the genesis of intellectual tradition," he writes, "is like the notion of such an explanation for the genesis of a style of painting. All attempts to give such explanations have foundered" (1971: 247). But this assertion provides at best ambiguous succor for the idea of human autonomy, since it seems likely that his reason for denying the causal explanation of norms of rationality reflects a belief that the task is empirically too complex and not that it is intrinsically incorrect. The issue is a moot one, however, as long as MacIntyre also sees the tie between the reasons stemming from norms of rationality and the actions of agents as causally necessitated. Moreover, even if the latter contention were jettisoned, as Hollis declares (with Peter Winch's converse contention in mind), "actors who are creatures of rules [or socially imposed norms] are still passive, however the tie between rule and action is treated." The "instructive moral," he concludes, is that "although an active self needs an alternative to causal explanation, not any alternative will do" (1977: 120). Greater attention must be given to the nature of the rationality set-off against causality.

Surveying the rationality assumptions employed in the interpretation of beliefs and the explanation of actions, Stanley Benn
and Geoffrey Mortimore suggest that most approaches can be identified with one of two broad conceptions of rationality: "practical
rationality" and "epistemic rationality."[9] Both conceptions have
their natural starting point in the realm of *Zweckrationalität*, and
both are interested in the question of whether an actor's reasons
for an action constitute good reasons. Each, however, interprets
this question in markedly different ways. In deciding whether an
actor's reasons were good ones, the exponents of a practical rationality require "that, given his beliefs, he had reasons for action
sufficient to pick out 'this' action as the one 'to be done' " (Benn
and Mortimore, 1976: 4). They are interested, in other words,
in the efficiency and/or consistency of the actor's reasoning process. They employ a strictly formal notion of rationality, concerned solely with the relation between premises and conclusions.
Yet somewhat incompatibly they restrict the scope of this rationality to the relative standards present within different groups or
fields of concern. Their conception of rationality is contextual,
then, as well as formal. The exponents of an epistemic rationality
are oriented to something more. They wish to know if the beliefs
the actor is calling upon to provide a rationale for his or her action are well founded in a sense that 'makes sense' for all. In part,
as indicated, they hold to this demand because only then will we
have a full explanation of an action by knowing whether it was
free or determined.

MacIntyre's views fall into the former camp, though admittedly
not in a very typical way, while Hollis squarely adopts the latter
perspective. Practical rationality, which is usually presented as
being essentially descriptive in nature is commonly employed in
the social sciences and history. Epistemic rationality, which is
obviously normative, is less frequently admitted to be a component
part of the social sciences. In the next chapter, however, it will be
argued that there really is no such thing as a merely practical or
descriptive argument from rationality.

IX.
Epistemic and Expressive Rationality

Epistemic Rationality as a Regulative Principle

With some justification most social scientists restrict their references to rationality to practical conceptions because arguments from rationality centred on epistemic standards are too methodologically demanding for common usage. Nevertheless, it should be recognized that no social scientific study can forego the formulation of some epistemic conception of rationality. The Australian philosopher Quentin Gibson captures this state of affairs well in a brief examination of the argument from rationality.

Explanations of actions based on the imputation of reasons, Gibson notes, are complicated by the fact that the beliefs about means attributed to actors may be different in form, and hence degrees of rationality. In some cases the beliefs that are attributed to the agents may be to the effect that an action will merely "contribute" to their ends. In other cases the belief attributed to the agents may be to the effect that their actions will be "sufficient" to bring about their ends or be the "necessary" step to the satisfaction of their ends. The most informative approach, however, entails invoking a fully epistemic standard of rationality and arguing that the beliefs attributed to the agents are to the effect that their actions constitute the "best ways" for them to achieve their ends (1976: 117-18). This approach is the most informative since as there is but one best way to accomplish any particular end, rational conformity to this way eliminates the need to pursue any further explanation of why a particular actor has done the action in question. There are a number of methodological problems posed by the best way approach, however, which appear to call its feasibility into question.

If the belief about means to an end is concerned with the best way to achieve an end, then in most social situations the actors have to be understood as weighing alternative possibilities. This, Gibson comments, "complicates the argument from rationality considerably" (1976: 199). For except in cases where the end in mind is simply obtaining the maximum quantity of something possible, this consideration of alternatives presents the inquirer with the problem of a "cost analysis." In life people have multiple ends, and this means that in deciding on any particular course of action, an actor is going to be oriented not so much to the accomplishment of any single end as to the obtaining of an optimum position vis-a-vis the harmonizing of his or her collective goals and interests. The best way of obtaining one end will be calculated with an eye to the costs entailed by any course of action in terms of the sacrifice of other ends. This means the investigator of any action must seek to know the actor's scale of preferences in order that he or she may schematize a hierarchy of the actor's priorities. From the perspective of the actor and the investigating social scientist, recognition of this state of affairs greatly expands the epistemic component of a rational action. The complexity of the situation suggests that "we end up with a somewhat rarified ideal picture of what it is to act rationally" (Gibson, 1976: 120), and hence equally of what it is to assess an action according to its rationality.

Even a fairly informal analysis[1] reveals that the problems faced by the argument from rationality are manifold. First, if a cost analysis entails a full accounting of all of the possible ends and means available to the actor, then the more complex the situation under scrutiny is the less likely it is that the analysis can ever be completed. Second, the more complex the situation, the harder it is to trace the possible relations of various ends and means, and hence the relative costs of acting in one way rather than another. Third, and accordingly, the more complex the situation, the less assurance there is that the actor will not overlook some cost consideration and act irrationally. And paradoxically, the more deviations from rationality recorded by using the argument from rationality, the less justification there is for assuming the actor in question to be rational in the first place. In other words, the application of the argument may undercut its own theoretical legitimacy. Lastly, as Gibson most effectively points out (1976: 122):

> ... even if the people we are considering were all to act in a perfectly rational manner, there would still remain a difficulty about our capacity, as social scientists, to reconstruct their reasoning. If they find comparisons of evidence difficult, so do we. And when it comes to their scales of preferences, we are in a considerably worse position.... It must be

remembered that, under the heading of 'wants,' we must here include not only explicit desires for ends but also various temperamental tendencies such as the store set on adventure or security. ... the store set on immediacy of satisfaction against long-range achievement. Such an all-embracing survey of a person's relevant desires and inclinations may be thought to be hardly a realistic undertaking.

Difficulties like these, lead social-psychologists like Robert P. Abelson (1976) to conclude that rationality simply may not be a useful concept when it comes to the study of human behaviour. The number and complexity of the cognitive tasks required of an individual to achieve full rationality in any given situation makes the pursuit of epistemic rationality a "grossly implausible... model or standard of human functioning." Furthermore, "the assumption of motivation strong enough to support [such a] cognitive effort seems gratuitous." It is too easy for people to live epistemically, though not practically, irrational lives. "Despite the seemingly obvious advantages in normal life adjustment of what clinical psychologists call 'reality testing,' it is not so clear what costs or punishments are incurred by individuals for being non-rational concerning remote events" (Abelson, 1976: 59). Even if attention is restricted to practical rationality, social-psychology poses problems, for it has established just how strong and pervasive the influence is of peers and authority figures on the behaviour of individuals. The balance sheet of the practical reasoner is always being irrationally biased in ways he or she knows little about or is aware of at all. Consequently, only a "limited subjective rationality" is recognized by social psychologists, and this rationality might be found in conjunction with "a personally distorted picture of reality" (1976: 62-63). Using Balance Theory, Dissonance Theory, or Attribution Theory, social-psychologists are content to orient themselves to people's fairly subjective "mental processing rules."

Likewise, as Gibson points out, other important scholars, fearful of the difficulties attendant on an epistemic standard of rationality, have sought to accommodate an account of rational explanation to a merely practical criterion of rationality. Hempel denys that in order to explain an agent's action in terms of their reasons, we must take into account whether the person's beliefs are well-grounded (Hempel, 1965: 464-65). In his study of the laws of history, William Dray argues that it is enough to know practically that an individual's means do not conflict with their beliefs and ends to judge their actions rational (1964: 125-26). While John Watkins has proposed what he calls "the imperfect rationality principle," whereby it is irrelevant whether or not the agent's appraisal of his or her situation is accurate, for an explanation of behaviour it is sufficient that "a person will act in a way appropriate to his aims and situational appraisal" (Gibson, 1976: 124) (Watkins, 1970: 172).

These perspectives are by no means incorrect. But they do little explanatory work. Their minimalistic standard of rationality amounts to the truism that for every action there is a belief with which it is in accord. This style of argument has the effect of rendering all actions rational short of those perpetrated by the mentally unstable. Though as the grounds for an action are irrelevant for explanations of this form, not even the latter type of action warrants being excluded. Gibson amusingly comments that arguments of this form enable us to explain and predict "that someone will lie down on the pavement from his belief that this is essential to his catching the bus" (1976: 126).

Most importantly, the simple reliance on a practical rationality deprives us of the special explanatory advantage of the epistemic approach. Gibson illustrates this advantage with the example of trying to explain the refusal of an employer to hire non-Aryans. To point to the practical rationality of not hiring non-Aryans by relating the employer's belief that non-Aryans do inferior work is not very illuminating. "It is evidently more satisfactory if we can say how the [employer] came to have [this] belief," and this entails asking a question about his epistemic rationality. As Gibson puts things (1976: 126):

> We assume there is good evidence for the belief that a person with more qualifications and experience does a better job, and we assume that the employer is aware of this. We therefore have an explanation ready to hand. But we have no such explanation for the belief that an Aryan does a better job. We have to look for a sociological explanation for such a belief in the same way we do for any other social fact, by delving into the employer's attitudes and background.

In general, reference to an epistemic understanding of rationality is instrumental to the inference of what a particular actor believes for even the weakest form of the argument from rationality.

> The fact is that what a person believes is often hard to discover directly. This remains true even if he happens to make autobiographical

statements about his beliefs. Our ability to infer the belief from the information he has at his disposal, on the assumption that he is epistemologically rational, is therefore almost indispensible (Gibson, 1976: 126).

Now it is precisely this insight that Hollis has developed into one of the essential supports of the argument from rationality.

In two of his most widely cited articles, "The Limits of Irrationality" (1967) and "Reason and Ritual" (1968), Hollis examines the classical problem of translating ideas from one language into another, especially in the context of the anthropological investigation of the religious and magical beliefs of primitive peoples. In this context, he argues convincingly that translators can break the circularity of all interpretative situations only by imputing a certain fundamental consistency to the views held by the members of their own culture and those of the culture they are studying. In effect, inquirers must attribute a common rationality to the thought of the two peoples. and only then can they choose, in some instances, to attribute inconsistent beliefs to one of the groups. The assumption of such a common or a priori rationality is instrumental to the very justification of any translation, Hollis notes, since "the best direct defence of an interpretation is that it makes the Other Mind more rational than its rivals do." In understanding others, whether of our own age and culture or another, there is no true recourse to anything other than an epistemic standard of rationality.[2]

In arguing that the hermeneutical circle can only be broken by imputing rationality, Hollis is not making the brash claim that humans are in the main rational creatures. On the contrary, in line with Abelson, Hollis declares: "Life is too short for constant Cartesian monitoring, even supposing that to be possible in principle." In fact, "mankind could hardly survive without beliefs which are incoherent, unlikely, disconnected or daft" (1982: 72). Rather. as is probably clear, the contention is merely that the identification of beliefs requires a "bridgehead" of beliefs taken to be universally true and rational. What this precisely entails, however, needs elaboration. To this end, it is worth quoting at length the following passage from "The Social Destruction of Reality" (1982: 73):

> An enquirer ascribes a belief to an actor. He does so by interpreting evidence. The evidence can, it seems. only be what the actor and others say and do. Their sayings and doings must have been rightly understood. Hence, apparently. every interpretation requires a previous

one. So how is identification possible? A tempting reply is that the air of paradox is spurious; each interpretation is provisional and subject to confirmation: a later interpretation can overturn an earlier one; so the need for a previous interpretation is genuine but harmless. But I retort, there are two reasons why there has to be more to it than the pragmatic assembling of a jigsaw. One is that even this pragmatic work presupposes internal relations among the beliefs–if you like, the existence of both a picture on the face of the jigsaw and a geometry to the shapes of the pieces–which are not discovered by the confirming process. The other is that, in addition to internal relations, there must be an external determinant which is also presupposed and not discovered. It would foreclose on a long dispute to call this simply 'the world' and I prefer to regard it as an a priori guarantee of overlap between the perceptual judgements of the enquirer and his informants. Putting internal and external constraints together, I submit that the enquirer must presuppose shared precepts, judgements, concepts and rules of judgement in making his empirical discoveries about beliefs. So, although some individual interpretations are adjustable later, adjustment cannot be so thorough as to overthrow the bridgehead of interpretations it relies on.

The reference to the world does not mean that Hollis has taken up the naive realism of the traditional empiricist. Rather, as he states, "the moral is not so much that there is a single, objective and neutral world as that translation needs to presuppose one." More specifically, as indicated, what must be presupposed is "some set of interpretations [of the world and humankind's response to it] whose correctness is more likely than that of any later interpretation which conflicts with it. The set consists of what a rational man cannot fail to believe in simple perceptual situations, organized by rules of coherent judgement, which a rational man cannot fail to subscribe to" (1982: 74). This set constitutes what D. P. F. Strawson called "a massive central core of human thinking which has no history" (Hollis, 1982: 75).

Even Abelson's mental processing rules, Mortimore points out, really equal only weak conditions of epistemic rationality. That is, they could not be identified in the first place without the prior postulation of some epistemic standard of rationality. Therefore, rather than shunning the use of rationality assumptions, out of a misbegotten effort to hold to the principle of value-neutrality, Abelson should actually endeavor to make the implicit standard undergirding his work explicit. But Abelson spurns the explicit stipulation of an epistemic notion of rationality, saying: "searching for the idealization that isn't there is a less productive strategy than finding out what 'is' there" (1976: 61). In other words, in a traditional inductivist and descriptivist manner he misses the point and fails to realize that in the human realm any strategy to find out what 'is' inevitably starts from what rationally and ideally might be the case.

Reiterating the point first made in Chapter IV. in terms of purposes and reasons, the isolation of mental processing rules does not provide us with an intellectually satisfying explanation of an action, because it does not push the analysis far enough. Through experimentation and interviews social psychologists may be able to discover the character of the processing rule at the heart of their subjects' systematic process of belief-formation. For example, Balance Theory postulates that "individuals will not believe that objects which they evaluate positively are 'bonded' to objects they evaluate negatively" (Mortimore and Maund, 1976: 21). Therefore. an individual confronted with a situation where two such objects are associated. will attempt to develop a rationalization whereby in this instance a pro-attitude can be justifiably ascribed to the negatively evaluated object or event. This is fine in itself. But in any particular case, the subjects' disposition to believe in the rationalization may be the product of radically different reasons for positively and negatively evaluating the two initial objects. To explore this deeper issue, in the last analysis, the subjects' beliefs will have to be checked for the degree to which they manifest an epistemic rationality. Unwillingness to pursue this matter, Mortimore and J. B. Maund conclude, "can... lead the theorist to ignore real explanatory questions. and to give a uniform theoretical account to cases which require radically different explanations" (1976: 21). Of course, in our case, it can lead to the lumping together of essentially free and unfree actions.

In conclusion, lest anyone think that the upshot of this fulmination about the necessity of operating with an epistemic standard of rationality has relevance only to those concerned to rescue human freedom. consideration should be given to a further warning issued by Hollis. Those students of human action. and particularly religious action. who attempt to work exclusively with a merely practical or contextually limited conception of rationality (i.e., to judge a culture or belief system strictly from within, according to its own standards). in order to prevent reductive and ethnocentric analyses, run the risk of doing far greater harm to the groups they are studying than could ever be done by the exponents of a rationalist monism. For when "Reason is dethroned" in favour of making it "an axiom of method" that social worlds are "always rational from within," it becomes "a contingent matter what criteria are in use among what groups of actors." The "objective furniture of the social (or indeed of the natural) world [becomes] accessible only through the actors' beliefs and can therefore be constituted in whatever way helps the final account hang together." This result not only damages the claim to a 'science' of human action, it throws the integrity of all belief claims into jeopardy. For by this account,

> both ontology and epistemology are relative to shared belief and, in principle, variable without constraint, beyond that of overall coherence. Since the criteria of coherence are themselves included in epistemology, however, it ought to follow, that there are no constraints at all. Indeed it does follow, I maintain, and only failure of nerve stops anyone who has gone this far drawing the conclusion. Moreover, since other cultures are, epistemologically, merely a case of Other Minds, there will no longer be any constraint on any interpretation of one person's beliefs and desires by another (1982: 82-83).

In other words, arguments for a contextual rationality give rise to a pernicious scepticism and not just a supposedly realistic and tolerant relativism.[3]

Underscoring the main point of the last two chapters, the identification and systematic assessment of free human acts requires the establishment of a principle of asymmetry in modes of explanation. This in turn necessitates operating with an epistemic standard of rationality. Yet the use of such a standard and hence the existence and viability of an asymmetry in modes of explanation is not dictated by the interest in human freedom alone. Rather it is a component of the very process of understanding itself.

An asymmetry in explanation, Hollis says (1982: 77),

> arises because beliefs are woven into a system by actors' beliefs about their beliefs. These are the actors' own reasons for belief and so their own explanations of why they believe what they do. Schematically someone, who cites p as his reason for believing q, believes not only p and q but also that p is good enough reason to believe q. One of the enquirer's tasks is to discover these connections, not merely because his list of actors' beliefs will be incomplete without them, but also because his list must add up to a system. But he must also produce his own explanation of why the actors believe what they believe. In doing so, he cannot fail to endorse or reject the actors' own reasons or, where the actors are not of one mind, to side with some against others.

Whether scholars care to employ an explicit standard of rationality or not, understanding and complete neutrality cannot go hand in hand. They must accept or reject interpretations, or the factual claims made by others, as final or not. They can do so either because they explicitly are willing to argue about the rationality or irrationality of the claims in a way ideally open to all, or impicitly because they deem the claims to be rational or irrational since they do or do not happen to coincide with their own basic beliefs.

Expressive Rationality as a Regulative Principle

The four points underlying Hollis' alternative mode of social scientific explanation, have now been established, at least at the abstract level of pure theory. A person is free to the extent that he or she has authentically taken on certain social roles, and authenticity is the result of making rational choices with regard to these roles. It makes sense to speak of rational choices and to attribute explanatory significance to them because an asymmetry in modes of explanation does exist in the social sciences. It exists because it is impossible not to invoke an epistemic conception of rationality when assessing the origins and significance of human action. The bottom line, as Hollis admits is an "insultingly simple" thesis (1977: 130): "[an action] done from good reasons is, in the ideal case, a fact needing no explanation; [an action] done from bad reasons is a different fact, needing an explanation." Is the ideal case specified in this simple thesis, however, too ideal? Despite all that has been said, the practical suspicion persists that the alternative mode of explanation offered by Hollis is so rarefied that it defies accurate application and is empirically vacuous.

Initially this might well appear to be the case, for the argument from rationality entails "two sets of true judgements, one by the actor, who must know exactly what he is about, the other by the enquirer who must see through the actor and then judge his action." But Hollis denies that this state of affairs poses any "outrageous" methodological demands. "Where [the demands of the ideal case] are not met in full," he comments, "the scope of a rational explanation is diminished to that degree. The actor is only partly revealed and the enquirer speaks tentatively; but the form [of the explanation] remains the same" (1977: 131). Furthermore, as pointed out by Mortimore in his refutation of Abelson, there is no reason for believing that an epistemic conception of rationality "cannot accomodate the ordinary notion that there are degrees of rationality in belief falling short of full rationality." The attribution of an epistemic rationality orients the actor and the inquirer to the best way of achieving an end, but failure to pursue the best way does not automatically lead to the action being deemed irrational and hence deterministically caused. Hollis is working already with degrees of identity and individuality, and we know that our conceptions of human freedom must be relational, therefore the judgements of rationality underlying claims to authenticity must also be understood in terms of degrees. This is an important point, one not properly appreciated even by Hollis (hence I will return to it in Chapter XI). But for the moment, completing the thought common to Mortimore and Hollis, it should be recognized "that the pervasiveness of deviations from full rationality does not imply, as many social psychologists seem to think, that the ... concept of epistemic rationality is heuristically expendable" (Mortimore and Maund, 1976: 20).

Leaving aside the plight of actors trying to judge the rationality of their own choices, the set of truth judgements required of the inquirer, though, do point to some formidable technical hurdles. Most obviously it has been specified that for an act to be authentic and free it is not enough for there to be good reasons for it, the reasons must be the actor's own reasons. Yet how are we to know when this is the case? It is reasonable to propose broadly that in recognizing good reasons for action that apply to them, actors will make those reasons their own. But in point of fact we are faced with the problem of 'other minds,' and only the actor is able to mysteriously "pass through the swing doors leading to [their] inner sanctum." We cannot know definitively what really motivated any action. And when this problem is situated within the more straightforward difficulties associated with the cost-analysis of human decisions (discussed in the previous section) it does appear that the argument from rationality is making unreasonable methodological demands.

Countering such a suspicion, Hollis asserts that the difficulties have been exaggerated, and his claim is supported by Gibson. Tackling the background issue of complexity first, Gibson begins by pointing out that against the span of human experience truly complicated decision situations "are fortunately rare." While decisions of "medium complexity" are often made to appear ominous "because in talking about alternatives and ends we are inclined to represent a person's reasoning as if it started from scratch" (1976:

122). But in fact an investigator can reasonably control the scope
of his or her analysis by close study of the actor's background situation. The actor's stock of knowledge and physical and social
circumstances will greatly limit and circumscribe the real options
open to him or her at any given time. Nevertheless, it remains
clear that the argument from rationality is used most effectively
in situations where "conflicting ends are manageably small in number and the evidence for beliefs is relatively simple and cogent."
But then a similar state of affairs holds equally for the application
of a merely practical standard of rationality or a causal mode of
analysis. Positivists and pragmatists (i.e, including social psychologists) want a science which makes sound predictions, but Gibson
notes: "It is a commonplace that prediction is difficult in the social
sciences. and this for reasons which have nothing to do with the
rationality or irrationality of human beings" (1976: 123) or the
character of the paradigm of rationality empolyed by the inquirer.

Complexity wreaks havoc on our ability to predict causally or
on the basis of any concept of rationality. But if one already knew
an actor's action. and was certain about their chosen end. could
one not derive a satisfactory explanation of the action simply on
the basis of our ability to infer the belief the actor must have in
mind without assuming anything more than his or her practical
rationality? The temptation to agree is strong, and curiously, raising the question speaks to our first problem – knowing the motive
for someone else's action – from a new angle. For as Hollis notes.
it reveals that those students of human action who would restrict
themselves to a practical understanding of rationality, have themselves neither avoided nor resolved the problem of 'other minds.'
They have simply assumed that suitable motives can be inferred
with hindsight. If the assumption is valid or just accepted regardless of its validity. then the concern of such scholars over the
outrageous demands of Hollis' position evaporates and once again
we see that in practice the analysis of decision situations is not as
complicated as it seems. As Hollis concludes. *"Zweckrationalität*
too is not wholly silent about motives and ends" (1977: 133).
Therefore, working with a merely practical conception of rationality (entailing such inferences) is not enough. As Gibson explains.
bringing Gellner to mind (1976: 127):

> ... a proper explanation requires that there be some reason for accepting
> the explaining facts which is independent of the fact to be explained.
> If the only reason for accepting that a person has a certain belief is
> that without it, given his ends. he would not have done what he did. it
> is hardly illuminating to mention the belief as part of the explanation
> of what he did. To do so would be to invite the comment that we

know that already, and have not increased our understanding of why
the action was performed.

Note that this comment conforms to Abel's classic refutation of
the explanatory adequacy of the *Verstehen* method (see Chapter
III). In both cases the point is: though all arguments are circular
and regressive, as Gellner warns, "re-endorsement theories" will
not do.

One can lose sight of this criticism and be content with the kind
of inferences of motive made with hindsight from actions (as commonly done by historians) because the ends of most actions can be
treated in classic *zweckrational* form as only intermediate means
to other ends. But, in principle, it is not enough simply to show
that an action is rational because it is the best means to attain
some relatively immediate end. The rationality of ends in a more
ultimate sense must also be drawn into the judgement. An actor
"has no good reason for doing in the best way what he will have no
good reason to have done. Indeed where there is good reason not to
have done something, there is good reason for not taking the best
means to do it" (Hollis, 1977: 133). This crucial point of principle,
however, does not eliminate the viciously regressive character of
all practical dealings with means and ends. Paradoxically the act
of rationally deciding between two goals which are supposedly not
means to further goals, transforms the goals into precisely means
for further ends or otherwise there could have been no grounds for
'rationally' deciding between them. To "elude" this regress, Hollis
offers a solution which parallels the insight underlying the general
thesis of the argument from rationality (i.e., some tautologies are
not empty): "we must make some goals desirable for their own
sake." Introducing this idea into the epistemic rationality of ends
which is called upon by the argument from rationality gives, as
Hollis typically understates, "a fresh sense to 'rational' " (1977:
135).

To draw his point out Hollis asks us to reflect on the problem
of the Determined Voter (1977: 135).[4]

This is the puzzling fellow who turns out in winter sleet to vote in
an utterly safe seat. He admits cheerfully that his candidate will lose
(or win) by twenty thousand votes or so. He agrees that his fireside
is snug and television enticing. But he votes just the same. No doubt
it is tempting to find him a further end. He might be hoping to save
the loser's deposit or to impress his neighbours. Perhaps he has to
face other party workers in the bar afterwards. No, he insists with the

smug humility of the good citizen, he voted solely on principle. Well, on what principle? He has no legal duty in Britian and we may coherently suppose that his mates see no moral duty either. But it explains nothing to credit him with a private principle that the good citizen always votes. This tells us merely that he votes because he thinks he should and that is precisely what we are trying to explain. Being one of these odd animals myself, I hope the 'because' is a rational one but I can find no instrumental reason. I desire to vote but that mere fact does not make the action rational. Does anything?

We are accustomed to understanding rational actions as ways of achieving things. But the act of the determined voter appears to be simply an act of self-expression. It is an act of expression, however, which to some degree characterizes the behaviour of most of the electorate. Therefore many political scientists have been moved to deem such an act of expression rational, if only out of embarrassment, because their science is founded on the premise that humans are rational. Such an association of rationality and expression clearly has some explanatory advantages: "cost-effectiveness is no longer crucial and men can act rationally from, for instance, honour, respect or gratitude without having to be found a goal rationally achieved" (Hollis, 1979: 13). But equally clearly, rationality cannot be just identified with acts of expression per se. It is acts of true self-expression alone which Hollis advances as candidates for rationality. In an immediate (though inexact) sense it is such acts which are the goals desirable for their own sake. In other words, harkening back to the conclusions of Chapter VII, it is those acts of identification with a role which are subject to the actor's retrospective judgement and which he has not found cause to regret which Hollis has in mind.

But, Hollis asks (1979: 12), can there not be role duties which an individual could act on, without regretting the result, which nevertheless it is irrational to have acted on? Is the murderous act of the Mafia hitman rational, for instance, because he does not regret it, but rather considers it an integral part of his "way of being and becoming, of expressing and developing the self[?]" Obviously it is not, and the question returns us, within the context of scrutinizing the concept of expressive rationality, to the lesson pointed out above to the exponents of practical rationality. It is not enough that the actor has taken on the reasons of some character or role as his or her own reasons and that he or she has retrospectively affirmed this act of identification. There must be

some external standard, open in principle to both the actor and
any observer, by which expressively rational acts and their component retrospective self-judgements can be assessed (within the
confines of the established overall point that there are no wholly
independent points of view). In other words, in light of what we
have learned about the need to refer to a rationality of ends, we
must, as Hollis chooses to frame things, decide whether an actor's
apparent acts of expressive rationality are truly in line with his or
her "real interests" and hence are in fact rational.

So now we see that the "goals desirable for their own sake" are
our "real interests" or, more immediately, those actions which are
in accord with or expressive of our real interests. But here the
central bind emerges; a bind with which we are familiar. Since the
ultimate goals towards which the actor is striving are locked deep
within his or her individuality, they are, in spite of the above comments, essentially inaccessible and ineffable. Therefore how are we
to determine what these real interests happen to be? Both of the
options which appear to be available eliminate the possibility of
human freedom from the start. Either we can locate our real interests in the realm of the atomic, pre-social individual, or we can
identify them with the ascribed rules and rationales of the social
system. The former point of view makes the adoption of one identity rather than another, and hence all later acts of self-expression,
an arbitrary matter. The latter point of view leaves us with the
passive agent who in fact has no true self, and hence cannot engage in distinct acts of self-expression. If we wish to proceed at all,
Hollis reiterates, then we must – an epistemological *must* – assume
three things: that persons are always "in some character on some
stage," no matter how private the stage may be (1977: 139); that
our real interests "are bound up not with what we want but with
what we are" (1979: 12); and that consequently, the only move
that can be made in support of the principle of human freedom is
"to invoke the idea of real interests which the actor acquires with
those characters in which he is himself" (1977: 137). Autonomous
action, in other words, should be seen as "rational self-expression
on the part of an essentially social man" (1977: 140); and the central tenet of the argument from rationality, namely that rational
action is its own explanation, can be restated as "True consciousness is its own explanation" (1977: 140).

This conclusion is dictated by more than a prejudice in favour of
human freedom. There is also, as indicated, an ethical component

to the position. The claim to have acted rationally must be tied
to the concept of real interests, and this concept in turn must be
realistically situated within the social nature of human existence.
Otherwise the hired underworld assassin could seek to rationalize
his actions idiosyncratically by saying 'I would not be me if I did
not murder this person.' Alternatively, if the claim to have acted
rationally (i.e., in one's real interests) is too closely identified with
the social character of our existence, then our hitman might "rationally" murder with enthusiasm citing that "orders are orders"
and what is more "he is happy in his work, has a proper career
structure, and enjoys the esteem of his peers." In the end, Hollis concludes, "rationality has to consist in identifying with some
set of principles neither merely because one wants to nor merely
because they are the going norms of one's station but because,
whatever it may mean to say so, they are in one's real interests"
(1979: 12-13).

Practically, where this lands us, as Hollis admits readily, is in
the realm of values (1977: 137):

> What starts as a search for an active model of man leads first to a
> demand for actions which are self-explanatory because fully rational,
> thence to an account of rationality in terms of real interests, thence
> into ethics and finally to that ancient problem about the nature of the
> Good Society. Yet it should come as no surprise that questions in ethics
> and politics attend an analysis of human nature. We cannot know what
> is rational without deciding what is best.

There is nothing distinct to the argument from rationality in this
situation, for as already established, even the exponents of a practical rationality cannot avoid an implicit ascent into this rarefied
realm in drawing distinctions between more or less preferable actions. "The point gets hidden," Hollis comments, "because ...
health, wealth and happiness are such popular goals. But to assume is not to eliminate. Passive conceptions too tell us what we
must do to be saved" (1977: 139).

Methodological acknowledgement of this fact sets a new agenda
for the scientific study of social actions. In an "ideal type of enquiry," Hollis argues, we must presuppose the autonomy of human
agents. Having made this assumption we must then exhaust the
channels of investigation made available by the normative structuralist approach in order to isolate all rule-governed behaviour
and hence, more importantly, what still needs explaining. Then
to deal with these latter questions we must switch our methodological caps, become methodological individualists and ask after

the actor's own reasons for having done his or her duty or presented it as he or she did. The answer we derive will take the form of *Zweckrationalität*, subject to assumptions about the rationality of certain ends. We may begin with the consideration of relatively immediate ends (i.e., what are really means to other ends), but sooner or later, as Hollis graphically states, we shall have to "lay our bets" about those things which are ends in themselves and the final criteria of rationality. Judging the action in question from this perspective it is actually unlikely that the actor's activity will appear fully rational, for the approach imposes extremely strong conditions. But this poses no problem as long as it is realized that we are dealing with an "ideal limiting case," while real cases will vary in degree of autonomy. Saying this, Hollis cautions, does not entail assuming that "all actors always act autonomously. Nor [does it imply] that all rules and institutions result from deliberate contracts." The approach may revert to a strictly passive and causal account at two junctures: either after the first application of the normative structuralist mode of application or, which is more likely, after assessing the rationality of an actor's behaviour. If the individual's actions are found wanting in rational justification, then the inquirer is free to depart fully from the initial assumption of this ideal type of inquiry.

The "laying of bets" sounds like a precarious base for social science, but the idea does not perturb Hollis (1977: 137).

> Both actor and enquirer must lay their bets but there is no reason to doubt that some bets are more shrewdly laid than others. It is not absurd to judge some actions more rational than others, while living with the possibility that the judgements may have to be revised.

In considering this statement it must be remembered that the argument from rationality as formulated by Hollis rests upon the broader epistemological argument for the necessity of the idea of "necessary truths" in the overall assessment of human actions. This point has been argued in slightly different ways in Chapter VI and the preceding discussion of the problem of other minds as analogously expressed in the difficulties of translating ideas from one culture and language to another. Hollis acknowledges that "there is no uncontentious way of distinguishing necessary from contingent – nor even of claiming that there is a distinction to draw ... " (1977: 170). Nevertheless, if there is to be any social science at all, then one must invoke the equivalent of an idea of necessary truth; and when applied to human actions it will be invoked in a *zweckrational* form. In a game of chess, for example, this principle is obvious. There is a best move to attain one's end and making this move is the rational thing to do. This move is knowable both a posteriori and a priori. If by chance the merits of this move are not known a priori, but only recognized a posteriori, this does not alter the necessary truthfulness of the move (i.e., does not render it contingent). In the social world the truth of this state of affairs is less evident. In the game of chess, unlike the social world, the ultimate end is clearly defined and the available means are limited both in number and kind. But logically, even in the much more complicated social world, it remains true that "the effect of making necessity prior to proof is to license a posteriori knowledge of necessary truths" (1977: 172). In practice, of course, the problem of actually elucidating "real interests" intrudes and leaves one making calculated guesses with regard to the behaviour of specific agents in specific circumstances. But, reiterating the simple but elusive point which frames all of our discussions, the laying of bets is not unique to the argument from rationality so much as the study of human action. "Natural science is spared such judgements and this is the epistemological difference" (Hollis, 1977: 183).

How the Plot has Thickened

Three overlapping tasks have been undertaken in the second part of this study: first, a space has been cleared amongst the traditional perspectives on the nature of scientific explanations in the study of human action for due consideration of the argument from rationality; second, the working assumptions of the argument from rationality have been clarified and situated (broadly) within a sociological framework of analysis (i.e., role theory); third, logical, methodological, and epistemological arguments have been advanced in justification of the central assumptions of the argument from rationality, namely that rational actions are there own explanation and that the assessment of the rationality of an action is a feasible social scientific undertaking. Each task has been undertaken with some acknowledgement of the intrinsic limitations of both the argument from rationality and Hollis' specific formulation of that argument.

The first task involved legitimizing the aspirations of the humanist perspective in sociology, as embodied in the presupposition of voluntarism, by breaking the hold on the social sciences of the soft positivist equation of explicability and causal analysis. This entailed both a negative and a positive procedure. Negatively, the insufficiency of the soft positivist equation was demonstrated, by as impartial means as possible, through a critique of the internal logic of the deductive-nomological and hypothetico-deductive formulations of the soft positivist position. Positively, it was argued that if the 'scientific' study of society is to be defended against the conceptual pragmatist implications of post-positivist philosophy of science, then the soft positivist equation should be replaced with a qualified idealist understanding of the principle of natural necessity underlying the logic of scientific analyses (natural and social). With the full elaboration of a new idealist philosophy of science (a task which Hollis leaves for another time and place), Hollis speculates that it might well become apparent that there are unique ways of conceptualizing domains of experience. On the basis of this point of epistemological speculation, it was then argued, by means of an examination of Tibbetts' reconsideration of the positivism-humanism debate in sociology, that the use of the idea of rational human agency in the explanation of human action probably is a conceptual necessity, and not, as Tibbetts proposes, a matter of mere preference. The necessity invoked, however, is more qualified than the necessity Hollis specifically advances in the general thesis of the argument from rationality (i.e., that all sciences depend on necessary truths knowable a priori). The qualification in question stems, in part, from consideration of the epistemological speculations presented in Gellner's *Legitimation of Belief*. Unlike the soft positivists or Tibbetts, and like Hollis, Gellner employs an epistemological and anti-conventionalist approach to the question of natural necessity (i.e., scientific explanation). But, in stark contrast to Hollis, this approach leads him to the formulation of a deterministic method of science which appears to dissociate proper scientific explanations from the use of any specific "model of man." As Gellner, however, does not apply his views directly to the problem of explaining human action, it is difficult to assess just what the precise implications of his method of science might be for the social sciences. Nevertheless, with the examination of his ideas one thing becomes apparent, since all theories of knowledge are at best prescriptive (including his own), the problem of human freedom cannot be conclusively resolved one way or the other through the simple application of logic. In other words, it is not possible to claim explicitly with Hollis that the principle of rational human agency is an a priori of social analysis. Yet, in the light of Hollis' and Nell's scrutiny of the pitfalls of classical micro-economic theory, it is hard to imagine how human actions could be explained without explicitly or implicitly invoking some principle of rational human agency. Therefore, while in the last analysis it seems impossible to view the notion of rational human agency as anything other than prescriptive, at present and for the forseeable future it also seems that the notion is best treated as a an essentially transcendental category of the explanation of human action.

The second task undertaken in Part Two involved examining sociological role theory in order to demonstrate further the relevance of the argument from rationality. The dramaturgical analogy at the heart of role theory is used to link the argument with the explanatory problems generated by the tension between the principles of autonomy and socialization in sociological accounts of human action. Criticising the logic of the normative explanations offered by role theory, Hollis argues that such explanations remain insufficiently conclusive because they fail to develop a consistent notion of the subject self, or actor, who inhabits the roles under scrutiny. To explain fully the actions of an actor, a role theorist must choose between passive and active conceptions of humanity and found his or her theory upon either the ideal type of a completely socialized actor or the ideal type of a completely rational actor. Implicitly, sociologists tend to choose the former option, but this choice undermines the heuristic value of the dramaturgical analogy and it raises the problem of accounting for social innovation. The latter option, however, poses the problem of identifying the actor's "real reasons" for adopting any role. To get at an actor's real reasons (as opposed to simply the professed reasons), Hollis argues that it is necessary to discover what he or she "essentially is," since real reasons are those which serve one's "real intersts." But to understand what someone essentially is, it is necessary to isolate strict criteria of identity – a task which has stymied the philosophers. To illustrate the need for such criteria, in a quick, simple and effective fashion, the debate between Young and Bernstein over the infinite regress of socialization was reviewed. Young, it was revealed, is hard pressed to defend the notion of human autonomy through simple reference to our capacity to distance ourselves reflectively from our socialized orientations. However, his attempt to work with a notion of "degrees of identity and individuality" can be used to support the notion of "Autonomous Man" if, as Hollis asserts, a more audacious tack is taken. The actor can be seen to find him or herself in socially assigned roles, or at least some roles, while remaining autonomous, if the roles in question are those he or she has "rationally" consented to accept. Ideally, the rationality of the identification functions as a substitute for strict criteria of identity and halts the infinite regress of socialization, for "rational action is its own explanation."

In the absence of strict criteria of identity, however, we get a peculiar notion of rational judgements: they are inherently retrospective and relative, if only because they are subject to indefinite future revision. Thus the onus of the argument shifts to the task of elucidating the nature and operation of these peculiar judgements of rationality, both as they are employed, for explanatory purposes, by social actors and by the social scientists studying such actors.

This third and final task of Part Two hinges on establishing the credibility of three basic methodological premises of the argument from rationality: asymmetry in modes of explanation, the epistemic character of all discussions of rational action, and the derivation of all rational actions from acts of self-expression on the part of an essentially social self.

The first premise, the asymmetrical nature of the explanations given to rational and irrational actions, was developed through consideration of three sub-issues: the relation of beliefs and actions, of reasons and causes, and of practical and epistemic standards of rationality. Refuting the soft positivist tendency to interpret actions simply in terms of behaviour, it was argued that it is a central feature of actions, and not just a contingent fact, that they are expressive of beliefs. Actions appear, that is, to be differentiated by their intentional character. In fact, however, while mere reference to behaviour is insufficient, so is mere reference to intentionality, for the relationship between actions and intentions is too circular. To break free of this circularity, more specific reference has to be made to the rationality of the beliefs informing actions. But for this reference to carry explanatory force it is necessary to have a clearer sense of how reasons generate actions. It is at this juncture that Hollis parts company with another prominent proponent of the principle of asymmetry – Alasdair MacIntyre. MacIntyre attempts to impart force to reasons by interpreting them

as causes of a type. Through a complicated discussion of the case
of post-hypnotic suggestion, he suggests that the condition of an
agent's "possessing a reason" for an action operates as a causal
connection subject to empirical testing and hence verification or
falsification. But his proposal is problematic in a number of respects. Foremostly, it was argued that if the reason for an action
is verified or falsified by reference to an empirical generalization
supported by tests, it does not necessarily follow that the relation
between the supposed 'cause' (i.e., the possession of a reason) and
the effect (i.e., the action) is law-like and transitive (i.e., truly
causal). Rather, as Hollis stipulates: "Knowledge of a fact is not
to be analysed as true belief caused by the fact. ... Admittedly
I know a fact only if there is such a fact. But the fact is not
the cause of a state of mind but the reason for judgement" (1977:
127). In fact, Hollis goes on to argue, using the example of a chess
move, "where good reasons do explain action, they also explain
any relevant general connection" (1977: 128). In other words, as
suggested in the critique of Tibbetts' position, actions from reasons are not testable. However, the explanations of such actions
can be criticized by questioning the underlying assumptions of the
norm of rationality invoked by the explanation in question. In his
own case, though, MacIntyre has preempted such a line of attack
by unnecessarily and unjustifiably restricting himself to a merely
practical conception of rationality.

Like most social scientists, MacIntyre ends up implicitly identifying rational actions with actions which conform to the relevant and given set of social norms of reasonableness. This view
is insufficiently strong, however, to support the principle of asymmetry. Hence MacIntyre is drawn into the convoluted task of
rendering reasons causes; an endeavor which actually only further
undermines the principle of asymmetry. To found the notion of
asymmetry, rationality must be equated with truth – an epistemic
standard must be invoked. Social scientists and historians resist
this conclusion in an effort to keep their work free of explicit normative commitments. But their efforts are not only futile, from
a practical perspective, they are theoretically misguided from the
start.

It is methodologically very demanding to work with an epistemic standard of rationality. It apparently leads one, for example, into the dilemmas of effecting a cost analysis of each action.
Hence the temptation is strong to restrict oneself to a merely practical conception of rationality, like the subjective rules of mental

processing delineated in the theories of the social psychologists. These approaches, however, turn out to be equally dependent, in unacknowledged ways, on some epistemic standard of rationality; and their explanatory capacity hinges, in the last analysis, on this fact. Reference to an epistemic understanding of rationality is instrumental to the inference of the beliefs of any particular actor. Hollis demonstrates this state of affairs through his analysis of the other minds problem as analogously revealed by the problem of translating ideas between cultures (especially widely disparate cultures) with different languages. Some bridgehead of universally valid propositions must be postulated if understanding is to be advanced. And it is these propositions which undergird the principle of asymmetry and hence the argument from rationality with all its implications for the systematic employment of the claim to human freedom. To believe that one can avoid invoking some such epistemic standard is to invite not just cognitive relativism but outright scepticism – to remove all constraints on the interpretation of beliefs and practices.

With these arguments in place, as concluded, the scaffolding has been erected for an alternative mode of social scientific explanation. A person is free to the extent that he or she has authentically taken on certain social roles. The authenticity of this activity is the result of making rational choices with regard to these roles. It makes sense to speak of rational choices and to attribute explanatory significance to them because an asymmetry in modes of explanation does exist in the social sciences. It exists because it is impossible not to invoke an epistemic conception of rationality when assessing the origins and significance of human action. Practically, however, the suspicion persisted that the argument from rationality makes excessive methodological demands and that it is empirically vacuous. While true to some extent, neither charge, when pressed, led to the specific condemnation of the argument from rationality. Soft positivist methods are equally plagued by the problems born of the complex nature of human actions and the mysterious character of the individual motives behind them. The study of these actions inevitably moves the inquirer from the formulation of the rationality of various means-ends relationships to the contemplation of the rationality of ends themselves. The pursuit of this endeavor, however, soon brings the inquirer face to face with yet another infinite regress (i.e., of ends which are always being transposed into means to other ends). To circumvent this regress, Hollis proposes that the argument from rationality should focus on those "goals desirable for their own sake," which he equates with true acts of self-expression (i.e., acts which fulfill one's real interests). Integrating the lesson of Chapter VII, in the abstract, an autonomous action is an act of rational self-expression on the part of an essentially social humankind.

To flesh-out this proposition practically it is necessary to "lay your bets" about the real interests served by rational self-expression. It is necessary to venture into the realm of values, in other words, and to form some notion of the Good Society; a risky undertaking, but one which underlies, in one way or another, even the most plebian and/or conservative accounts of human actions. It is these root judgements and their logical and natural consequences which must be assessed and debated to discern which potential formulation of the argument from rationality most shrewdly explains any given action. The feasibility of indulging in such assessments is in turn underwritten by the qualified idealist premise that there are indeed certain necessary truths about the nature of the world and the operation of human beings within it. Such assumptions and the evaluative bets which build upon them are not unique to the argument from rationality, but rather to social analysis as a whole. The argument from rationality just renders the situation explicit by giving unequivocal expression to the ideal typical character of the larger explanatory framework within which social analyses must be undertaken and hence rational and causal explanations, free and determined actions, sorted out.[5]

Having thus delineated the context and nature of the argument from rationality, and at least partially justified it through philosophical analysis, we are now in a position to answer two additional questions. How could students of the academic study of religion benefit from a working knowledge of the argument from rationality? Is Hollis' formulation of the argument satisfactory, or could the feasibility of the argument be advanced through the introduction of certain basic modifications? These are the questions to be addressed in the third and final part of this study.

Part Three
The Problem of
Transcendent Elements

It is not the 'actual' interconnections of 'things' but the 'conceptual' interconnections of 'problems' which define the scope of the various sciences. A new 'science' emerges where new problems are pursued by new methods and truths are thereby discovered which open up significant new points of view.

Max Weber, page 68 of
"Objectivity in Social Science and Social Policy,"
The Methodology of the Social Sciences, E. A. Shils and
H. A. Finch trans., New York: The Free Press, 1949.

X.
The Argument from Rationality and Religious Studies

The Reductionism Dilemma

If one accepts the identification of authentic religious acts with free acts (at least ideally), then to the extent that the the credibility of the argument from rationality has been established, a link has already been forged between Hollis' ideas and the social scientific study of religion. In addition, however, there are interesting parallels between the methodological hurdles tackled by Hollis and those dominant in the methodological debates of religious studies. When the latter are examined with the former in mind, it becomes apparent that the reasoning underlying the argument from rationality can have a direct bearing on the choice of a method of science for the social scientific study of religion.

As noted in the Introduction, in the academic study of religion a humanist majority and a social scientific minority contend with each other, and their disagreements echo the traditional struggles between religion and science. Recognizing this state of affairs, some students of religion have realized the need to ground their studies in more explicit insights from the philosophy of science (cf. Whaling. 1984). On the whole, however, in religious studies, unlike sociology, anthropology, and even psychology, scholars have been slow to realize the value of seeking redress to fundamental methodological dilemmas at this level of analysis.[1] The positivism-humanism debate in sociology, for example, is being reworked with developments in the philosophy of science in mind. Debate in religious studies over the parallel issue of reductionism has yet, though, to be affected significantly by such ideas.[2] Consequently, scholars in the field continue to debate the reductionism issue with an excessively restricted understanding of the epistemological options available. In this chapter, by way of partial adjustment of this state of affairs, one element of the reductionism debate: whether the social scientific study of religion can or cannot legitimately accomodate some 'references to the transcendent', will be examined, in the light of Gellner's and Hollis' contrasting conceptions of the foundations of science.

Obviously neither Gellner nor Hollis deal directly with the question of whether references to the transcendent can be incorporated into the scientific study of religion. But as noted in the Introduction, on the one hand, Michael Cavanaugh has used Gellner's understanding of science to criticize stringently the anti-reductionist attempt to found religious studies on a 'kind of technical competence about religion' which could 'rule out extra-religious claim testing'(Cavanaugh, 1982: 110). In other words, he has used Gellner to provide new legitimation for a hard reductionist science of religion. This science categorically rules out any explanatory consideration of the references made by the religious to the transcendent, by blocking the inclusion of any 'references to the transcendent' in the discourse of the scientific study of religion. On the other hand, some of the epistemological insights developed by Hollis can be used to provide valuable methodological support for Donald Wiebe's programmatic suggestions for a soft reductionist science of religion: one which not only permits but necessitates the inclusion, at least initially, of the espoused references to the transcendent of the religious in the complete and scientific assessment of religious phenomena.[3]

As outlined in the introduction, those scholars in religious studies which can be roughly grouped (according to their methodological sympathies) with the humanists in sociology, claim that the truth of religious experience requires something other or more than social scientific understanding. Seeking to guard the specific nature of religion from explanations which, it is thought, in the end explain it away, the scholars of this tradition stress the *sui generis*, esoteric, and self-interpretative character of religious beliefs. Yet unlike some contributors to the positivism-humanism debate in sociology (e.g., Winch. 1958 and Simon, 1982), these scholars have not gone so far as to exclude religious phenomena from scientific analysis per se. Rather they have chosen to fashion a new science which fits their subject matter: a nonreductionist, phenomenological descriptivism (R. Otto, 1917; Van der Leeuw, 1938; W. B. Kristensen, 1960: C. J. Bleeker, 1954, 1975; Mircea Eliade, 1963, 1969; W. C. Smith, 1959, 1962). One of the objectives of this approach, an objective shared with the humanistic agenda in sociology (e.g., Peter Berger, 1963 and Paul Filmer et al., 1972), is to remain true to the perceived open-ended character of the actions and experiences under study. The science in question has been rendered, however, without significant recourse to either the philosophy of science or even the philosophical phenomenology of Edmund Husserl (see George A. James, 1985).

Consequently, other scholars, while equally leery of the pejorative implications of many of the classic theories of religion (e.g., Tylor. Durkheim, Freud), think that the nonreductionist option simply constitutes poor science. To fashion a true science of religion, these scholars argue, the demands of science must be given precedent to those of the subject of study. Therefore the spectre of reductionism probably cannot be avoided (e.g., H. Penner and E. Yonan. 1972; R. Segal, 1980, 1983; D. Wiebe, 1979, 1981, 1984b). But in this instance as well, the force of the criticism is undermined by a failure to truly provide a satisfactory formulation of the standard of science being invoked. Instead, the work of these critics only refers, on the whole, to certain basic principles associated with traditional inductivist and/or deductive-nomological conceptions of science. Yet it is only with reference to a more specific model of science that a reasonable decision can be made as to whether giving precedence to the demands of science necessarily entails, as both parties to the dispute seem to assume, accepting a reductionist method or, to be more specific, a reductionistic linguistic grid for the study of religion.

The exponents of the science-before-subject policy tend not to see reductionism as a problem, especially in the limited sense of excluding references to the transcendent from scientific accounts of religious phenomena. Like Tibbetts with regard to the question of free-will talk, they think that the reduction in question is strictly theoretical and not ontological.[6] Penner and Yonan give voice to this view in their oft cited article 'Is a Science of Religion Possible?' (1972: 130-31):

> As we have shown. reduction is an operation concerned with theories or systems of statements, not with phenomena, data, or the properties of phenomena. ... None of the scholars we have examined ... states that reduction wipes out, levels, or demeans, the phenomena or data being explained. On the contrary, reduction in the sciences implies an *explanation* of one *theory* by the use of another in the same discipline (or, different disciplines). The sole purpose of reduction is to offer adequate theoretical explanations and to provide for the continued progress of scientific knowledge.

Cavanaugh, we will see, holds to an essentially similar view.

Those who lay claim to the irreducible nature of religious beliefs and practices are suspicious of this distinction, however, though they are rarely very methodologically articulate in stating their case.[7] The wholesale deductive reduction of explanations framed in religious terms to ones framed in terms applicable to psychic and/or social structures and processes entails, they implicitly argue, the displacement of religious claims as such from the universe of truly significant discourse. In other words, as I will argue, so-called theoretical reductionism does result in ontological reductionism. But what is more, from the vantage of Hollis' epistemological insights, it is clear that the acceptance of this theoretical reductionism might well be at odds with the actual procedure by which scientific fields of discourse are shaped and knowledge advanced.

There is no need to choose categorically between faithfulness to the perceived nature of one's subject matter (i.e., the traditional nonreductionist position) and commitment to the supposed standards of sound scientific practice (i.e., the traditional reductionist position). The true lesson learned from the philosophical demise of the positivist conception of science, it must be remembered, is that no statement is simply analytical (i.e., abstract, theoretical) or simply synthetical (empirical, ontological). When pressed all statements are in some sense a complicated blend of the two elements. And by extension, no phenomenon susceptible in part to scientific study (e.g., human references to the transcendent) can be treated categorically as either beyond all possible knowledge (i.e., absolutely transcendent) or wholly the subject of phenomenal knowledge. Subjects such as this, which are close to the heart of the human condition, vary in manifestation and nature by a matter of degrees, and they cannot be neatly divided into exclusive kinds of reality. Recognition of this fact does not warrant, however, methodological anarchy. We do obtain servicable knowledge of all aspects of our world and how this occurs, by design or accident, can be systematically examined. This is precisely what Gellner and Hollis have done, though they have arrived at contrary conclusions.[8] But Hollis, to a greater extent than Gellner, and Gellner to a greater extent than Cavanaugh, seems to have appreciated the need to build a measure of openness into the method of science used to treat such essentially open-ended phenomena as those human claims which have metaphysical roots yet a daily significance. In *Models of Man*, the groundwork is laid for a systematic methodological openness to the possibility of human freedom. Something similar can and should be done vis-a-vis the treatment of human references to the transcendent. The possibility will hinge, once again, on the role assigned to certain axiomatic terms of reference in the delineation of a field of study.

By way of initial elaboration of this point, let it be noted that the debate over reductionism in religious studies has been complicated by a sometimes explicit, more often implicit, political aspiration: to secure disciplinary status for the field of religious studies. What being a discipline entails is itself a very thorny issue. But it is safe to say that disciplines are demarcated by distinctive modes of discourse and methodological axioms which indicate (the acceptance of) the relative autonomy of a specified subject matter (e.g., economics, psychology, organic chemistry, and so on). Consider, for example, Durkheim's effort in *The Rules of Sociological Method* (published in 1895) to establish the *sui generi* character of social facts and hence a distinct set of methods and terms for their analysis. In religious studies the quest for disciplinary autonomy has been embodied in two discussions: the attempt to resolve the relationship of religious studies and theology (e.g., C. J. Bleeker, 1971; A. D. Galloway, 1975; Schubert M. Ogden, 1978; J. M. Kitagawa, 1980; and several of the references from endnote one of the Introduction), and the attempt to resolve the relationship of the phenomenology of religion with, on the one hand, the history of religions, and on the other, the social scientific study of religion (e.g., E. R. Goodenough, 1959; U. Bianchi, 1972; R. J. Zwi Werblowsky, 1975; K. Rudoplh, 1981; and several of the references from endnote one of the Introduction). The aspiration to demarcate a distinct realm of study, I think, is valid (cf. Paul Wiebe, 1984). The discussion in religious studies, however, has proceeded in an introverted fashion. Debate has centred on specific historical and methodological differences, while largely ignoring the general epistemological and practical steps involved in the establishment of the existing social sciences. In particular, the role played by the creation of a consensus metalanguage has been neglected. But the methodological proposal developed here, on the basis of Hollis' ideas, pinpoints the significance of this factor. It does so by arguing for the philosophical feasibility of using the the concept of references to the transcendent to formally demarcate and focus religious studies as a discipline.

Before this argument can be developed a few important qualifications must be stipulated. In the first place, 'references to the transcendent' is being employed in this discussion to impose certain specific controls. The referent of the phrase is the noun 'the

transcendent'. That is the focus is not 'transcendence' in its relative adjectival and verbal forms, as in 'Niebuhr stressed the unique
capacity of humans to constantly transcend their circumstances'.
Religious activities, I am implicitly specifying, are distinguished
on the whole from other kinds of activities by a specific language
usage, namely by conceptual reference, explicitly or implicitly, to
a dimension of reality that is beyond and different from that of
our ordinary, daily existence. Nothing more is being specified,
however, than a purely ostensive differentia. My use of the phrase
'references to the transcendent' is not meant to entail any absolu-
tizing or unifying tendencies. The precise and contrasting character of the transcendents to which different believers refer remains
unknown and is not immediately relevant to this discussion.

Second, it is also not relevant whether the transcendent to
which the religious refer truly exists (whatever that precisely
means). In this chapter, I am talking about the formal employment of a category, talk of the transcendent, to frame the subject
matter of the academic study of religion. It is an argument, that
is, for the justification of a certain metalinguistic convention; an
argument which recommends itself precisely because it provides a
partial solution to the hoary old problem of reductionism in the
scientific study of religion without becoming liable to the charge
of engaging in a crypto-apologetic endeavour. (Perhaps this would
be clearer if the phrase were changed to 'references to a transcendent', substituting an indefinite article. But this change might
well only increase the likelihood of being misunderstood in the
manner addressed by the third qualification given below.

In broad outline, the argument to be advanced for the formal use of references to the transcendent in the scientific study
of religion consists, predictably, of a logical extension of Hollis'
arguments for the instrumental use of 'free-will talk' in the social
sciences as a whole. The advantages of this tack is the point to be
clarified through the methodological and epistemological analysis
of the views of Cavanaugh and Wiebe, in the light of Gellner and
Hollis. But as should be apparent, the argument to be advanced
does not represent an attempt to use the epistemological ambiguities born of the demise of simple inductivism and Logical Positivism to bolster the ontological plausibility of any claims made
by religious individuals or groups. Such negatively formulated arguments (i.e., focusing on the limitations and deficiencies of the
scientific method) cannot be used, as Gellner and Hollis agree, to

establish positive ontological propositions. The use of such arguments is philosophically dubious and only serves to widen the gap
between religious explanations of religious behaviour and scientific
explanations of the same behaviour by discrediting the methodological investigations of those students of religion who are striving
to remain sympathic to the religious viewpoint, through their very
method of study.

Third, and in a similar vein, the phrase specifically reads 'references (in the plural) to the transcendent', in order to avoid the
implication of support for any particular mono-view. The category
may be applied to the study of the beliefs and actions of polythe-
ists and monotheists. In fact, I would argue for its application to
almost all religions, including most populist forms of Buddhism
(Spiro, 1970). But to actually apply this terminology to atheistic
religions like Buddhism and Confucianism, and perhaps even to
primitive belief systems, would require more argument than can
be accomodated here. Therefore, side-stepping the issue for the
moment, the proposal offered may be limited to the study of the
mainstream religious traditions of the West alone. The objective
is to begin to see an old methodological problem in a new light, to
point out the promise of a different perspective, and not to draw
definitive conclusions.

Fourth, it must be cautioned, that this study is not intended as
an investigation of the overall problem of reductionism. The issue
is too ramified to be adequately treated here [4]; and to some extent,
a thorough discussion of the philosophic debate over reductionism
is precluded by the manner in which the problem has been treated
in religious studies. With rare exceptions (most notably with regard to the views of Freud, and perhaps Durkheim) the struggle
over reductionism in the academic study of religion has not been
about the substantive reduction of religious phenomena to non-
religious phenomena. The situation is not fully comparable, that
is, to the classic debate over the reduction of biology as a science
to chemistry and physics (though the consequences of this latter
debate, with regard to conceptions of human consciousness, does
have an obvious bearing on the truth or falsity of a wide range of
religious ideas). Rather, the debate over reductionism in religious
studies has been about the restrictions which can or cannot be
placed on scientific discourse about religion and/or the need to be
religious to understand the discourse of the religious.[5] The pertinent concern, that is (though rarely identified in these terms), is

the continued (but usually indirect) debate over the Logical Positivist attempt to eliminate metaphysics and unify the natural and social sciences through the reduction of scientific discourse to a phenomenalistic (i.e., sense-data) linguistic grid.

As admitted earlier, dyed-in-the-wool positivists are now a very rare breed. Yet, most social scientists continue to employ a method of science which is largely informed by the positivist project. And scholars concerned about reductionism in the scientific study of religion almost invariably identify the social scientific study of religion with a positivist method of science. With this state of affairs in mind, the present study is limitedly designed to suggest two things: first, that contrary to the implicit working assumption of most discussions of the issue in religious studies, the epistemological and linguistic framework of science need not be intrinsically reductionistic, at least with regard to the elimination of 'talk of the transcendent' from scientific accounts of religion; second, that nevertheless, unless careful attention is paid to the precise formulation of the epistemological and linguistic framework employed in the scientific study of religion, an unacceptable and perhaps even derisive ontological reductionism may be effected, though theoretically none is intended.

To properly frame the issues at stake and the alternative options advocated, let us first to set the stage of the debate by delieneating the basic elements of the nonreductionist position.

The Argument for Nonreductionism

In prolonged reaction to the early 'nothing but ... ' theories of religion of Freud, Durkheim and others, many students of religion have argued that a true social science of religion is impossible. The inner experience of what Wilfred Cantwell Smith calls "faith," they reason, constitutes the essence of religion and it is not susceptible to the empirical probings of the outside observer. The best that the scientific study of religion can aspire to is the accurate recording and comparative study of the external trappings of religious practice, the elements of what Smith calls "tradition" (Smith, 1962). But the study of the external expressions of religion must not be mistaken for a true knowledge of the reality of religion. True knowledge stems from an appreciation of the uniqueness of religious experience, hence to know religious reality one must have a direct experience of at least some form of faith.

Understanding and explanations can only grow out of a natural empathy for the consciousness of the religious believer. The detached and rationalistic consciousness of the traditional scientist simply misses the mark.

This turn of mind is made explicit in the opening comments of Rudolf Otto's classic *The Idea of the Holy* (1917: 8):

> The reader is invited to direct his mind to a moment of deeply-felt religious experience, as little as possible qualified by other forms of consciousness. Whoever cannot do this, whoever knows no such moments in his experience, is requested to read no further; for it is not easy to discuss questions of religious psychology with one who can recollect the emotions of his adolescence, the discomforts of indigestion, or say, social feelings, but cannot recall any intrinsically religious feelings. We do not blame such a one, when he tries for himself to advance as far as he can with the help of such principles of explanation as he knows, interpreting 'aesthetics' in terms of sensuous pleasure, and 'religion' as a function of the gregarious instinct and social standards or something more primitive still. But the artist who for his part has an intimate personal knowledge of the distinctive element in aesthetic experience, will decline his theories with thanks, and the religious man will reject them even more uncompromisingly.[9]

Most students of religion are not willing to go so far as to make personal religious experience a prerequisite for meaningful participation in the academic study of religion. They recognize that such a demand runs the risk of differentiating the study of religion from the study of other social phenomena by reidentifying religious studies with theology.[10] Some eminent scholars, however, express such a marked sympathy for the rationale of Otto's warning that the line separating their own position from his is so fine as to leave the distinction in doubt (e.g., M. Eliade, 1963, 1969; W. C. Smith, 1959, 1981; C. Davis, 1975, 1984). Consider the following statement by Smith (1959: 43):

> Non-Christians might write an authoritative history of the church but however clever, erudite, or wise they can never refute Christians on what the Christian faith is. The only way that outsiders can ever ascertain what Christianity is, is by inference from Christian work or art or deed; and they can never be better qualified than those Christians to judge whether their inferences are valid. Indeed, some Christians have maintained that in principle no one can understand Christianity who does not accept it. We do not go so far, but we recognize substance in this contention. We recognize also that a similar point applies to all religions. Anything that I say about Islam as a living faith is valid only in so far as Muslims can say "amen" to it.

It is this attitude that has led many scholars in Europe and North America to adopt a methodological platform something like that formally developed by the Dutch phenomenologists of religion (e.g., Gerardus van der Leeuw, W.B. Kristensen, and C.J. Bleeker). This platform, as I read it, has four planks. First, in the phenomenology of religion "judgement is suspended." The Husserlian notion of the *epoché* is applied, in the sense that the question of the truth or falsity of religious claims (especially metaphysical postulates) is "bracketed" and set aside (Bleeker, 1975: 6). Attention is turned solely to the description of religious phenomena. Second, the attention concentrated on this task is directed to "the search for the *eidos*, that is the essentials of religious phenomena." In Bleeker's words, "every religion has its own distinguishing factors," yet overall, "the number of ways in which religious belief expresses itself is relatively limited" and the world-over religions conform to certain essential forms and structures (1975: 9). Third, as Bleeker further asserts, "religion is *sui generis* and cannot be explained by non-religious factors" (1975: 9). Fourth and last, this means that "in order to understand the believer, [the phenomenologist] must take his words seriously when he declares that he has encountered God" (1975: 7). On at least two occasions, Bleeker recommends that students of religion should harken to the advice of Kristensen (Bleeker, 1975: 6 and 1959: 106):

> Let us not forget that there is no other religious reality than the faith of the believers. If we want to make the acquaintance with true religion, we are exclusively thrown on the pronouncements of the believers. What we think, from our standpoint, about the essence and value of foreign religions surely testifies to our own faith or to our conception of religious belief. But if our opinion of a foreign religion differs from the meaning and the evaluation of the believers themselves, then we have no longer any contact with their religion. Not only our religion, but every religion is, according to the faith of the believers, an absolute entity and can only be understood under this aspect.

The practical implications of this methodological advice are far from clear.[11] Yet it appears that the phenomenological method aims to render religious studies an autonomous discipline by establishing the autonomy of its subject matter. Religion is to be (somehow) understood according to its own logic.[12]

Those scholars influenced by this kind of 'internalist' account of the logic of religious studies have found themselves looking for what Smith has called "a decisive new principle of verification" (1976: 163). The objective is to legitimize the claim to the autonomy of religious studies by delineating a method of science which harmonizes or better yet transcends internal and external perspectives. Smith has proffered his own new principle of verification in the essay "Objectivity and the Human Sciences: A New

Proposal"(1976), and the principle he has in mind is "corporate critical self-consciousness." Formally he defines this principle as follows (1976: 163):

> By corporate critical self-consciousness I mean that critical, rational, inductive self-consciousness by which a community of persons, constituted at a minimum by two persons, the one being studied and the one studying, but ideally by the whole human race, is aware of any given particular human condition or action as a condition or action of itself as a community, yet of one part but not of the whole itself; and is aware of it as it is experienced and understood simultaneously both subjectively (personally, existentially) and objectively (externally, critically, analytically; as one used to say, scientifically).

Spelled out less abstractly, and in relation to its application, this principle entails agreement on two points. In the first place (1976: 164):

> No statement involving persons is valid ... unless its validity can be verified both by the persons involved and by critical observers not involved.

Secondly (1976: 164, 177):

> ... all humane knowledge (that is all knowledge of man by man) is in principle a form of self-consciousness.
> The process of knowing is a process of becoming. It is not a matter of using means, but of assimilating ends.[13]

The objective of this line of thought is valid, I think. It certainly would serve to keep the scientific study of religion formally open to references to the transcendent, if not much more. But, as Cavanuagh and Wiebe agree, the question of an appropriate method requires a more perspicacious treatment. Judgement will be reserved, however, until we have had a chance to peruse the diametrically opposed perspective presented by Cavanaugh.

The Argument for Hard Reductionism

Formally, with the demise of positivism as an operative philosophy of science, the threat of reductionism posed by the unified language thesis has dissipated. But in his article "Pagan and Christian: Sociological Euhemerism Versus American Sociology of Religion," Cavanaugh invokes the epistemological insights of Gellner to advance a new rationale for exclusively restricting the language of the scientific study of religion to matters open to empirical verification. In fact, taking up the Gellnerian theme of an inherent tension between the demands of valid cognition and human self-identity, Cavanaugh argues further that the scientific

study of religion must inevitably undermine the viablity of religious self-understanding as it can have no truck with claims to
knowledge entailing reference to the preterhuman.

In recent years, Cavanaugh points out, "a raft of briefs" have
been submitted for "an anti-reductionist imperative" in American
sociology of religion.[14] Mistaking the demise of strict empiricism
for an opportunity to "readmit religious metaphysics into knowledge" , the authors in question, he states, offer a "religious realism" which "holds religious phenomena to be self-demarcating
and idiomatic"(Cavanaugh, 1982: 109-10). But sound sociological
practice, he counters, is "euhemeristic".[15] It can neither be shown
that there is a definitive and idiomatic religious consciousness, nor
that the endorsement of such a consciousness is a necessary qualification for understanding religion. In our post-positivist age, "both
religious and scientific claims are messy social constructions and
... there is neither empyrean nor clairvoyant knowledge". In the
last analysis, "euhemeristic disenchantment is a necessary condition for analytic power because *thought remains sharp in measure
as it remains disconsolate*" (Cavanaugh, 1982: 110-11).

The dispoilers of religious realism par excellence, Cavanaugh
proposes, are Weber and Kant. Weber disrupts the romaticism of
religious realism with the sweep of his sober assessments of religion
in societies both ancient and modern, eastern and western.

> Weber's great service was to remind scholarship that any general con-
> ception of religion must be broad enough to cover what is innerworldly,
> ascetic, rationalist, churchly, stimulating, and world-rejecting, as well
> as what is otherworldly, mystic, mytho-poetic, sectarian, opiating, and
> world-accepting. This very breath should obviate ideas like ... 'symbolic
> realism', which portray religion as uniformily idiomatic or otherworldly
> (Cavanaugh, 1982: 112).

More importantly, Kant has "press[ed] the difference between
noumena and phenomena in such a manner that ... concepts [like
religious realism] become ... oxymoronic". At one time, phenomena, as merely sensible, were thought to "bar knowledge of intelligible reality". Kant demonstrated, however, that the intelligibility of all things is rooted wholly in the phenomenal world.
All knowledge is the product of perception. But perception is,
as Cavanaugh says, "simultaneously logico-empirical". Sensory
data are rendered intelligible by categories and concepts which
form an irreducible component of the process of perception itself.
Therefore, the act of knowing occurs "strictly within this world

of historically constructed experience." This means "by *noumena* we no longer mean *that which is not visible*, but rather, *that which we cannot know*." By definition then, "the objects of our knowledge and discourse cannot be non-phenomenal, non-empirical, or other-worldly"(Cavanaugh, 1982: 113).

If Kant's account is correct, and recent philosophy supports it, then religious realism is untenable. It is inadequate, moreover, for the same reason that undermines its nemesis, Logical Positivism. The latter "has been judged uncritical for regarding observation as primordial and naive. Religious realism is equally uncritical for regarding claims to non-empirical experience the same way" (Cavanaugh, 1982: 118). No matter how one attempts to equivocate, Cavanaugh concludes, since all religious phenomena entail reference to preterhuman phenomena, the claims of religions cannot be endorsed – at least not as self-understood. Religious apologetics, he asserts, have no place in social science, the consolation of religious realism must be stoically placed aside in favour of sociological "paganism".

Specifically, Cavanaugh suggests, sociologists should interpret religious phenomena with three conclusions in mind (Cavanaugh, 1982: 115-16). First, "the claims of modern sociological paganism are epistemic before they are ontic." Sociological paganism does not argue that gods do not exist, only that we cannot know them and hence preterhuman indeterminacy should not be permitted to muddle phenomenal explanations. Second, modern sociological paganism does not "relegate religion to non-rational or preintellective status. ... Modern paganism takes religious claims not as utterly false, but as *distorted communication* ... [it] recognizes the social reality of religion and seeks to explain that reality, including its distorted self-images, as a human product." Third, "the values of modern paganism are built into the structure of the sociological interpretation of religion". For the sociologist as sociologist there is no "extrinsic requirement for a realist conception of *religion*"; hence there is no methodological reason to work with anything other than a nominalistic and, in some instances, explicitly reductionistic conception of religion. The concern is not with religion per se, but with the role of religious variables in the social and historical life of humanity. Accordingly, "*religion* is not some predemarcated thing to which we then adjust our concepts. Rather, *religion* (like totemism) is merely the name we give to a congeries of phenomena with rough family resemblances" (Cavanaugh, 1982: 117).

In sum, Cavanaugh states, religious realism is but a "species of what Gellner identifies as 'the concordat' between post-modern thought and enchantment"(Cavanaugh, 1982: 113). The realists are reverting to re-endorsement theories which cannot truly advance our knowledge. Worse, Cavanaugh warns, they are "bound to produce an habitual and assiduously cultivated sociological gullibility", sanctioning every belief someone is committed to and labels religious. And, ironically, this gullibility begs the case of those religious adherents who "would vehemently deny the realist proposition 'religion is true' precisely in order to protect the truth-claims of their diverse religions" (1982: 122).

These comments logically lead us back to a consideration of the adequacy of Smith's "corporate critical self-consciousness." Is Smith's approach guilty of such a gullibility? In many respects it would seem that Cavanaugh's suspicions are warranted. In the first place, does not Smith's injunction to have claims about religions validated by both those involved in the religions and critical observers result in a science of religion which is little more than descriptive? As indicated above, with such a method of validation it would be difficult to verify even the general proposition that 'There is an essential veracity to the religious experience of humanity.' Second, Smith's new principle does not allow for any significant means of independently assessing the accuracy or worth of the judgements made by believers about their existential situation. Yet, if anything has come from the myriad of empirical studies undertaken by sociologists and psychologists of religion, it is the recognition that many religious beliefs and practices are the result of fear, anxiety, and ignorance, and not the result of any positive value commitments. Thus, while social scientists must strive to learn about religion from the religious, when they learn that the religious have avoided questioning their beliefs and practices, then, as social scientists, they must also accept a responsibility to inform the believers about the possible limitations or even harmful effects of their beliefs and practices. Methodologically the right to potentially challenge the reasonableness of a subject's faith, through the formulation of uncomplimentary explanations of that faith, should not be foreclosed to the student of the academic study of religion. No appeal to authority can be final in the work of critical reflection.

Referring to more innocuous matters, Smith calls the wisdom of his own proposal into question when he acknowledges two of many complicating factors. First, in the text of his essay he notes that though religions develop, few believers recognize this fact. Consequently, it is implied, the accounts they give of their religion may be out of touch with reality. Second, in a footnote he further comments, that of course the insider can speak with final authority only for himself (1959: 42-3). Yet neither of these problems, nor the many other complications Smith acknowledges but leaves unspecified, lessen his confidence. "On the fundamental point," he surprisingly insists. "I have no qualms."

Third and lastly, Smith's new principle of verification is too epistemologically ambiguous. Validity cannot be equated with mere agreement between, for example, a devote Moslem and a sceptical social scientist. It is the grounds for agreement that are interesting, and whether these grounds can be standardized. If the grounds are idiosyncratic to the situation or the issue, or if the two parties agree to some statement for different reasons, then the mere fact of agreement reveals little. It is the pattern which might emerge from many such agreements that bears some significance. Afterall, if standardized grounds for agreement can be specified, then justification probably exists for verifying other statements regardless of whether they meet with the agreement of both the Moslem and the social scientist. In any case, the bottom line is that Smith's rendering of the nonreductionist option does not allow us to skirt Cavanaugh's assertion of the need to choose between "disconsolate knowledge" and "unjustifiable consolation." The demands of cognition and identity remain in tension.

The Argument for Soft Reductionism

The values of "modern paganism", contrary to what Cavanaugh thinks, are not "built into the structure" of the social scientific study of religion; and references to the transcendent are too central to the conceptualization of religious beliefs and practices to be categorically excluded from any systematic study of religious phenomena. These are the claims of the soft reductionist option born of the linkage of some of the epistemological principles of Hollis' argument with some of Donald Wiebe's methodological suggestions for the scientific study of religion.

In his numerous writings on the fundamental methodological tensions of the academic study of religion, Wiebe has struggled to overthrow the existing pernicious polarity of views. Wiebe denys, in effect, the need to choose between "disconsolate knowledge" and "unjustifiable consolation" and argues both that the reductionists must drop their out-moded identification of empiricism with knowledge in *toto* and that the nonreductionists must abandon their epistemologically regressive claims to privileged access. The critical study of religion, Wiebe argues, presses on all fronts for well-grounded ideographic and nomothetic accounts of religious phenomena, while explicitly acknowledging the metaphysically and scientifically open-ended character of the religious studies enterprise.

A sense of what this means is provided in the following passage from Wiebe's critique of Robert Segal's article "In Defense of Reductionism" (1984a: 157-158):

> Despite an essential methodological agreement with Segal regarding the role of explanation and theory in the study of religion, I find myself forced to dissent from an important, even if largely hidden, element of his argument. He argues, it seems to me, for the a priori validity of a reductionist account of religious phenomena and in doing so himself adopts, although in a negative register so to speak, the same stance as that of the nonreductionists. On the metaphysical issue at stake in religious claims he comes down firmly on the side of the sceptic and against the devotee. And like his opponents, he does so without benefit of logical assessment or philosophical argumentation. "Whether or not reductionistic interpretations themselves preclude the reality of God," he writes, "nonbelievers by definition do not accept that reality and so cannot employ interpretations which presuppose it" (1983: 116). But in proceeding in this fashion Segal attempts to prove more than he needs to prove in his defense of reductionism in the study of religion; all he need have shown is the 'possibility' of reductionist accounts of religions and not their necessity. Consequently, I will suggest that the establishment of a framework for the scholarly and scientific study of religion requires neither a defense of the devotee over against the sceptic nor vice versa, but rather merely an agreement that methodological assumptions in such a study prescind that metaphysical debate altogether.

In his article Segal complains that the nonreductionist approach places too much emphasis on understanding religions in terms of how they are meaningful for religious believers. When faced with a methodological position like that of Mircea Eliade, he argues, the issue literally becomes "whether the true meaning of religion is its conscious meaning for believers" (Segal, 1983: 103). Nonreductionists acknowledge, in Smith's words, that "the observable part of man's religious history ... is an open question so far as scholarship is concerned" (Smith, 1962a: 155; cited by

Wiebe, 1979: 4). But they undermine the significance of this admission by further contending, in Smith's words once again, that "... the whole path and substance of religious life lies in its relation to what cannot be observed" (Smith, 1962a: 136; cited by Wiebe, 1979: 4), and that consequently a basic principle in the academic study of religion "is an ability to see the divine which I call faith" (Smith, 1962b: 46; cited by Wiebe, 1979: 4). Claims of this sort, Segal charges, have the effect of tying the understanding of religion to a prior "religious understanding" and reducing the concepts and categories of theories about religion to those indigenous to the religious communities under study. Under these circumstances the study of religion loses all pretense to objectivity and becomes synonymous with "endorsing" or even "reduplicating [sic]" religious beliefs. Does not the claim that it is necessary to appreciate the meaning of a religious belief as it is experienced by the believer amount, Segal asks, to the acceptance of the belief in question by the nonbelieving inquirer? If so, then the social scientist is being asked to accept in advance the truth of the very things which it is his business to test.

There is substance to this line of argument, but when it is pressed, Wiebe points out, problems arise. "Implicit in this argument lies an assumption on Segal's part that there is an asymmetry between his defense of reductionism and Eliade's defense of nonreductionism." The burden of the argument rests with the suggestion "that nonreductionist accounts of religion are possible only for devotees ... whereas reductionist accounts are possible for both devotees and sceptics (because devotees, presumably, can be helped to recognize not only the distinction perceived by the sceptic [, between the true meaning of religion and its conscious meaning for believers,] but the truth of the sceptic's alternative explanation)" (Wiebe, 1984a: 159). This assumed asymmetry, however, depends on a purely logical and circular argument which when scrutinized is both logically and psychologically deficient. True, Wiebe notes, for sceptics there is no alternative to employing reductionist interpretations of religion, "if they are to remain nonbelieving interpreters." But this argument "cuts both ways" since for devotees there is no alternative to nonreductionist interpretations of religion, "if they are to remain believers." By definition one is as much the case as the other, and there is no reason for Segal to presume that the psychology of commitment is any different or better founded for the sceptic than for the devotee.

This being the case, Wiebe suggests that we are confronted
with two possible methodological conclusions. On the one hand,
"if the only concepts the sceptic can use in understanding religion
are external to the religious discourse of the studied community
while the devotee's understanding is entirely in terms of concepts
that are internal to that discourse and community, then, surely, the
two discourses are incommensurable" (1984a: 161). This would
mean, of course, that a unified discipline or even academic study
of religion is impossible. On the other hand, if the possibility of
"apostasy" on the part of the devotee is to be entertained seriously as a component of the method of religious studies, as Segal's
reasoning implies, then presumably the modes of discourse of the
humanist-devotee and the scientist-sceptic are not truly incommensurable. In which case it must be possible to conceive of the
sceptic "going native." At least such must be the case if Segal
is held to the self-refuting logic of his strictly logical argument.
Interestingly, however, Segal rejects the first conclusion and fails
to consider the second.

Acceptably Segal rejects the first conclusion because he sees
the two discourses as incompatible but not incommensurable. Unacceptably he does not entertain the second conclusion, Wiebe
speculates, because he has already assumed that religion is false
and therefore it must be explained in terms of concepts not rooted
in religious self-images. But this assumption, Wiebe charges, is
"a cavalier adoption of rather momentous philosophic conclusions
without the benefit of philosophical argument (even by way of authority)" (1984a: 162). Suffice it to say, amongst philosophers the
falsity of religious beliefs remains problematic and even the implicit invocation of such a judgement is counter-productive. It can
only serve to bring about an equally unwarranted reentrenchment
of the nonreductionist position as the sole method appropriate for
religious studies.[16]

Ultimately, Wiebe asserts, the metaphysical question of the
truth or falsity of religious beliefs is "one of great importance in
coming to a theoretical understanding of the nature of religion"
(1979: 7). We do know more about a religious belief and those
who believe it, we have a better description, in fact a sufficient
explanation of the belief, if we can not only say that A believes 'p,'
but that 'p' is a true belief (Wiebe, 1981: 3). But, Wiebe stresses,
"to admit this is not to capitulate to the wholly different claim that
the very study of religion requires a conclusive ... answer [to this

question] before it can be embarked upon" (1979: 7). The question is still subject to dispute and to explicitly or implicitly take-on an ontological commitment (e.g., to declare that religious phenomena are *sui generis*) is to contradict the intent and the logical scope of the principle of the *epoché*. A proper suspension of judgement would leave the academic study of religion equally open to both the 'possibility' of reductionist explanations and the 'possibility' of nonreductionist explanations. In other words, in terms of the categories of Chapter VI, Wiebe advocates the adoption of an epistemological as opposed to an ontological approach to the root metaphysical issue of religious studies.[17]

Wiebe still wishes to conclude that "the reductionist approach shows a great deal of promise for the future of the academic study of religion" (1984a: 164). He hopes that contrary to the existing trends in religious studies greater attention will be given to the "microtheoretical" analysis of those limited areas of human religious behaviour "that can more easily be tested against empirical reality" (1983: 304). But he also points out that even the sceptic, the nonbelieving interpreter, must be "willing ... to move in counterinductive and counterintuitive ways when well-trodden paths seem to lead nowhere" (1984a: 164). The present lack of consensus about the theories of knowledge that normally undergird reductionist analyses of religion has created what Wiebe calls a "breathing space" in which attention can and should be turned to developing some of the "counterinductive procedures" suggested in the "rival religious (nonreductionistic) explanations" (1984a: 163).

As things stand in the field of religious studies this open-ended policy is epistemologically more responsible than Cavanaugh's. Cavanaugh is correct in suggesting that the first principle of a sound method for the study of religion is the realization that its claims "are epistemic before they are ontic." Like Segal on the one hand, and the phenomenologists on the other, however, he fails to appreciate the full extent of this principle. By identifying epistemological insight simply with Kant he, in effect, passes an ontological judgement when he further concludes that all preterhuman claims are illegitimate and consequently all religious claims are but distorted communications of social realities. He does not understand the degree to which, to use Berger's phrase, the "relativizers have been relativized" (1969: 43ff.); which is a peculiar failing for a sociologist. Unlike his mentor, Gellner, he does not seem to understand that Weber relativized not only the religious realists but Kant as well. The Kantian edifice cannot remain impervious to the onslaughts of sociologists of knowledge and conventionalist philosophers of science without reverting to something truly like the notion of synthetic a priori truths. But Cavanaugh, ironically true to Gellner's perspective, ignores this latter possibility. Within his sharply dichotomized scheme such a notion bears too close a resemblance to the claims of the nonreductionists. Yet formal openness to the 'possibility' of a priori-like truths, or to nonreductionist explanations of religion, does not constitute a "concordat with enchantment." Nor, Wiebe would assert, does such formal openness constitute an abandonment of the critical edge of "selector theories" in favour of a strategy of "reendorsement."

To be convincing on this score, however, Wiebe needs to anchor his criticisms of existing methodological approaches in religious studies in a positive alternative formulation. As one of his critics has commented, to be enlightening he must move beyond polemics and the "passionate pursuit of denounced error" (Davis, 1984: 394). The philosophers of science Karl Popper, Thomas Kuhn, Imre Lakatos, and Larry Laudan have all stressed the importance of positive and detailed alternatives in generating progressive paradigm shifts (Popper, 1963; Kuhn, 1970; Lakatos, 1970; Laudan, 1977). In his writings Wiebe makes reference to Popper, Lakatos, and Gellner, as well as such other philosophers of science as Carl Hempel, Michael Polanyi, Alan Ryan, and Richard Rudner. For the most part, however, these references are insubstantial and it remains unclear what his model of science is, let alone his alternative paradigm for the academic study of religion.[18] Nevertheless a survey of his work reveals that he has made three methodological suggestions which point to the possibility of constructively integrating his views with the epistemological and methodological insights of Hollis' argument from rationality. The first of these suggestions displays a congruence with elements of the general thesis of the argument from rationality, while the remaining two relate the quest for a method of science for religious studies to the development of the special thesis of the argument from rationality.

In the first place, unlike most students of religion interested in promoting the scientific study of religion (e.g., Michael Cavanaugh), Wiebe has argued for the use of a substantive/real and not a functional/nominal defintion of religion (Wiebe, 1981: Chapter I). After acknowledging the very real problems standing in the

way of defining such an elusive phenomenon as religion, he states
that "nevertheless ... unless some preliminary definition ... some
kind of intuitive understanding of the nature of religion susceptible of verbal formulation, is possible, no study of religion can
ever be launched." But if the definition one chooses is to escape
the "indictment of irrationality" a reason must be specified for
including and excluding different materials. And the specification
of this reason, Wiebe suggests, always involves one "in providing a
'real' rather than a merely 'operational' [(i.e., nominal)] definition
of religion." Writing in response to Robert Baird's well known
criticisms of real definitions of religion as unscientific indulgencies
in an "essentialist-intuitional method" (Baird has Eliade in mind),
Wiebe comments (1981: 12):

> In a sense, Baird's complaint is justified. It seems to me, however,
> that there is really no possibility of distinguishing, in an absolute way,
> real or essential definitions from operational ones. This distinction is
> useful only if it is remembered that it is a pragmatic one. ... The
> point of the distinction ... is that the operational definition is held
> open to further revision, whereas, at least as presently understood, the
> essentialist definition is not.

Recognizing this Wiebe notes, Baird's criticism can be evaded by
simply specifying "that the definition is not meant to locate once
and for all the essence of religion so much as to make certain assumptions about the type of phenomena that are to 'count as'
religious" (1981: 13). These assumptions may be stipulative, to a
degree, but through the application of certain criteria they can be
shown to be anything but arbitrary. In this regard, Wiebe cites
two sets of criteria. Melford Spiro proposes the two criteria of
"cross-cultural applicability" and "intracultural intuitivity" (i.e.,
the assumption cannot be counterintuitive). Fredrick Ferré suggests the three criteria of "responsibility of public intelligibility"
(i.e., a parallel to Spiro's intracultural intuitivity), "responsibility
of scope" (i.e., Spiro's cross-cultural applicability), and the "responsibility of cruciality." The latter criteria, Ferré states (cited
by Wiebe, 1981: 13), takes into consideration the fact that

> ... there are discoverable uniformities or resemblances in our experi-
> ences, with various degrees of pervasiveness, obviousness or importance
> for shared human interests. These are the uniformities which have been
> given names by having general terms applied to them, and it is at ma-
> jor intersections of such uniformities that we are likely to find our most
> crucial interests delineated.

Consequently, if an assumption taps into these crucial interests,
and is satisfactory on the other two counts, then it must be taken
to be fundamental and informative in some sense and not entirely

arbitrary. Definitions in logic and mathematics may be truly stipulative, but Wiebe concludes, "it is still the case that in other contexts definitions can be actually either true or false" (1981: 16). In
words which call Hollis to mind, Wiebe states that in these other
contexts all studies begin with certain "necessary assumptions"
about the delimitations of the subject matter. Therefore, in a
subtle but very important way, Cavanaugh is wrong in suggesting
that our concern need not be with religion per se. Methodologically, whether we choose to respond to the situation in a positive
or a negative manner, explicitly or implicitly, we do proceed as if
religion were "some pre-demarcated thing to which we then adjust our concepts," at least with regard to certain fundamental
concerns.

Cavanaugh has merely responded to this long standing, though
perhaps always implicit, fact of life of the academic study of religion in a negative manner. He has reacted against it, that is,
because he believes that he must in order to hold the social scientific study of religion to a strictly epistemological viewpoint (i.e.,
avoid unwarranted ontological commitments). Wiebe knows that
this end can be served better by adopting a less extreme and more
positive reaction. While he has not articulated his position in this
manner, it seems to me that he has realized that there can be an
autonomous study of religion because 'conceptually' religion is at
root an autonomous subject.

Elaborating on this let us look at the substantive definition of
religion offered by Wiebe (1981: 15): "The three elements that
jointly make a cultural phenomenon a religious one," he proposes,
"are transcendence, human limitation, and and salvation" (1981:
15).[19] In this approach the most significant component, he admits,
is reference to the transcendent. But he carefully stipulates (1981:
19):

> To see religion as involving a belief in the transcendent or even the
> supposition of an experience of the transcendent is not to endorse the
> truth of such a belief or assumption but only to recognize the "cultural
> postulation" of such a being or entity.

This statement is accurate enough. But since it is not anchored
in a clearly delineated and complementary method of science I
do not think that it carries enough persuasive force to safeguard
the academic study of religion from slipping back into either the
theistic ontological commitment of the phenomenologists or the
atheistic ontological commitment of the hard reductionists.

Yet by extending Wiebe's position, I think it is possible to maintain the autonomy of religion and establish the autonomy of the discipline of religious studies through an instrumental use of the category of 'references to the transcendent', without thereby pre-determining the very thing which ultimately religious studies is about, namely the truth of transcendent references. But following Hollis, I would argue that this entails finding an epistemological base for a method of science which does not fall squarely into either the humanistic or the positivistic camp. As Wiebe has asserted, it is unacceptably self-validating to simply declare, as the phenomenologists do, that religious phenomena are *sui generis* and can be interpreted in terms of their own principles of self-understanding. But openness to the possibility of a transcendent referent in explaining religious phenomena can be legitimately maintained because the field of discourse of religious studies is necessarily conceptualized and demarcated in terms of such a referential activity. The notion of references to the transcendent in religious studies is on a par with that of references to the principles of lawfulness and the truth in the demarcation of science itself.[20] Or even more closely, it is on a par with references to rational human agency in a field like neo-classical micro-economics. These references are conceptual primitives, givens, which can be deleted systematically from the analysis of religious phenomena only at the risk of losing the implicit intersubjective (though perhaps only linguistically so) base of ordinary and scholarly discourse. Only when this is appreciated will the academic study of religion be protected from the distorting effects of the covert ontological commitments of the nonreductionists or the hard reductionists. This is how I have chosen to read the challenge set out by Wiebe when he stipulated that even the sceptic, the nonbelieving interpreter, must be 'willing ... to move in counterinductive and counterintuitive ways when well-trodden paths seem to lead nowhere'(Wiebe, 1984a: 164).[21]

To reiterate (see Chapter VI), this view of matters is 'counterinductive' for it rests on recognizing that, if the first lesson of post-positivist philosophy of science is that all systems of thought are conceptually self-referential and rely on certain base assumptions that are apparently tautological, then the second derived lesson is that not all tautologies are empty. In the Kantian spirit of Hollis' suggestion that there are probably unique ways of conceptualizing domains of experience, it can be argued that religious data can be approached as religious by virtue of the fact that formally the identification of religious phenomena inevitably entails reference to references to the transcendent. I do not think this insight is counterintuitive; it only initially appears so. Hence it is in conformity with the criteria of Spiro and Ferré, as specified by Wiebe. (Regrettably, since Wiebe has not striven to fashion a true alternative to the positions of which he is critical, he has overlooked the need to harmonize the claims he has made on the pertinent issues in different places and at different times).

The process of acquiring knowledge in religious studies undoubtedly resembles the process elsewhere: practically it is a kind of piecemeal, perspectival feedback process, a *gnosis* in the hermeneutical circle. But for every hermeneutical process there has to be a unifying background. What is this background for the hermeneutical process as applied to religious action? Wiebe's critics (e.g., W.C. Smith, Charles Davis) seek this unifying background in the subjective experience of faith and accuse Wiebe of being deficient in this vital mode of preunderstanding. But with Wiebe I would say that such an orientation can only continue to invalidate the academic study of religion in the eyes of the other disciplines. What is required is formal openness to the transcendent, philosophically justified, and not personal contact. And the methodological embodiment and guarantor of this insight is the use of 'references to the transcendent' as a metalinguistic convention to demarcate the subject matter of the academic study of religion.

It must be acknowledged that Wiebe might object to this interpretation and extension of his ideas. The appearance of a connection with Hollis' ideas, however, is strengthened (in the absence of a more detailed statement of his method of science), through consideration of the two other methodological suggestions made by Wiebe.

A significant parallel can be detected with Hollis' ideas in Wiebe's discussion of the nature of truth and its relationship to "religious truth." In opposition to the phenomenologists, Wiebe argues that in the pursuit of explanations there can be no avoiding the truth question in studying religion. But, as indicated, he also rejects the tendency of social scientists to close off the issue prematurely (in a negative manner) by holding to a strictly naturalistic perspective. Questions must be asked about the truth of religious phenomena, but we should not expect the answers to be straightforward. The very notion of truth itself is obscured by a proliferation of distinctions: scientific truth, historical truth, philosophical truth, metaphysical, ontological, poetic, symbolic, extrinsic versus intrinsic, relative versus absolute, higher versus lower, personal or lived truth versus objective, and so on. With regard to religion, for example, it is common for believers and others to claim that the truth that counts is noncognitive and existential. But when Wiebe sifts through these claims in *Religion and Truth*, he finds that the bottomline remains clear (1981: 176):

> By 'truth' ... one means that something is in reality as one perceives it to be and to say otherwise is to play games with words. Being is *real* rather than true and it is our *knowledge* of being that is either true or untrue. The concept of truth, consequently, amounts to a matter of the truth or falsity of propositions purporting to tell us something about the world around us.

For all the talk of correspondence versus coherence versus pragmatic theories of truth (Wiebe, 1981: 176-180), to question the truth of something is to examine 'statements' about the 'reality of something.' But one additional component must be taken into consideration. As Michael Polanyi argues, in listening to a truth claim it is the tacit assertion of something that one picks up on and not merely the content of the claim. Although truth is a matter of correspondence between statement and state of affairs, it must be spoken of in terms of the asseration of a sentence because of what Polanyi calls "the personal mode of meaning" (i.e., in the last analysis, the nature of linguistic designation is not mechanical but idiosyncratic). In light of this we must learn to accept the risks of semantic indeterminacy and see that only words of indeterminant meaning actually have any bearing on reality. Recognition of this situation, however, does not plunge us into a subjectivist conception of truth, whether in the mode of the prosecutors (e.g., Nietzsche) or the defenders (e.g., Kierkegaard) of religious truth. There is. as Wiebe says, "a decided existentialist ring to [Polanyi's] conception of truth," but it remains founded in "the idea of correspondence and the objective nature of truth" (1981: 183).

Working with this conception of truth, Wiebe concludes that when it comes to examining 'the truth of religion' we are in fact talking of the truth of religious beliefs and doctrines. Religions are complex phenomena involving numinous experiences, feelings and emotional states, ritual actions, and moral practices, but the *truth* in any graspable sense resides in the "metaphysical claims" made by religions. And "if truth in other branches of knowledge ... calls for critical assessment involving the laborious process of collecting, sifting and analysing the evidence then it must require the same in religious matters" (1981: 187). But what can this mean when we know that religious claims are not verifiable in any ordinary sense? How might it make sense to identify the process of explaining religious phenomena with an assessment of their truth? Drawing on proposals advanced by Raeburne Heimbeck (1969), William Christian (1964), and Ninian Smart (1970), Wiebe suggests "that transempirical statements, such as 'God sentences,' can be made checkable or falsifiable in an indirect way"(1981: 188).

It has already been amply demonstrated that in statements of significance about the human condition metaphysical and non-metaphysical claims are intricately interconnected. This certainly holds true for the basic suppositions of the human sciences. It also holds true, according to Heimbeck, Christian, and Smart, for the basic suppositions underlying the claims of religious doctrine. Recognition of this fact is what makes it possible to speak of 'God sentences' or asservations of human freedom as indirectly subject to systematic assessment. They can be assessed, that is, provided it is also recognized, Wiebe points out, that a distinction can be drawn between 'criteria' for a truth statement and 'evidence' for the same (1981: 188).

> It is a different matter for something to be the case than for one to know or have reasons to believe that it is the case. 'Criteria' concern the conditions determining the meaning of a cognitive sentence; and 'evidence' concerns the conditions under which the truth or falsity of the statement is ascertained. It is possible thus to state what the truth conditions of a sentence are, independently of the availability of evidence. Such criteria can be derived from entailment or incompatiblity relationships such transempirical sentences have with more directly empirical statements.

Of course, this procedure by no means provides us with what Smart terms "knock-down arguments" in favour of one reading of the truth of a religious claim over another. But as Christian suggests, at the very least it does allow one to show that one view is as consistent and well grounded as another, and at the most that one view might actually be more consistent and well grounded than another. It is this possibility, Smart notes, which sensibly underlies "the fact that men argue about religion" (Wiebe, 1981: 191).

Here then we find Wiebe advancing a procedure for dealing with the problem of transcendent references in religious studies which is parallel to that advocated by Hollis for dealing with the problem of human freedom in the social sciences as a whole. The connection of beliefs to actions is essential; beliefs must be treated in the identification and assessment of actions. Yet the precise nature of the connection cannot be pinpointed. An instrumental reference to rationality seems to provide the best means of relating beliefs to actions and vice versa, and this opens up the possibility of some actions being free because they are rational. But the pursuit of the practical introduction of rationality judgements leads us ultimately to the "laying of bets." Likewise it is not possible to explain (as opposed to merely describe in a relative sense) religious phenomena without ultimately raising the question of their truthfulness. And in terms of the identification and assessment of religious phenomena this means invoking some reference to the idea of a transcendent dimension. But the reference need be, and in fact to avoid unwarranted biases, should only be formal in nature. So how are students of religion, in practice, to judge the truthfulness of the claims to transcendence which they encounter? They are to check the content of the actual claims they encounter for their consistency and compatibility with more directly empirical statements. In other words, on the basis of the limited knowledge of such ultimate things available the students of religion are also to 'lay their bets,' just as in a less critical manner all religious believers and "autonomous men" do in their daily activity.

Finally, an even closer link can be forged between Wiebe's and Hollis' methodological orientations by noting a direct but never developed reference by Wiebe to the argument from rationality. In questing after an adequate mode of explanation for religious studies, Wiebe dismisses in order: Carl Hempel's deductive-nomological model, the empathetic rendering of the *Verstehen* method, and the 'causal' explanation of human behaviour as a whole (1981: 63-72). Citing William Dray, he points out alternatively that the best model of social scientific explanation is that of "rational explanation." Only this model, he states (like Hollis), permits us to maintain "a distinction both common and of great significance," namely that "between the explanation of ordinary behavior and extraordinary or abnormal behavior" (1981: 66, 68). Accordingly, Wiebe endorses Keith Dixon's conclusion that "all explanations of human behaviour involve reference either directly or parasitically to the concept of what it is deemed 'rational' for men to engage in." He declines, however, to pursue the question of how it is that we should determine the rationality or irrationality of any action. Instead he merely uses this information to bolster his argument for the necessity of employing an "enlarged understanding of explanation" in any 'science of religion'; one which takes into consideration both the views of the 'insider' and the 'outsider' (1981: 69-79).

In fact in the conclusion to his discussion, the role of rationality assumptions in social scientific explanations is overlooked
altogether. "The question we are left with," Wiebe concludes, "is
quite simply, How is the science of religion to proceed?" In response to this question, Wiebe just reiterates the two conclusions
with which we are already familiar. Somehow, in order "to be
scientific the study must be critical as over against theological ...
and yet, if it is to do justice to its subject matter, it cannot adopt
a priori, a reductionistic framework." This in turn means that
the phenomenological bracketing of the truth question must be
abandoned. "An explanation of religion as illusion will be vastly
different from the explanation of religion as a true picture of reality." Therefore philosophical arguments for and against theism
and atheism must be taken into consideration. And "in this sense,"
Wiebe declares in his final sentence, "philosophy remains a key
factor in the scientific study of religion" (1981: 70-81).

Quite true; but from a procedural perspective, the social scientific study of religion entails philosophy even more fundamentally
because it rests on the argument from rationality. As Hollis stipulates in "Reason and Ritual" (1968: 239):

> In short, although it is an empirical fact that [religious believers] hold
> any beliefs and have any language at all, and although it is a matter
> of hard work and huge expertise to discover what forms they take, the
> [student of religion] needs conceptual tools before he can even begin.
> When packing his tool box, he is a philosopher.

And the most useful tool to be packed in this box is the argument from rationality (with it various applied forms), since it tells
us more about 'how' we should actually proceed in studying religious actions. It directs our attention more concretely to the
epistemological arguments that justify the continued use of 'talk
of the transcendent' in identifying and assessing religious actions.
In other words, it provides less contentious grounds for permit-
ting some 'religious explanations' to stand as true alternatives (in
a practical sense) to the reductionistic accounts of conventional
sociology and psychology.

In sum, a compounded form of the ideal typical approach recommended by Hollis for the study of social action in general offers
us an epistemologically defendable and highly appropriate method
of science for the academic study of religion. The method is a
compounded one in the sense that the intial assumption of human
freedom is complemented with an initial assumption of the relative

viability of references to the transcendent. With regard to both assumptions, the student of religion is simply being equipped with sound reasons for adhering. in these realms of endeavour, to the dictum 'innocent until proven guilty.'

XI.
The Argument from Rationality and Value-Neutrality

An Empty Argument?

In the last analysis, Hollis acknowledges, assessing whether a human action is free or not requires both the actor and the inquirer to shift their thinking about actions from the level of *Zweckrationalität* to that of *Wertrationalität*. In other words, it not only requires a shift from a practical standard of rationality to an epistemic standard, but a shift into the realm of values. In defences of human free will, such a shift is common. Reflective moral choices are among the human phenomena most resistant to explanation in terms of deterministic causes. As Tom Campbell observes (1981: 238):

> The experience of actually making moral choices is hard to reconcile with the idea that we always act in accordance with our strongest desire. Most people believe, at least sometimes, that they ought to do things they do not wish to do, and often they act on such beliefs: temptation, it appears, can be resisted.

But more importantly, as Campbell further notes:

> ... if moral values are independent of human choices and moral judgements can be true or false, then this provides a basis for an important type of interpretative explanation of human conduct (for it must then be accounted rational to do what is right and choose what is good).

In conclusion, though, Campbell notes, "there is ... no more open question in philosophy than that of the epistemology or truth-value of moral judgements" (1981: 239). Practically, for social scientists, all dealings with questions of value remain steeped in subjectivism. Hence the presence of a value judgement at the heart of explanations based on the argument from rationality arouses resistance to the approach. Amongst most social scientists, the preference persists, with some justification, for methods of science which are at least supposedly value-free.

Hollis removes much of the sting of this problem, as we have seen, by pointing to the inevitability of some crucial degree of value dependency in any social scientific analysis, and more will be said on this subject below. But his attempts to deny that the

kind of "theoretical evaluations" entailed in conceptualizing free
actions involve any pejorative value dependency do not eliminate
the troubling element of 'decisionism' at the base of the argument
from rationality (Hollis, 1977: 179-83). This problem of decisionism exists because Hollis' resolution of the problem of freedom is
too transcendental and formal, and consequently insufficient information is provided about the criteria of decision social scientists
should actually employ in determining the rationality of actions.
Therefore, despite all that has been said, the positivist-like suspicion understandably persists that his theory is empirically vacuous, because at heart it is too open-ended.

In a review of *Models of Man*, Gary Trompf zeroes in on precisely this deficiency. The line of thought developed by Hollis,
Trompf states (1980: 338),

> ... is certainly a stimulating rebuttal against moulders of Plastic Man,
> and it is a nice legitimation of impractical, dyed-in-the-wool academi-
> cism, but it does not appear to be so significant for social scientists as it
> may for philosophers, since it only very slightly impinges on the practice
> of social science (with its various traditions). Hollis seems happy just
> to show us that we are oftimes free, not so much because of higher crit-
> ical knowledge (Habermas) or awareness (W. Barrett), the ambiguity
> of our language (Wittgenstein), the fluid indeterminate nature of being
> (Heidegger), or the workings of our moral will (W. James) ... but be-
> cause we can be self-expressive. That is an important affirmation, yet
> researchers trying to understand the course of human affairs are only
> likely to note it (hopefully with relief), and pass on to the business of
> trying to explain why social events happen.

At the very least, it seems true that while Hollis presents a convincing argument for the necessity and value of assuming the applicability of some form of argument from rationality, the inquirer
is still left without significant guidance in the most important task
– choosing the specific criteria of rationality that could be used to
put the theory to work in a non-prejudicial way. Trompf's worry
is that the bet which Hollis is likely to lay, with regard to his
operative criteria of rationality, will be so indebted to the philosophical terms of reference of the European tradition that it would
force us to "write off most of the discrete 'belief-systems' of the
world ... as 'mostly' or 'mainly' irrational" (1984: 509). Whether
this "inference as well as ... intuition" is warranted is a subject for
debate. But the important point is not whether Hollis' actual conceptualization of rationality would be "open-textured enough" to
allow acts of revenge, perpetrated by the members of the Melane-
sian tribes Trompf has studied, to be viewed as rational. Rather,

the important point is the fact that his conception is so open-textured, in a different sense, that this very doubt can be readily and tellingly raised.

To bring the issue into direct relation with our primary concern, religious belief-systems as a whole (that is, in addition to the link established by the free nature of authentic religious acts), it should be noted that Hollis has suggested that the possibility of identifying and assessing religious beliefs and practices rests necessarily with the potential for viewing religious conduct as rational. It is common and appealing to speak of religious phenomena as embodying, in the language of Susanne Langer (1942), a non-discursive presentational symbolism which imparts its meaning like music. Ritualistic acts and objects, for example, are metaphorical; they require a different mode of "understanding." But Hollis states, "claims to have identified the metaphorical uses of words and gestures must be rationally justified. This involves cashing the metaphors and therefore the notion of 'metaphorical use' never has any explanatory force" (1970: 238). To have a science of religion or just a theory of religion, it is necessary to be able to discriminate between religious beliefs that are 'intelligible' and those that are not. It is necessary to be able to pass judgement on the rationality of the phenomena to determine the subject and scope of such a science or theory. Of course, in the past this necessity was denied by the likes of Feuerbach, Marx, and Freud, by simply identifying religion *tout court* with irrationality. But such an orientation just begged the question, for understanding then made it necessary to divine the rhyme and reason of the irrational. "The conceptual problem," Hollis points out, "... is that of putting ritual beliefs into a form in which they can be classed as rational without ceasing to be the beliefs in question" (1970: 236). As in the instance of the theologian, a paradigm of rationality is needed which permits the mysteries of the Catholic faith to remain mysteries without thereby being deemed senseless or irrational. But with the social sciences in mind, this paradigm must place these beliefs in a form which facilitates critical and comparative analysis, and is free of either the specific ontological commitments of the theologian or the reductive instrumentalist/functionalist assumptions of those social scientists who have been willing to discuss such a possibility since the days of Tylor and Frazer.

Now the question, once again, is: Has Hollis actually equipped us with the paradigm of rationality to accomplish this reorientation? No, as Trompf surmises, in any straightforward sense he has

not. Yet, in agreement with Hollis, it will be argued that we have
neither arrived at a *cul de sac*, nor have all of our labours been
for naught.

Over and again we have encountered the need to overcome various infinite regresses through the postulation of certain a priori
constraints. It is the interlocking network of the results of these
investigations which constitute the foundations of the argument
from rationality. First, Hollis argues that the infinite regress of
conceptual pragmatism must be halted, if there is to be something like science, by accepting the existence of certain a priori
conceptual constraints which demarcate realms of possible experience and hence appropriate modes of explanation. Second, Hollis
points out, in particular the regress of premises and *ceteris paribus*
clauses in the social sciences comes to an end only with acknowledgement of the model of rational human agency as a conceptual
a priori. Third, he suggests that the regress of socialization that
interfers with making sense of the notion of human agency can
only be halted by conceiving of personal identity as the product of
retrospective rational choices on the part of an essentially social
being. Fourth, in tracking down the nature of the rational choices
which undergird our autonomy, Hollis argues that the regress of
the translation situation (i.e., the hermeneutical circle) is broken
of necessity by postulating the epistemological unity of humankind
(i.e., working with an epistemic standard of rationality). Fifth, the
infinite regress of means and ends associated with the rational assessment of human actions is resolved by resorting to the notion
of 'expressive rationality.' This resolution leads us directly, however, to the sixth and most problematic regress: the debate over
which values are universally ultimate. It is a regress which might
return us, for example, to Chapter II and the choice between individualistic and communalistic sentiments on the degree of order
required to bring human freedom into harmony with the needs of
human communities, thus creating the Good Society. In the face
of this choice, it appears that Hollis' well of a priori conceptual
constraints has run dry, and we are confronted with the following predicament: in order to put the argument from rationality
into practice, the sociologist must introduce a crucial substantive
value judgement and that judgement carries the method beyond
the bounds of proper scientific procedure (i.e., because the judgement is not open to sufficient intersubjective assessment).

In fact, however, the critical point is that the constraints invoked by the argument from rationality, despite Hollis' claims, are

not really or simply a priori, and recognition of this fact curtails the degree to which an unusual and unacceptable decisionism is present in the argument from rationality. With a change in the precise formulation of the general thesis of the argument, it can be demonstrated that logically the infinite regress of epistemological debate (between empiricists and idealists) that has led social scientists to assume that all substantive value judgements, of whatever configuration, must be deemed extraneous to proper scientific procedure can also be halted.

In other and simpler terms, the element of decisionism in the argument from rationality can be reduced significantly if the epistemic standard of rationality invoked by Hollis is reinterpreted as being transcendental in a reduced sense (relative to Kant). This can be accomplished, without moving beyond the framework of Hollis' thought, by readjusting the balance between the two central formal principles of Hollis' new sociological metaphysics: the 'transcendental' status of rationality and freedom as categories of social analysis, and the 'relational' character of the same two categories as tools of social analysis.

In the polemical context of Hollis' theory, namely the debate over cognitive relativism in philosophy, anthropology, and sociology, it is the transcendental component of the argument from rationality which Hollis has emphasized (i.e., the fact that it is not only possible but necessary to use explicit standards of rationality in the social sciences). But in conformity with the evidential base and, one might say, the theoretical momentum of Hollis' actual argument, it is the relational component, most specifically the relational character of rationality, which needs to be developed. This entails bringing the element of decisionism under greater control when "laying bets" (at least in principle) by doing two things, both of which develop suggestions within Hollis' work for a more nuanced and operable conception of rationality. In the first place, in spite of Hollis' protestations, the criteria of rationality to be used in the social sciences should be naturalized (i.e., they should be rendered empirical hypotheses, though of a peculiar sort). Second, in line with this, judgements of rationality should always be thought of as a 'matter of degree.'

These modifications, it will be argued, can be introduced without sacrificing the explanatory force of Hollis' epistemological (i.e., transcendentalist) understanding of the nature of social scientific explanation. Yet they place a hedge against "the problem which faces any transcendentalist approach, that particular concepts, once elevated to the status of categories, will be treated with excessive respect and resist attempts to transcend and relativize them" (Outhwaite, 1983: 33). These modifications productively open up the argument from rationality to the results of investigations into what Robin Horton (1982) calls "primary theory" and Avrum Stroll (1982) "primordial knowledge" – empirical and theoretical research, ranging from Jean Piaget to Jürgen Habermas, into the apparently universal empirical bases of reasoning processes and rationality standards. Such research provides a conception of rationality with sufficient substantive form and meaning to assure the viability of science and the analysis of free actions, while paying due attention to the evolving and incremental nature of our understanding of what is rational, and hence either scientific, free, or authentically religious. Thus such a reinterpretation of the basic premises of Hollis' theory does much to reduce the open-ended character of the argument from rationality (i.e., its dependence on inaccessible value judgements).

A Natural Matter

To begin with, let us be certain that we have correctly grasped Hollis' position. In "The Social Destruction of Reality," Hollis reiterates that in the face of the plunge into scepticism lurking behind both conventionalist philosophies of science and the "strong programme" in the sociology of knowledge [1], social scientists have but two options: "[o]ne is to retrieve the given, to restore the independence of facts ... [t]he other ... is to place an a priori constraint on what a rational man can believe about his world" (1982: 83). For reasons already addressed, the former option is untenable, especially in the context of the social world. Even though the reasons for wanting to smuggle empiricism back in are patent, Hollis comments, it simply cannot be done credibly. Therefore, we have to place our faith in a transcendentalist solution: "there has to be that 'massive central core of human thinking which has no history' and it has to be one which embodies the only kind of rational thinking there can be." And lest anyone mistake the tenor of this conclusion, Hollis stresses:

> The 'massive central core' cannot be an empirical hypothesis, liable in principle to be falsified in the variety of human cultures but luckily in fact upheld. Otherwise, as Sextus Empiricus remarked in ancient praise of scepticism, 'In order to decide the dispute which has arisen about the criterion, we must first possess an accepted criterion by which we

shall be able to judge the dispute; and in order to possess an accepted criterion, the dispute about the criterion must first be decided.' To escape Sextus, the existence of a core must be taken as a precondition of the possibility of understanding beliefs.

The trouble is, as Hollis acknowledges,

> such reflections yield at most an existence proof. What has to be in the core? Notoriously not everything which Kant said about the categories of human thought has remained intact. ... It is tempting to respond by making the core all form and no content, by assigning to it only the formal properties of coherent belief, and leaving all particular beliefs about what there is to empirical enquiry. But this line of division between the necessary and the contingent does not give enough to stop the rot [of scepticism]. ... Hence the plain snag remains. Without specifying the core, I cannot make this paper cogent. But neither can I make it short. So I simply enter a plea for metaphysics.

The task of specifying the core is an onerous one which we too will leave for other more ambitious studies. But there is no reason to rest content with a plea for metaphysics, whatever that might entail. Hollis is reluctant to render the criteria of rationality mere empirical hypotheses because, like Kant, he fears the scepticism born of making the constructor of reality a part or product of the construction. Yet like most of his contemporaries, while he wants to think in terms of the world taking its form from our imposition of order upon it (because this view accords with our experience), he finds it difficult to conceive of the knowing subject simply as transcendental. Hence, as will be remembered: his commitment to the epistemological perspective on natural necessity is couched in the language of conditional propositions (see Chapter VI); and when transferring the lessons of the general thesis of his argument to the realm of the special thesis, he never identifies the values called upon in passing judgements of rationality with an objective or transcendent order. He stops short of such an identification even though it would appear to be the logical outcome of stipulating that the constraints on scepticism are synthetical a prioris. (Of course, it is possible that his plea for metaphysics points towards a full-fledged idealism; in this regard see "The Social Destruction of Reality," page 85.)

In like manner, the "bridgehead" of propositions required to break the hermeneutical circle (if only relatively) are treated ambiguously by Hollis. Certainly his formulation of the nature of this set of propositions does not remove them from the natural realm.

> The set consists of what a rational man cannot fail to believe in simple perceptual situations, organized by rules of coherent judgement, which a rational man cannot fail to subscribe to.

Are not these simple perceptual situations and our responses to them open to empirical inquiry? Cannot the rules of coherent judgement associated with these situations be tracked down through cross-cultural analyses? Need the massive central core of human experience literally be without a history?

The propositions of the "bridgehead," and by extension the so-called a priori constraints on social scientific analysis, are, in the last analysis, naturalistic phenomena which can be clarified and ramified through developments in the very research they underwrite. Such is the view of one of Hollis' closest colleagues, Steven Lukes. Lukes agrees that understanding necessitates the existence of a bridgehead, and its existence is an a priori truth. But, he asks, "Is the bridgehead fixed or floating?" As indicated at the end of Chapter VI, the latter option seems more likely. The bridgehead is but a part, albeit a crucial and neglected part, of Gellner's raft, for as Lukes asserts: in all practical instances "what must be presupposed for the interpretation of beliefs and belief systems is in a sense an empirical matter, or at least revisable in the light of experience" (1982: 272). Such is the case, because we cannot circumvent the fact of fallibilism: we can neither rule out the possibility that we might be able, with new information, to make assertions which at present we cannot. nor conversely, the possibility that assertions which we presently are warranted in making may have to be recast or discarded in the light of new information. (i.e., to put matters in a more concrete context, as pointed out by Horton (1979: 236), Lukes (1982: 272) and Skorupski (1985: 348), we cannot rule out the possibility that we might encounter an operative culture whose language and ways resist our attempts to establish a bridgehead).

The ambiguity of Hollis' position stems from his mistaken assumption that a naturalistic orientation must always entail some undesirable combination of causal realism and cognitive relativism (i.e.. in essence: determinism and scepticism). On the basis of this assumption he seems to have concluded that any alternative method of social science must rest upon an idealist foundation. But he is unwilling to argue for a true idealism because as a post-positivist thinker he is unable to disregard the fallibilism which roots all contemporary claims to knowledge in a naturalistic framework. Hollis' "existence proof" significantly adjusts the apparent consequences of this situation. But the bottom line is that fallibilism also constitutes an insurmountable conceptual constraint on the social sciences – one which Hollis has not adequately taken into account.

This disturbing ambiguity in Hollis' argument can be resolved, however, through the introduction of several insights advanced by the British philosopher John Skorupski. These insights develop points implicit to Hollis' work which can be used to make his argument consistent with a naturalistic framework (i.e., with fallibilism), thereby rendering it a more cogent logical alternative to the existing methodological extremes in the social sciences.[2]

In "Relativity, Realism and Consensus" (1985), Skorupski advances an argument which suggests (indirectly) that the true logical consequence of Hollis' choice of an epistemological approach to the question of natural necessity is to found the argument from rationality on a general thesis of what we will call *epistemic naturalism*. At first glance the term epistemic naturalism may appear to be oxymoronic. But this is only superficially the case. Seeing through the apparent paradox, however, entails fully appropriating the epistemological lesson of Chapter VI. It must be realized that the epistemic orientation at work in Hollis' thought can be distinguished from idealism by the fact that it constitutes a thesis about 'cognitive content' and is not a 'theory of truth.' Borrowing terms from the previous chapter, it is an orientation, that is, which reduces questions of truth to "asservations" about the "criteria" of knowledge claims, to asservations about the "conditions determining the meaning of a cognitive sentence," and not literally about the truth of knowledge claims. In other words, in the light of the fact of fallibilism, it is a thesis about statements of the type 'The assertion of Y is warranted' and not of the type 'Y is true.'

Now it is the case that with the framing of an epistemic conception of cognitive content, from the perspective of the practice of the social sciences, a kind of definitional equivalence is established between 'The assertion of Y is warranted' and 'Y is true.' The two statements become, in effect, *cognitively* equivalent. Thus we find Hollis talking peculiarly about the derivation of "real definitions" from a "definitional" conception of necessity. It remains the case, however, that these two statements are not *semantically* equivalent; and this distinction, though fine, is of crucial importance. For it is this distinction which makes it possible to speak of an epistemic approach which is naturalistic and a naturalistic approach which is epistemic. It is this distinction, in other words, which offers us the opportunity to make the argument from rationality

meaningful for the practice of the social sciences by opening the
criteria of rationality (at least in principle) to empirical investigation and specification, while simultaneously protecting the force
of human claims to freedom (i.e., to rational action) by main-
taining that even these empirical investigations are, nevertheless,
circumscribed by certain methodological assumptions (e.g., rational human agency) of a necessary, if not truly a priori nature. This
distinction extends the sensible conclusion reached by Wiebe, with
regard to metaphysical issues in religious studies, to the foundations of social science itself: the establishment of a framework for
the scholarly and scientific study of social action requires neither
a defense of a humanistic idealism over against a dehumanizing
naturalism nor vice versa, but rather merely an agreement that
methodological assumptions in such a study prescind that metaphysical debate altogether.

Still, the claim to be able to distinguish cognitive and semantic
content, though intuitively apparent, is contentious and requires
further argument. Here, however, pursuit of this argument is for-
closed to us by the breadth and complexity of the issues at stake.
Therefore, we can only point to the debate surrounding the seminal work of Jürgen Habermas. It is Habermas, more than any
other contemporary thinker, who has kept the distinction intact
by arguing three things: the immanent *telos* or function of speech
itself is 'understanding': understanding is premised on the idea of
an ideal consensus of views (i.e. the views arising from an ideally spontaneous and undistorted collaborative inquiry); and it is
this ideal consensus which is the regulative principle of theoretical (encompassing scientific) discourse. Unpacking the cognitive
content of the pursuit of truth in such a manner, Habermas has
struck the kind of balance of so-called a priori and naturalistic
considerations which needs to be infused into the argument from
rationality. Countering relativism, such an orientation recognizes,
as Skorupski points out, that "to defend a statement seriously
(i.e. on grounds other than tempermental preference) is to commit
oneself to the claim that consensus could be reached, in an 'ideal
speech situation,' as to its truth-value, and that it would survive
(at least in its essentials) in such a consensus" (1985: 357). Yet
the notion of an ideal consensus is in large measure open to the
empirical investigation of its developmental-psychological and social conditions. And it is these conditions which constitute, in the
most interesting sense, the "massive central core of human thinking." Only, from this vantage it is apparent that these conditions

do have a history, at both the phylogenetic and the ontogenetic levels.

Turning to Habermas at this juncture entails acknowledging that the argument being advanced for epistemic naturalism is only progammatic. Following Skorupski's lead, however, a few more things can be said by way of clarifying the position and demonstrating that it is at least consistent with Hollis' reasoning and objectives. Given the theses of the under-determination of theories by evidence and the epistemic conception of the nature of knowledge claims, it becomes clear, as Hollis argues, that our understanding of the cognitive content of a sentence is determinate only relative to a theoretical context and the rules of ampliative inference built into that context (see Chapter VI). Yet from this state of affairs we cannot move to the conclusion that the assumptions of the context are synthetical a prioris. We cannot do this because "we cannot exclude the possibility of a community which develops a system of beliefs different from our own [–entailing different ways of applying fundamental predicates to experience, and different rules of ampliative reasoning –] but which ... is as effective from our point of view as ours is, not only by the test of predictive adequacy, but by the test of all those standards of good explanation which we would accept, taken as a whole" (Skorupski, 1985: 350). In other words, as naturalists bound by fallibilism, the grasp of the fundamental rules structuring our realms of experience can neither be the result of "the intuition of a Platonic realm of non-natural relations between propositions, nor [an articulation of] Kantian 'forms' of reasoning and perception." Rather, Skorupski suggests, our grasp of such things "can rest only on a spontaneous agreement, within the speech community, as to the application of certain fundamental predicates to experience, and of certain fundamental rules of reasoning to the experiential data."

This conclusion, Skorupski stresses however, does not land us in the conventionalist camp, thereby undermining the argument from rationality (1985: 350).

> This does not mean that the agreement is 'conventional,' and that the rules on which we agree are 'conventions.' Conventions are arbitrary. They are appropriate where there is more than one acceptable solution to a co-ordination problem – in this case, the co-ordination problem involved in collective theorizing about the world. But basic rules of reasoning are not felt as arbitrary. We have no insight into, or feel for, alternative ways of going on (though we cannot rule out acquiring such insight in a wholly unexpected context). The crucial point is that the

agreement is one of *reactions*, and not of *choices*. We find that we agree
in feeling constrained to 'go on' in certain ways; we do not experience
it as a matter of decision.

This line of reasoning captures more accurately the nature of
the conceptual constraints to which our thought is actually subject. And though such a formulation of matters does not definitively exclude the possibility of relativism, as Skorupski concludes,
"to concede that much is not to concede a great deal" (1985: 354).

> There are innumerable possibilities which we cannot definitively ex-
> clude, but which we have no ground at all to take seriously. In prac-
> tice, what is known historically and ethnographically of other cultures
> abundantly supports two points. First, there is indeed a fundamental
> 'epistemological unity of mankind,' in Martin Hollis's phrase: a practi-
> cal agreement on basic modes of reasoning. Second, by comparison with
> the cosmologies of primitive societies, or of traditional civilizations, the
> scientific ideas developed in the West have, since the seventeenth cen-
> tury, had a striking advantage in explanatory adequacy, and since the
> second half of the nineteenth century an even more obvious advantage
> in technical control: to the point of transforming the material base of
> Western and almost all other societies in dramatic and irreversible ways.

Returning to first principles, to this need only be added, lest Gellner rule the day, that the triumph of the methods of the natural
sciences only tells half the story. The other half, lying within the
realm human relations, rests with the universal viability of the
other supposition which historically also reached its apothesis in
the West, what Habermas calls the "supposition of responsibility."
Normatively, that is, it is assumed that to interact with an individual is to interact with a subject; and this entails supposing that
an individual knows what they are doing and why, that they inten-
tionally hold beliefs and pursue ends, and that they are capable of
supporting their beliefs and actions with reasons if necessary. In
many instances such a supposition may prove to be counterfactual,
yet it remains fundamental to the structure of human relations,
if only because, as Habermas concludes, "on this unavoidable fic-
tion rests the humanity of intercourse among men who are still
men" (1971b: 120).

In sum, then, it is by following through on Hollis' epistemological approach to the question of natural necessity that a satisfactory answer can be found to "the root question," which Hollis
acknowledges, threatens to undermine his perspective: Can necessary truths be shown importantly distinct from contingent truths
without making them empirically vacuous? Yes, from the perspective of an 'epistemic naturalism,' they can. But this conclusion

removes only a measure of the decisionism present in the argument from rationality – it opens up the broad framework of the method to piecemeal criticism and change. Can the specific value judgements which social scientists must make to apply the argument in particular instances also be opened to some systematic assessment? It is the second of our proposed changes, viewing judgements of rationality as matters of degree, which at least partially ameliorates the concerns raised by this question.

A Matter of Degree

The most immediate objection to the argument from rationality stems from its reliance on an epistemic standard of rationality which is normative. In other words, the objection stems from the assumed identification of science and moral neutrality. While it is reasonable, however, to assume that the natural world is morally empty, such is not the case for the human social world. If one attempts to remove norms from the latter realm, in order to disqualify them from the causal nexus, sociologists would in fact be left with nothing to explain. For, as previously argued, the attempt to elude the noncontingent connection between actions and beliefs merely leads one to the problem of linguistic behaviour, which can be explained only through reference to the shared norms and standards by which it is governed. But does this then mean that we are fated to operate within a dualistic ontology: the world consists of a morally empty nature over against a morally constituted human sociation? If the answer to this question is yes, then the way is barred forever to the formal unity of the sciences, and the principle of value-neutrality is rendered a non-starter as a foundation for objection to the use of the argument from rationality to explain social actions.

On first appraisal it might seem that Hollis, with his dualism in modes of explanation, has himself taken refuge in just such a radical ontological split. But in fact he has argued that the simple equation of modes of explanation and realms of data is illusory. Instead, it will be remembered, he carefully stipulates that his rejection of the orthodox conception of social science is not intended to clear the way merely for "a rampage in hermeneutics" (1977: 41). Rather, he states, "[t]here is still a need for causal laws, even though they do not wholly explain social action; hermeneutics offer much but not all" (1977: 19). In principle, Hollis argues, all

social action should be approached with the argument from rationality in mind. But in fact only rational actions will be explained
completely by such a procedure. The great residue of irrational
actions will require further causal explanation. But what precisely is the nature of this causal explanation? The importance of
this question is acknowledged by Hollis on several occasions (e.g.,
1977: 45 and 65; 1982: 82), but to date he has not pursued adequately it or its consequences. Do causal explanations truly differ
in form, in a post-positivist (i.e., post-Humean) context, from explanations based on the rationality of an action? If in essential
ways these modes of explanation do not differ, then for even the
limited dualism underlying Hollis' argument to remain methodologically relevant its *raison d'être* must be cast in a new light.
Here it will be argued that the appropriate reinterpretation rests
with understanding that Hollis' criticisms of the positivist distinction between analytic and synthetic truths, and hence the nature
of causal laws, points logically to a supposition of epistemic naturalism. In fact his analysis of this distinction points logically to
the methodological embodiment of this epistemological position in
a conception of rationality as a matter of degrees.

    In Chapter VI, the epistemological viability of the formal unity
of the sciences was established on the basis of the collapse of the
positivist distinction between analytic and synthetic truths. At
that juncture, however, it was suggested, following Hollis' mistaken talk of "definitional necessity" giving rise to "real definitions," that the positivist distinction had really collapsed, contrary
to the reasoning of the pragmatists, because the key theoretical
(i.e. analytic) terms of reference of the various disciplines are, in
a sense, actually synthetic in kind. Yet conversely, at an earlier
juncture, it was established that the supposedly synthetic predictions of the deductive-nomological form of soft positivism are in
fact just analytic suppositions. Both discoveries play an essential
role in clearing a methodological space for the argument from rationality, but if the appearance of contradiction is to be dispelled
the logical inference must be drawn to an overarching epistemic
naturalism. From this perspective it is clear, from the start, that
all knowledge claims are simultaneously analytic and synthetic in
nature, and that consequently, the distinction between analytic
and synthetic propositions should be read as a referring to a difference in *degree* and not *kind*.

    In line with this reasoning, the philosopher of science Newton-
Smith suggests that it is still both convenient and necessary for

science to draw a "rough pragmatic distinction of degree" between the theoretical and the observational, even though the positivist formulation of this distinction has been discredited. Specifically, he proposes that an observational term corresponds to a term towards one end of a rough spectrum of terms determined by the following principles (1981: 27):

> (1) The more observational a term is, the easier it is to decide with confidence whether or not it applies.
>
> (2) The more observational a term is, the less will be the reliance on instruments in determining its application.
>
> (3) The more observational a term is, the easier it is to grasp its meaning without having to grasp a scientific theory.

By the same logic, the difference between causal and rational explanations of actions is actually one of *degrees* and not *kind*. In light of the difficulties traditional empiricists and positivists have in establishing a connection, through tests, between empirical generalizations and the causal laws which are suppose to explain them, Hollis turns to a definitional conception of natural necessity. This move, however, seems logically to have the effect, though Hollis chooses not to pursue the matter (see Hollis, 1977: 65), of aligning his views with the unorthodox understanding of causal laws advanced by Roy Bhaskar in *A Realist Theory of Science* (1975). Bhaskar conceptualizes these laws according to the following reasoning (1975: 105):

> Reflect, for a moment, on the world as we know it. It seems to be a world in which all manner of things happen and are done, which we are capable of explaining in various ways, and yet for which a deductively justified prediction is seldom, if ever, possible. ... It is true that the path of my pen does not violate any laws of physics. But it is not determined by any either. Laws do not describe the pattern nor legitimate the predictions of any kind of events. Rather, it seems they must be conceived, at least as regards the ordinary things of the world, as *situating limits and imposing constraints on the types of action possible for a given kind of thing.* [Emphasis added.]

Bhaskar argues that the laws of nature should be understood as "normic and transfactual" statements "analogous" to the "rules" of a game, where empirical events are analogous to the actual play of the game on some occasion (1975: 92). Such a definition of causal laws draws out the similarity in form between explanations in terms of causes and those in terms of reasons. Yet it does not exonerate MacIntyre, since the the conceptions of causal explanation in question are radically different and in this instance the form of causal explanation is assimilated to that of rational explanation and not the reverse. Nor, by the reasoning of Skorupski specified above, does it put us in league with the pragmatists and conventionalists. Rather it simply establishes that causal analysis is inherently a mixed undertaking involving both analytic and synthetic components blended together in such a subtle and constantly changing manner that the isolation of either component is unlikely with regard to even the simplest of events or actions.

In sum, in pursuing the argument from rationality it has become apparent that the intertwined questions of personal identity and authenticity can be resolved at best into questions of degree. Consequently, in the practical employment of the argument a transcendent reason is hitched to a relational freedom and rationality itself becomes a matter of degree. Now it has also become apparent that this situation is not merely the result of a regrettable practical limitation. In principle as well as practice both judgements of rationality and causality are simultaneously analytic and synthetic in nature. Therefore Hollis' attention should rightly have turned to the formulation of the criteria of the spectrum upon which both rational and causal modes of explanation are situated.

In "The Social Destruction of Reality," Hollis specifies the initial and most obvious sense in which explanations of social action should be viewed as matters of degree (1982: 84):

I have argued that the sociology of knowledge must distinguish the true-and-rational from the false-and-irrational. Without the former there is no entry into a system of beliefs and the actors' world cannot be seen from within. Without the latter, there is no accounting for intellectual change. Thus the sociology of knowledge advocated here starts with beliefs which are held for the good reason that they are true and advances by identifying beliefs which are held for the fairly good reason that others are true. It is then ready to deal with beliefs held for the indifferent reason that others are held. Thence it enters the realm of beliefs held when there was better reason not to hold them; and a fresh form of explanation is needed. With false beliefs irrationally held the divorce between identification and explanation is complete; they are identified on the pretense that they are true and rational and explained in the recognition that they are neither. The two missing classes thus require a mixed explanation, from within to the degree to which they resemble one ideal type and from without for the rest.

But secondly, it must also be recognized that there is not a simple relationship of identity between the spectrum separating the two modes of explanation (i.e., the rational and the causal) and the polarity of analytic (theoretical; ideal) and synthetic (observational; empirical) orientations. Delineation of the true-and-rational ideal type, which is the necessary assumption of social explanation, is itself a matter of degree. In fact it is the same question of degree addressed by Newton-Smith, with the addition of a substantive focus on the "marks of rationality" as revealed by the work of ethnologists, developmental psychologists, anthropologists, linguists, and philosophers. It is with the filling-in of the criteria of this latter spectrum that a process of amelioration is set in motion which offers an effective counter to the charge of vacuity and the fear of decisionism. The elaboration of even the most basic criteria of this spectrum must be left, however, to another occasion.[3]

But if rational and causal explanations are formally similar, it might be asked, what sense is to be made of Hollis' fundamental assertion of a principle of asymmetry? At heart both rational and causal explanations are about the imposition of a theoretical order on the world of experience, an order which constitutes a form of natural necessity in the sense of "situating limits and imposing constraints on the types of action possible for a given kind of thing." Through a series of theoretical evaluations, that is, each mode calls into being sets of foundational concepts which, from a traditional perspective, are what Steven Lukes calls "essentially contested concepts" because, in the last analysis, they are "ineradicably value-dependent" and open in principle to modification through the introduction of new information (Hollis, 1977: 179). In behind each, however, also lies an essential semantic reference to the truth; and the crucial difference in degree between rational and causal explanations stems from the fact that explanations from rationality are founded on tautologies, that it is necessary to assume are not empty, which relate directly to the reflexive processes of a human consciousness. Causal explanations, on the other hand, are not limited to these tautologies because their reference to the reflexive processes of a human consciousness, namely ours, is once removed and secondary. In other words, as best as we can tell, reason is ultimately its own object in all types of explanation. It is just more immediately and exclusively so in explanations from rationality.

This distinction is very subtle. Therefore, functionally, the argument from rationality is applicable whenever and wherever the decisive element in determining an action has been the presence of a mediating human consciousness. Causal analysis then, explains those actions and natural events which would have transpired as they did whether or not a human mind was involved. It is this functional division of labour that comes to the fore in Hollis' proposal, in the closing pages of *Models of Man*, that the argument from rationality be thought of as an attempt to conceptualize "skill" (1977: 180):

> What, then, is special to theoretical evaluation in social science? It is, I submit, that social scientists are conceptualizing skill. Actors have natural, social and rational powers, whereas the sciences of nature are concerned only with powers of the first kind. Thus the genetic effects of thalidomide depend on the powers of the drug and the task of theory is to isolate these powers with models to distinguish lawlike from unlawlike connections. The actions of Themistocles, by contrast, depend also on two further kinds of powers. This is not to deny that natural powers, both his and those of people and things about him, come into it. But he also had the powers conferred by being the Athenian general facing a Persian invasion. These were partly those of a social position which enabled some courses of action while constraining others, partly those of command over a fleet of ships against a Persian force of mixed talent far from home and partly those of the respect which his fellows might not have given a different incumbent of his position. These natural and social powers were premises of a calculation whose outcome depended on his rational powers. History credits him with a nice judgement of what it was best to do, given his own capacity to carry it out, and Salamis has always had a place among the great naval victories. If it was truly thanks to him not only that the Athenians won it but also that they fought it at all, instead of defending Athens, and had the ships to fight it in, instead of using the product of the Laurium silver mines in other ways, then skill is a crucial factor

Caution must be exercised, however, lest this comparatively reliable criterion of the spectrum of modes of explanation be over-interpreted, as Hollis is inclined to do, and turned into the criterion of a division of kind between the two modes of explanation. The distinction, it must be remembered, is functional (i.e., heuristic, though not nominal). If over-interpreted as a distinction of kind and not just degree, a wholesale return is made to the problems of vacuity and decisionism.

Conclusion

The Moral of the Story

> He who jumps to his death has cause. He who leaps
> purpose. Always Remember I leapt.

Such are the lines of the suicide note left to a son by his father in
the opening pages of Timothy Findley's novel *Famous Last Words*.
A simple, even comical, play on words. Yet the father's parting
message is clear and, as the son will go on to learn in his own
tragic life, full of significance. Like the terse suicide note, our
dealings with freedom have an inarticulate precision about them.
We generally assume ourselves to be free, and as these lines convey
with brutal economy, to be free matters. But social scientists have
not known how to respond to this situation. One pivotal question
has remained problematic: Is the consideration of human freedom
compatible with the demands of a 'science' of human action? Here,
following Hollis, I have endeavored to argue that the two are indeed
compatible, if both the freedom in question and the science in mind
are properly conceived.

In an obvious sense, the insights generated by the investigation
of this issue have a special relevance for religious studies. In the
great religious traditions of the world, the most important and
authentic religious acts are free acts. Thus to the extent that
the latter can be systematically identified and assessed, a door is
opened to the more rigorous and nonreductive treatment of the
human context of religious actions. In a less obvious, but perhaps
even more important sense, however, the two concerns are linked
by the fact that the epistemological argument used to turn science to the consideration of human freedom can also be used to
accomodate science to religious references to transcendence. Both
developments work to narrow the gap between religious explanations of religious behaviour and social scientific explanations of the
same behaviour.

The development of each of these concerns, we have argued,
depends upon the conceptualization of rationality as a category

of social scientific analysis – everything hinges on what we have
learned about what it means to identify an act as rational (from
the perspective of an actor and an observer of his action). To say
that an action, or a belief for that matter, is rational is to invoke
an explanatory framework. based on a qualified idealism, that is
internalist, epistemic. and normative, yet subject to modification
in the light of new empirical information. Let us now, then, reca-
pitulate the moral of the story by briefly reviewing each of these
components of this theoretical framework.

Humans are not necessarily rational creatures, and hence they
are not necessarily free. But, in line with Hollis, we have argued
that the notion of rational agency is an intrinsic and constitutive
component of the framework on which we rely in identifying and
explaining human actions. Therefore to assert that rationality and
freedom are transcendental categories of social analysis is not to
assert a philosophical or psychological hypothesis about the mechanisms of human thought and activity. Rather it is to specify an
important set of formal constraints on the formulation of historical, sociological, and psychological hypotheses and explanations.
In the explanation of human actions the first crack must be given
to the humanists with their presupposition of voluntarism. In the
application of this presupposition a limit might well be reached
where particular inquirers may decide that they are ready to formulate and accept a causal explanation for the actions in question.
They might make such a decision because they think that it is impossible to say if there are any fully rational courses of action,
or because they think that the actors in question have failed to
grasp the best course, or simply because in the instances under
consideration they are unwilling to lay any bets. But. as Hollis
concludes. at whatever point the inquirers change from an active
to a passive orientation. they cannot avoid determining what still
needs explaining. "The residue is always a departure from an ideal
type" (1977: 140).

Judgements of rationality are internalist in the sense that they
are tied to the satisfying of real interests known only to the agent,
and not the maximizing of externally posited universal ends (e.g.,
profit). They are also internalist in the sense that the detection
of an irrational action depends on the actor being aware or at any
rate being made potentially aware of an inconsistency between an
action and his or her real interests. Rationality is linked, that
is, to the monitoring of actions, in the service of the indefinite

retrospective assessment of one's self-formative process. Internal coherence, then, is one of the crucial elements of judgements of rationality, though the judgement is based upon a floating notion of the actor's authentic self and interests.

There are, however, external constraints on judgements of rationality, though of a particular sort. For the actor and the observer, the very conditions of belief-ascription (including the actor's self-ascription of role expectations, etc.) entail the formulation and reliance on both a 'bridgehead' of general epistemic principles and of specific propositional 'bets.' By conventional standards, both sets of ideas appear normative. But since it is difficult to imagine how social actions could be explained without at least initially calling upon an ideal type of rational human agency, then the normative character of these ideas is best accepted as a fact and not a defect of social scientific analysis.

Appearances to the contrary, this does not mean that the social sciences (relative to the natural sciences) are condemned, in either theory or practice, to the vicissitudes of decisionism. For the charge of decisionism depends upon a dualism of kinds of explanation within the realm of human action. The criticism makes sense, that is, only if there is a mode of explanation (like causal analysis) which is applicable to human action in a manner which is definably different from and more certain than the argument from rationality. Hollis appears to be susceptible to the charge of decisionism because he employs a dualistic terminology in his writings. In fact, however, by the logic of his own refutation of the soft positivist option, it was revealed that there is no clear and definitive way to distinguish causal and rational explanations of human action. The difference between them is not one of kind, but of degree. Both modes involve a blend of analytic and synthetic, epistemic and practical, normative and descriptive considerations which it is impossible to completely differentiate and subject to methodological control. Both modes of explanation are but human impositions upon the world; they are heuristic devices.

But to say this does not undermine their explanatory value or the viability of drawing a distinction between them. Rather it merely redirects our attention to the real line of division: actions mediated by the reflective monitoring of human consciousness should be addressed from the perspective of the argument from rationality; they might well prove to be rational and hence self-explanatory, and in most cases they can be explained partially

through reference to reasons. If, however, they cannot, then the
analysis moves to another level, where no direct reference is made
to reflective consciousness, and the search begins for cause and
effect relationships. But a pure manifestation of either heuristic
form will be a rare occurence. In most instances, the scholar will
be called upon to decide a question of degree.

But what does it mean to decide that an action is rational?
What are the criteria by which this judgement shall be guided?
Hollis never really tells us, and we cannot begin to present a convincing presentation of probable criteria here. Every causal analysis links an idiosyncratically specific set of causes and effects.
Every argument from rationality links an even more idiosyncratically specific set of real interests and actions. The former linkage
is structured by and depends upon the laws of probability. The
latter linkage is structured by and dependent upon asservations
of what we are warranted in thinking an essential human interest. It is a matter of apparent necessity that the argument from
rationality be initially applied to all human actions. Its application, however, entails the use of criteria of rational action which
are essentially contestable – the product of empirical research into
the principles, processes, and patterns of thought underlying our
operative paradigms of rational activity. Our bets as social scientists will be shaped by our knowledge of these phenomena, and
these phenomena will in turn be changed by the results of the
research stemming from our bets. At all times we are suspended
between our ideals of rational human interests and causal laws,
and between these ideals and the heuristic orientations actually
employed by actors and institutions in social life – each endlessly
conditions the other. But for the sake of order, every social scientist must select and and identify a set of initial assumptions. To
this end it would be helpful if we could at least begin to delineate
a graduated paradigm of what it means to act rationally (i.e., an
act is more rational if ...). Such a conclusion, of course, says both
too little and too much. But it is difficult to speak with precision
about matters that are so complicated and perhaps intrinsically
vague. To overlook the task, though, is to abdicate an essential aspect of the social scientist's obligation to better understand his or
her subject matter and fashion a logic of inquiry which more fully
captures its nuances; and to do so without adequate philosophical
justification.

Such is the first moral of the story. But I might just as well
say the moral of the story so far, for each element of the formula

presented can be studied further and needs further substantiation. What is the precise status of concepts like rational human agency? An answer has been indicated here, but the intricacies of this epistemological problem need to be treated more exhaustively. Similarly, in the context of developing the argument from rationality, more detailed philosophic thought must be given to the nature and delimitation of causal analysis, the concept and people's sense of their 'self,' and the circular relationship that holds between the values we live by and the formulation of social scientific methods. Practically there is the need to attempt to formulate a graduated paradigm of rationality, to operationalize the argument from rationality. Once this has been done, then the argument needs to be subjected to the only test that counts: it needs to be applied to observed situations. None of these formidable tasks is worth undertaking, however, unless the indifferent or sceptical attitude of the social scientific community begins to change. Here I have sought to encourage this change by arguing that the the argument from rationality is part and parcel of the conceptual infrastructure of the social sciences and as such it warrants being more seriously investigated. One on one we take ourselves seriously as free and rational beings, and collectively, on the whole, we still place our faith in science as the most reliable source of knowledge. Is it not time that we abandon the illusion that these two points of trust are either inimical or wholly separate?

Similarly, it is time to end the debate over the formal incorporation of references to the transcendent in social scientific accounts of religious phenomena. The metaphysical issue underlying the debate cannot as yet be resolved in a manner favourable to either the reductionists or nonreductionists. Yet the demarcation of religious studies necessarily entails working with the concept of references to the transcendent. Focusing the analytic framework of religious studies on these references to the transcendent constitutes the first step towards deferring the threat of reductionism, in both its substantive and linguistic forms, and hence deflecting disciplinary entropy. Formally, talk of references to the transcendent is as epistemologically and methodologically legitimate for the academic student of religion as it is for the believers they study. The position, to borrow and adapt a category employed by A. R. Peacocke, is one of 'epistemological anti-reductionism' (Peacocke, 1976). 'References to the transcendent' is being treated as a conceptual primitive. It is neither a *sui generis* given in all supposedly religious contexts, nor a merely vacuous analytical construct

to be filled-in, in a relativistic manner, with distinct descriptions
of the objects of different soteriologies. It is a delimiting principle
of the field of religious studies, and as such it must initially figure
in all explanations advanced in that field. Its nature, to use the
Logical Positivist terminology once again, is neither synthetic nor
analytic, but a complicated blend of the two.

Contrary to Peter Berger's suggestion (1967: 177), then, the
choice between the use of a substantive and functional definition
of religion does not fall under the maxim *de gustibus*. The precise
working notion of the references to the transcendent called upon
and studied by a student of religion at any one time, in any one
context, however, does conform after a manner to such a maxim.
To borrow the phrase used by Hollis in reference to judgements
of the rationality of an agent's actions (i.e., in judgement of an
act's degree of freedom), in each concrete analysis the student of
religion must 'lay his bets' about the nature, effects, and viability of the references to the transcendent at issue. But hopefully
the configuration of the bets laid will be fleshed-out through feedback from the continued philosophical and empirical study of the
apparent and claimed manifestations of that which is deemed transcendent. Following the lead set by Skorupski, we must look for
those features of references to the transcendent that give rise to
an agreement or consensus based on "reactions" and not choices.
Let us search out those widely distributed features of the transcendent that appear to constrain our conceptualization of the transcendent. The existence of such constraints implicitly undergirds
the activities of both the student of religion and the missionary,
just as the presumption of a universal rationality undergirds the
growth and spread of science.

Ironically, of course, such a line of inquiry carries us back to
the seminal insights of Otto. When situated within a more ethno-
graphically informed and qualified philosophical and methodological framework, *The Idea of the Holy* still has much to offer. But
where Otto attempted to differentiate the religious sense of the
concept of the transcendent from the Kantian, I wish, by rein-
terpreting the Kantian perspective, to proceed by small steps of
reasoning from the latter to the former. The idea of the holy,
Otto asserts, is a complex category combining both rational and
non-rational components (i.e., the rational ideas of absoluteness,
completion, necessity, substantiality, and the good as an objective
value; the non-rational feelings of awefulness and majesty, mystery,
fascination, and dependency); and in both respects it is a purely

a priori category. Yet the religious *numinosum*, he declared, is something more than Kant's noumena (1917: 113-14).

> The proof that in the numinous we have to deal with purely a priori cognitive elements is to be reached by introspection and a critical examination of reason such as Kant instituted. We find, that is, involved in the numinous experience, beliefs and feelings qualitatively different from anything that 'natural' sense perception is capable of giving us. They are themselves not perceptions at all, but peculiar interpretations and valuations, at first of perceptual data, and then – at a higher level – of posited objects and entities, which themselves no longer belong to the perceptual world, but are thought of as supplementing and transcending it. And as they are not themselves sense-perceptions, so neither are they any sort of 'transmutation' of sense-perceptions. ... The facts of the numinous consciousness point therefore – as likewise do also the 'pure concepts of the understanding' of Kant and the ideas and value-judgements of ethics or aesthetics – to a hidden substantive source, from which the religious ideas and feelings are formed, which lies in the mind independently of sense-experience; a 'pure reason' in the profoundest sense, which, because of the 'surpassingness' of its content, must be distinguished from both the pure theoretical and the pure practical reason of Kant, as something yet higher or deeper than they.

Nevertheless, Otto acknowledges, the numinous "of course comes into being in and amid the sensory data and empirical material of the natural world and cannot anticipate or dispense with those ...." But this does not mean, he stipulates, that it arises "*out of* them, but only *by their means*" (1917: 113). This latter supposition is neither adequately proved nor, we have argued (following Wiebe), necessary. The academic student of religion benefits from a due acknowledgement of the relative viability of talk of the numinous because it helps to demarcate and make sense of the field of study. He or she does not need to know, however, from whence the experience refered to ultimately arises. The work done within the field of religious studies will have a bearing, in the last analysis, on the determination of this final question. But no metaphysical commitment must be undertaken in advance in order to get on with that work. To suggest otherwise is to substitute a theological reductionism for its more infamous empiricist counterpart.

Rather, as indicated by Otto's references to Kantian introspection and transcendental analysis, for the present it is sufficient to know that the notion of the transcendent or the numinous is a constantly recurring referent of 'talk of religion.' Like references to rational agency, references to the transcendent, I suspect, will always resist the full disenchanting thrust of rational inquiry. But

we cannot know this, so in the interim I think we are obliged
to identify and systematically study the elements of phenomenal
objectivity associated with references to the transcendent from
Otto's *mysterium tremendum* to Weber's charisma.[1] A new and
more sophisticated phenomenology of religion, of espoused dealings with the transcendent. must be undertaken. The task may
seem hopelessly ideal. but in attenuated form every serious student of religion (and not just some historical, social, or literary
sub-specialty) is explicitly or implicitly engaged in some measure
in the collective construction of an ideal typology of references
to the transcendent. Here, however, I have argued for something
much more limited and preliminary: the philosophical feasibility
of using the concept of references to the transcendent to formally
demarcate and focus religious studies as a discipline.[2]

Endnotes

Introduction

[1] Some sample references from 1970 on: F.J. Streng, "The Objective Study of Religion and the Unique Quality of Religiousness," *Religious Studies* 6, 1970: 209-19; Robert Bellah, "Between Religion and Social Science," in his book *Beyond Belief*, New York: Harper and Row, 1970; 237-59; John Y. Fenton, "Reductionism in the Study of Religion," *Soundings* 53, 1970: 61-76; Eric J. Sharpe, "Some Problems of Method in the Study of Religion," *Religion* 1, 1971: 1-14; Hans H. Penner and Edward A. Yonan, "Is a Science of Religion Possible?" *Journal of Religion* 52, 1972: 107-33; Reinhard Pummer, "*Religionswissenschaft* or Religiology?" *Numen* 19, 1972: 91-127; I. Hammet, "Sociology of Religion and the Sociology of Error," *Religion* 3, 1973: 1-12; Ninian Smart, *The Science of Religion and the Sociology of Knowledge*, Princeton: Princeton University Press, 1973; Ralph W. Burhoe, "The Phenomenon of Religion Seen Scientifically," in Allen W. Eister, ed., *Changing Perspectives in the Scientific Study of Religion*, New York: John Wiley, 1974: 15-39; Robert Baird, ed., *Methodological Issues in Religious Studies*, Chico: New Horizon Press, 1975; Charles Davis, "The Reconvergence of Theology and Religious Studies," *Studies in Religion* 4, 1975: 205-21; W.C. Smith, "Objectivity and the Humane Sciences: A New Proposal," in W.G. Oxtoby, ed., *Religious Diversity - Essays of Wilfred Cantwell Smith*, New York: Harper and Row, 1976: 158-80; K.K. Klostermaier, "From Phenomenology to Metascience: Reflections on the Study of Religions," *Studies in Religion* 6, 1977: 551-64; C.W. Kegley, "Theology and Religious Studies: Friends or Enemies?" *Theology Today* 35, 1978: 273-84; Ninian Smart, "Beyond Eliade: The Future of Theory in the Study of Religion," *Numen* 25, 1978: 171-83; E. H. Pyle, "Reduction and the 'Religious' Explanation of Religion," *Religion* 9, 1979: 197-214;

Donald Dougherty, "Is Religious Studies Possible?" *Religious Studies* 17, 1981: 295-309; N. Ross Reat, "Insider and Outsider in the Study of Religious Traditions," *Journal of the American Academy of Religion* 61, 1983: 457-76; Robert Segal, "In Defence of Reductionism," *Journal of the American Academy of Religion* 61, 1983: 97-124; Donald Wiebe, "Theory in the Study of Religion," *Religion* 13, 1983: 283-309 and "The Failure of Nerve in the Academic Study of Religion," *Studies in Religion* 13, 1984: 401-422; Bruce Alton, "Method and Reduction in the Study of Religion," *Studies in Religion* 15 (1986): 153-164; Hans H. Penner, "Criticism and the Development of A Science of Religion," *Studies in Religion* 15 (1986): 165-176.

2 For example, on an a priori basis and without significant argument, C.J. Bleeker asserts: "Religion is *sui generis* and cannot be explained by non-religious factors"; in part because there is a unique spiritual dimension to each religion which "cannot be explained anthropologically" (1975: 9 and 11).

3 For discussions of the integration of religious studies and the scientific method in the sociological literature – all of which raise the question of human freedom at some point – consult: William L. Kolb, "Images of Man and the Sociology of Religion," and the response by and exchange with Talcott Parsons, *Journal for the Scientific Study of Religion* 1, 1962: 4-29, 214-19; the R. Bellah - S. Klausner and B. Nelson exchange over "symbolic realism" in the *Journal for the Scientific Study of Religion* 9, 1970; William C. Tremmel, "The Converting Choice," *Journal for the Scientific Study of Religion* 10, 1971: 17-25; Joseph H. Fichter, "The Concept of Man in Social Science: Freedom, Values and Second Nature," *Journal for the Scientific Study of Religion* 11, 1972: 109-21, and the responses and discussions in this and the next issue; Robert W. Friedrichs, "Social Research and Theology: End of Detente?" *Review of Religious Research* 15, 1974: 113-27; Morton B. King and Richard A. Hunt, "Moral Man and Immoral Science?" *Sociological Analysis* 35, 1974: 240-50; Benton Johnston, "Sociological Theory and Religious Truth," *Sociological Analysis* 38, 1977: 368-88, and discussion in *S.A.* 39, 1978.

4 Dagfinn Follesdal (1982: 302-3) points out that Donald Davidson has "most vigorously ... argued that in order to understand man and attribute beliefs. desires and actions to him,

we have to assume that he is rational." William Dray, on the other hand, has more limitedly only asserted that an assumption of rationality is necessary in order to know what beliefs, purposes, goals, and motives others hold. Even more modestly, Carl Hempel looks upon "the assumption that man is rational as merely an empirical hypothesis," which is most useful but "presumably may be false."

5 Such a perspective is also fundamental to the work of Jürgen Habermas and of Karl-Otto Apel. For an introduction consult the essays reprinted in Fred R. Dallmayr and Thomas A. Mc-Carthy, eds., *Understanding and Social Inquiry*, University of Notre Dame Press, 1977. The possibility of developing a set of universal rational interpretations is also explored, from a different yet easily accessed angle, in Max Black, "Why Should I Be Rational?" and Avrum Stroll, "Primordial Knowledge and Rationality," in *Dialectica* 36, 1982: 147-68 and 179-201.

Chapter I

1 For the Christian perspective, for example, see Karl Rahner's entry under "Freedom" in the *Encyclopedia of Theology*, New York: Seabury, 1975. Rahner stipulates that in the documents of the magisterium, freedom of choice has always been regarded as "an inalienable and essential part of man's nature," the existence of which "can be known by the light of natural reason." In Theravadin Buddhism, to provide another example, a belief in human freedom is displayed in the Buddha Gotama's opposition to the fatalistic teachings of the Ajivaka leader Gosala; see D. J. Kalupahana, *Causality: The Central Philosophy of Buddhism*, Honolulu: University of Hawaii Press, 1975, and K. N. Jayatilleke, *Early Buddhist Theory of Knowledge*, London: George Allen and Unwin, 1963.

2 In the hard sciences the full determinism born of the Newtonian revolution no longer reigns. In contemporary Quantum Physics indeterminism is the order of the day. This indeterminism is rooted in an appreciation of the infinite and open character of all natural systems. Nevertheless, the categorical placement of chance in science has served to return feasibility to the commonsense assumption that some parts or aspects of the world are more determined than others, even though none is really fully determined. As Karl Popper says, clouds are less

predictable than clocks; see "Of Clouds and Clocks" in Popper's *Objective Knowledge*. Oxford: Oxford University Press, 1972.

3 The figures which spring immediately to mind in this regard are Emile Durkheim and George Herbert Mead. For example, in *The Division of Labour in Society* (New York: The Free Press, 1964: 350), Durkheim states: "it is a self-evident truth that there is nothing in social life which is not in individual consciences. Everything that is found in the latter, however, comes from society." Two of the classic protests written by sociologists against this tendency are: George Homans, "Bringing Men Back In," *American Sociological Review*, 1964, reprinted in A. Ryan, ed., *The Philosophy of Social Explanation*, Oxford: Oxford University Press, 1973, and Denis Wrong, "The Oversocialized Conception of Man in Modern Sociology," in L. Coser and B. Rosenberg, eds., *Sociological Theory*, London: Macmillan, 1964.

4 This does not mean that they must solve the metaphysical problem of human freedom. It means merely that the problem must be given serious consideration, and on the balance of the evidence, social scientists must, as Hollis says, lay their bets as to whether humans are or are not free. The scientist is to remain open, however, to the possibility of being persuaded by new evidence or argument to change his of her preference. Nor does the inability to completely shirk questions of quasi-fact, of normative analysis and praxis mean that the discussion must be situated in the realm of the sociology of knowledge (in any strong sense). Epistemological and conceptual matters can be adequately separated from their social and political implications to permit a rewarding discussion of general methodological principles.

5 By 'soft positivism' I have in mind a methodological position that entails broadly subscribing to a naturalistic, empirical, inductivist, and verificationist perspective, while acknowledging that none of these criteria of knowledge have proved to be philosophically satisfactory.

6 Ideally the issue of the treatment of the problem of human freedom in sociological thought should entail specific reference to the views of such influential figures as Karl Marx, Max Weber, and Talcott Parsons. Limitations of space and expertise, however, necessarily leave us shy of the ideal. Whatever comments

have been made about the views of these theorists in the discussions to follow have been carefully restricted for three reasons: (1) the complex and controversial nature of the diverse interpretations which have been given of the ideas of each of these authors, especially with regard to their ambiguous pronouncements about the conceptualization of human freedom, weighs against any but the most detailed treatment of their views; (2) perhaps because of this, while the influence of these writers has been great, in the sociology of religion it has been confined largely to a generalized use of the basic tenets of their theoretical systems; (3) though it can be assumed that the authors which I do cite are responding in some sense to things said by Marx, Weber, and Parsons, none of them dwell directly on such comparisons.

Chapter II

1 See for example, Talcott Parsons, *The Structure of Social Action* (1937); Leon Bramson, *The Political Context of Sociology* (1961); L. A. Coser in K. H. Wolff, *Emile Durkheim et al.: Essays on Sociology and Philosophy* (1964); R. A. Nisbet, *The Sociological Tradition* (1967); Percy S. Cohen, *Modern Social Theory* (1968); all cited by Dawe (1970: 216). To this list can be added: Ronald Fletcher, *The Making of Sociology*, (two volumes), New York: Scribner, 1971, and Tom Campbell, *Seven Theories of Human Society*, Oxford: Clarendon Press, 1981.

2 Hollis clearly sees Dawe's approach as instructive, for he uses the same scheme (without reference) in the review article "Meaning and Method." *Philosophy* 55, April 1980: 239-48.

3 As indicated by Sherry B. Ortner in "Theory in Anthropology Since the Sixties." *Comparative Studies in Society and History* 26 (1984): 126-66. social scientific interest in the question of human freedom and the conflict of system and action oriented perspectives is not restricted to sociologists. The anthropological theory of the of the eighties, she declares, will be characterized by a turn to the neglected question of how "society and culture themselves are produced and reproduced through human intention action" (158). Building on the work of Berger and Luckmann, the issue has also proved to be relevant to recent theological concerns. Consider, for instance, Hugh Jones

paper "The Spirit of Inquiry and the Reflected Self: Theological Anthropology and the Sociology of Knowledge," in *The Scottish Journal of Theology* 31 (1978): 201-16.

Chapter III

1 Philosophically such a view was championed by Rudolf Carnap, *The Logical Structure of the World* (1928), translated by Rolf A. George, Berkeley: University of California Press, 1967. In the social sciences it was advanced by Clark L. Hull, *Principles of Behaviour*, New York: Appleton-Century-Crofts, 1943, amongst others.

2 See Part I of Weber's *The Theory of Social and Economic Organization*, translated by A. M. Henderson and T. Parsons, New York: The Free Press, 1964, especially pages 98-100. Then consult the criticisms offered from opposed philosophical perspectives yet along the same lines by Peter Winch (1958: 111-16), and Russell Keat and John Urry (1975: 145-51).

3 It should be kept in mind that positivist naturalism (i.e., the doctrine of an essential unity of methods between the sciences) has existed in two forms. The naturalism of early positivism might be called "reductionism," because it posited an identity of subjects as well as methods. While the naturalism of later, more sophisticated versions of positivism might best be called "scientism," for they merely denied any important differences in methods, whether or not it was possible to identify the subject matters of the two sciences (Bhaskar, 1978, 2).

Chapter IV

1 The situation with Weber is highly problematic. It depends on the relative weight assigned to the contrasting emphasis found in his earlier and later methodological writings (e.g., " 'Objectivity' in Social Science and Social Policy" (1904) in Max Weber. *The Methodology of the Social Sciences*, translated by Edward Shils and Henry Finch, New York: The Free Press, 1949, and Part 1 of *The Theory of Social and Economic Organization*, op. cit.). Here the resolution of the true nature of Weber's position is not as important as the very fact that his understanding of the explanatory role of an assumption of causal regularity in the operation of the social 'sciences' is problematic.

2 Most specifically, Hollis goes on to assert: "Any theory makes men [passive], to my mind, if it regards action as the effect of causal antecedents working in a too law-like manner" (1977: 32). This statement, however, is open to serious misinterpretation. For on first reading the statement might be taken to mean that Hollis, like many humanists (e.g., Winch, Louch, and Simon), is flatly opposed to all causal, or more simply all law-like, explanations of social action. But as indicated, by adopting a dualistic stance Hollis grants a proper, though proscribed, place to causal and hence law-like analysis within a science of social action. All irrational actions, which encompasses a great deal, are subject to such a mode of explanation. The unfortunate phrase "in a too law-like manner" should be read as but a protest against the crude yet common tendency to associate scientific knowledge with the discovery of the (natural) laws of a mechanistic causal regularity in this world that is all-inclusive.

3 Until a distinction is drawn between two understandings of freedom, all appeals to the obvious "social reality" of human freedom are ambiguous and run the risk of misinterpretation. This holds true for Chapter I of this study. However, as I think that the ontological character of my concerns about freedom were clearly expressed even in that context, it would appear that the ambiguity of the two conceptions of freedom is implicitly appreciated even in our everyday references.

4 See Hobbes, *Leviathon* and letter to the Marquis of Newcastle, Moresworth edition, 4: 272-78; Spinoza, *Ethics; A System of Logic*, Book 6; and Ayer, "Freedom and Necessity" in *Philosophical Essays*-all cited by Hollis (1977: 33). For Locke's similar views see *An Essay Concerning Human Understanding*, Book 2. Chapter 21.

5 In Chapter VI of *Models of Man*, 108-12, Hollis argues effectively that the teleological mode of explanation based on the citing of purposes for actions fails to provide a real alternative to causal explanations. His position parallels closely the views developed by the neo-positivist philosopher Ernest Nagel in *The Structure of Science* (1960).

Chapter V

1 Contrary to what is often thought, the inductive-statistical or simply probabilistic variant of this method of science does not

manage to elude these same problems; see Hollis and Nell, 1975: 75-79 and Russell Keat and John Urry, 1975: 12-13.

2 When speaking of cognitive relativism I have in mind the "strong programme" in the sociology of knowledge advanced by David Bloor and Barry Barnes (1982). The term anarchism comes. of course, from Paul Feyerabend's (1975) notorious work in the philosophy of science: though now he prefers to be referred to as an epistemological Dadaist and not an anarchist.

3 In an attempt to strike a compromise between the positions of Hempel and Feyerabend. Thomas Kuhn for example, offers us five ways of selecting a good scientific theory. Roughly speaking. he stipulates that a theory should be accurate, consistent, have broad scope. be simple, and fruitful of new findings (Kuhn, 1977: 321-22). But as Hollis notes, while such approaches "make good sense of scientific practise" they "have no warrant in Positivist epistemology" (1977: 48). In fact, as Kuhn ultimately acknowledges, these criteria have no true epistemological warrant at all. They are "values" to which the scientist may appeal with persuasive force because of their general acceptance in the scientific community.

4 Hollis points out that there are much more elaborate formulations of the nature of natural and causal laws in contemporary philosophy. In this regard he cites J. L. Mackie's definition from *The Cement of the Universe* (Oxford: Oxford University Press. 1974): a cause is "an insufficient but non-redundant part of an unnecessary but sufficient condition" (1977: 45). He commends this definition and notes that there is no conflict. "unless this definition requires a different theory of perception." But in general he thinks that the root idea remains the same in all available definitions of causal laws.

Chapter VI

1 In other words, there is insufficient warrant for the positivist and Weberian differentiation between a subjectively influenced "context of discovery" and an objective "context of justification."

2 For an interesting. though long-winded. logical refutation of the epistemological import of Knorr-Cetina's argument, consult Joseph Agassi's review of her book *The Manufacture of Knowledge* (1981) in *Inquiry* 27: 1 (1984). 166-72.

3 As brought to my attention by Keat and Urry (1975: 255), an influential argument for the proposition that it is necessary to invoke the concept of necessity to characterize scientific laws is presented in W. Kneale, "Universality and Necessity," *British Journal for the Philosophy of Science* 12 (1961), 89-102. The argument is effectively restated in G. Molnar, "Kneale's Argument Revisited," *Philosophical Review* 78 (1969), 70-89.

4 See Nicholas Rescher, "Lawfulness as Mind-Dependent," in A. R. Anderson et al., eds., *Essays in Honour of Carl G. Hempel*. Dordrecht, Holland: D. Reidel, 1969. Rescher summarizes the points of his argument as follows (1969, 194-95):

(1) The concept of scientific explanation is such as to require 'lawfulness' in the generalizations employed.

(2) Lawfulness requires the factors of nomic necessity and hypothetical force.

(3) Nomic necessity and hypothetical force both in significant measure go beyond the sphere of what can be established by observation and experiment.

(4) Lawfulness thus can never be wholly based upon an observational foundation. Rather, it represents an 'imputation' that is (or should be) well-founded upon evidential grounds. (The factors in this well-foundedness are the 'correspondence-to-fact' aspect of empirical evidence and the 'systematic-coherence' of filling the generalization into a fabric of others that in the aggregate constitute a rational structure, an integrated body of knowledge that constitutes a "branch of science.")

(5) Laws are therefore in significant respects not discovered, but made. A law, unlike a simple assertion of regularity, involves claims (viz., of nomic necessity and hypothetical force) that are mind-dependent and cannot be rested simply upon objective matters of observed fact.

(6) Our position thus has the character of a qualified idealism. Lawfulness is not 'just' a matter of the observable facts, but involves–through reference to the factors of nomic necessity and hypothetical force–an essential element of transfactual imputation, and thus is in a crucial respect mind-dependent.

5 Against positivism as a whole, and in line with J. L. Austin (1970), I would argue that words and distinctions enshrined in our ordinary discourse, having survived for many generations the competitive struggle of alternative linguistic forms, in general provide a clear and subtle insight into the important distinctions to be observed in the world around us. Common prudence suggests that these words and distinctions should receive initial favour until severe doubt can be cast upon them.

I do not believe that the concept of freedom has met this fate yet. Against Tibbetts in particular, I would argue that if the questions of human freedom and rationality cannot even be raised sensibly as a subject for study, then, in the contemporary neo-positivistic climate of opinion, the free-will linguistic grid cannot be on an equal footing with the deterministic-causal linguistic grid. The supposed freedom of social scientists to choose between the two theoretical viewpoints is a sham.

6 A proponent of Tibbetts' perspective might interject at this point: "To criticize positivists and determinists for their account of human behaviour as not contributing to our understanding of human action misses Tibbetts' point that 'human action' and 'human behaviour' belong to different linguistic grids. How could the one contribute to the other given its radically different paradigmatic assumptions, objectives, puzzles and so on?" To this the humanist might respond that it is irrelevant that human action and human behaviour belong to different grids. The point is that the former grid is primary to the task of the discipline of sociology (which is Tibbetts' focus); only it provides a full and intellectually satisfying explanation of human social activities (not as a substitute for causal analysis, but as an extension and embellishment of reductive nomological accounts). In line with Michael Simon, he might further argue that 'action' is a logical primitive. There is "no eliminative account of action... that does not abstract from those features of social phenomena that give them their peculiarly human character" (1982: 7). Therefore, it must be recognized that sociology as the science dealing with social actions enjoys a 'descriptive autonomy' similar to that enjoyed by chemistry, for example, vis-a-vis physics. But this autonomy does not equal an incommensurability which blocks all extension of information developed in one context into another.

7 The method of study should not be allowed to dictate, so categorically, the reality and scope of the subject of study—especially when the method itself is so questionable.

Chapter VII

1 The term "relational" is more appropriate than "relative" in characterizing human freedom. It captures the socio-historical

reality of our free acts without bringing to mind any epistemological implications about the rational accessibility of free acts
to systematic study.

2 Complications enter the picture by virtue of the fact that a
lack of dependence in one way can often be accompanied by a
greater degree of dependence in another way (e.g., in societies
with an advanced division of labour there is a trade-off between
individual liberties, intellectual freedoms, etc., and the degree
of individual economic self-sufficiency).

3 The identification of freedom with autonomy has become such
a staple of Western thought, Dauenhauer interestingly points
out (1982: 81, note 8), that even those who wish to deny the
claim to human freedom do so by arguing that humans cannot
be free because they cannot be radically autonomous.

4 Using William Jame's famous discussion of the nature of the
self in *The Principles of Psychology* as a gross pointer to problems, Hollis undertakes a survey of the complicated responses
of philosophers to the problem of personal identity. It is this
philosophical endeavor that plunges off into the deep end of
epistemology before any effective resolution is reached.

Chapter VIII

1 It might be argued that ascriptions of rationality and irrationality in the human sciences are undermined by the theory-
dependent character of all supposed facts. Hollis denies this,
noting that Thurber's story is not spoiled "if unicorns and
tulips are theory-dependent." Presumably, even for the confirmed conventionalist, it is not "a matter of indifference
whether to send for a psychiatrist or a zoo-keeper. So there
is a distinction of reality from illusion, which the [convention-
alist] needs as much as anyone" (1982: 76).

2 Arguments for this point can also be found in A. I. Melden,
Free Action (1961) and Alvin Goldman, *A Theory of Human
Action* (1970).

3 In his discussion of the role of rationality assumptions in interpretation and the explanation of action, Dagfinn Follesdal
(1982) makes a similar point, while rebuffing the assertions of
the behaviourists (1982: 309):

> It has long been popular among economists studying so-called "re-
> vealed preference" to hold that the only way of determining a person's

beliefs and values is to examine his actual choices, there is no non-choice source of information concerning a person's beliefs and values. This gives us a very small circle. We explain a person's choices by appeal to his beliefs and values, and we attribute beliefs and values to him on the basis of his choices.

4 Hollis offers some interesting but undeveloped speculations about these matters (see 1977: 116).

5 The question of the relationship between reasons and causes has been the subject of heated and complicated debate in the philosophical theory of action since the late 1950s. I have no intention of surveying these sophisticated analyses here. A good overview of the basic issues is provided by Keith S. Donnellan's discussion in *The Encyclopedia of Philosophy*, Paul Edwards ed., New York: Macmillan and The Free Press, 1967, Vol.7/8: 85-88. More detailed and recent surveys are provided by Donald Gustafson, "A Critical Survey of the Reasons vs. Causes Arguments in Recent Philosophy of Action," *Metaphilosophy* 4 (October, 1973), and Lawrence H. Davis, *Theory of Action*, Englewoods Cliffs, New Jersey: Prentice-Hall, 1979.

6 In "The Social Destruction of Reality" (1982), Hollis (calling to mind MacIntyre's comments on the noncontingent connection between actions and beliefs) extends this insight into a more general criticism of social scientific practice. He argues that the presumption underlying so much social science that "social and intellectual systems can be separated and then related as cause and effect" is equally misleading. For here too all rests on the questionable assumption that social phenomena and the ideas of men can be described in isolation from each other. Yet the truth of the situation is quite contrary (1982: 70):

There is a fusion in the identities of the actors, who can be treated neither as walking beliefs, nor as bipeds whose beliefs are accidents. ... Consider, for instance, Catholicism ... no doubt the beliefs and the social life of priests (or of laymen) vary systematically between New York, Dublin, and Warsaw. Yet a priest is not essentially the occupant of a social position who just happens to hold Catholic beliefs. Nor is he a universal believer who just happens to live somewhere. His flock have social relations with their father confessor and his spiritual journey takes him through the streets and offices of a social world.

To treat beliefs as independent units is a proper and useful device. But it is precisely that, and it should not be allowed to generate a reification of intellectual systems or even single ideas. In like manner, it is helpful to present social relations as

social structures, external to and exercising coercive power on
actors. But such phenomena owe their existence and power to
the fact that they are recognized in the minds of individuals.
Consequently, while social and intellectual systems, like actions
and beliefs, can be distinguished, "the distinction is ... got by
abstracting in two different ways from the same charivari." We
must remember that what is two for the sake of thought, is
usually lived as a single thing with two aspects, each identified
with the aid of elements from the other (1982: 70).

7 It is for this reason, amongst others, that MacIntyre's argument
for an asymmetry in modes of explanation is rejected by the
Realist social theorists Russell Keat and John Urry (1975: 206-
11).

8 MacIntyre's position in this instance is very difficult to understand in light of his well known opposition to the cognitive
relativism of Peter Winch. In fact in the second section of
"Rationality and the Explanation of Action" he takes up this
critique, arguing again that the interpretation of alien beliefs
necessitates thinking in terms of 'the' criteria of rationality and
not 'ours' and 'theirs'. "Rationality is nobody's property", he
states.
Further, confounding his separtion of the questions of rationality and truth, he begins this same section of his essay with the
following response to Bryan Wilson's "neutrality thesis" for the
sociology of religion (i.e., the sociologist should remain neutral
as to the truth and reasonableness of the beliefs he studies):

... for reasons I have already given, the question of the truth or falsity
of the belief studied is to some degree independent of the question of
its rationality; but, although this distinction must not be ignored, truth
and rationality are both conceptually and empirically related. For to
advance reasons is always to advance reasons for holding that a belief
is true or false; and rational procedures are in fact those which yield us
the only truths of which we can be assured. Thus, to recognize a belief
as rationally held is to lay oneself open to at least the possibility of its
truth (1971: 249).

But if this is so, what serious justification does MacIntyre have
for criticizing the late Victorians for confusing the issues of rationality and truth? When the concluding comments of this
section of his essay are also taken into consideration, his position becomes quite inconsistent and untenable.

One final footnote to this section of the argument: the community of
shared rationality to which I have argued that all recognizably human

societies must belong must of course also be a community of shared beliefs to 'some' extent. For there are some commonsense beliefs (about day and night, the weather and the material environment generally) which are inescapable for any rational agent.

Here MacIntyre has dissolved his distintion between the realm of truth, concerned with the content of what is believed, and the realm of rationality, concerned with how things are believed.

9 I have taken some liberties with Benn and Mortimore's terms and have conceptualized the contrast in a slightly different way.

Chapter IX

1 The analysis given is informal in the sense that no attempt has been made to go into the very elaborate and technically specific discussion of these matters undertaken in the field of decision theory. For an excellent brief discussion along these lines consult Chapter VII, "Technical Models of Rational Choice," in Benn and Mortimore, *Rationality and the Social Sciences* (1976). Benn and Mortimore conclude that though studies of praxeology (derived from economic marginal utility theories) reach a high level of logical and mathematical sophistication, their payoff in terms of successful predictions and satisfactory explanations is disappointingly low. The problem seems to lie with putting values to the variables and functional constants used, and more generally, in translating qualitative relationships into symbolic formulae. Hollis and Edward Nell come to similar conclusions in their detailed critique of neo-classical technical models of rational economic behaviour; see Chapter V of *Rational Economic Man* (1975).

2 Donald Davidson, one of the dominant figures of the philosophy of action has argued forcefully that in order to even attempt to understand humans, and attribute beliefs, desires, and actions to them, it is necessary to work from the assumption that they are rational; for example, consider Davidson's essay "Psychology as Philosophy," especially page 237, in D. Davidson, *Essays on Actions and Events*, Oxford: Clarendon Press, 1980.

3 This point is established with great clarity in John Skorupski, "Relativity, Realism and Consensus," *Philosophy* 60, 1985: 341-58.

4 This point is developed by Hollis in greater detail and with much humour in "Rational Man and Social Science," the lead

essay in Ross Harrison, ed., *Rational Action*, Cambridge: Cambridge University Press, 1979. In this instance Hollis elaborates his perspective using the example of the differing responses of three neighbours to a municipal request to save water during a drought.

5 The method of science developed by Hollis is very Weberian in its format (i.e., it entails formulating and comparing 'ideal types'). However, for reasons already partially indicated, little effort has been made to develop the connections between the Hollis' and Weber's ideas. Weber's discussions of three relevant subjects are simply too problematic to be pursued here: the nature and justification of the use of ideal types and their relationship to causal modes of analysis; the nature of rationality, both as a subject of sociological analysis and as a tool of the same mode of analysis; and the relationship of his ideas on both of these topics to his conceptualization of social action and its explanation. Weber's views on all of these concerns are in many respects paradigmatic (as demonstrated in Susan J. Hekman, *Weber, the Ideal Type, and Contemporary Social Theory*. Notre Dame, Indiana: University of Notre Dame Press, 1983). But in each case his comments are also, incomplete, incidental to other concerns, conceptually diversified and at points even inconsistent (see Rogers Brubaker, 1984: 49). In terms of this study the major difficulty is co-ordinating the methodology of ideal types with Weber's confusing array of conceptions of rationality: formal and substantive rationality, subjective and objective rationality, *Zweckrationalität* and *Wertrationalität*. These distinctions are not clearly ordered with regard to one another, and the latter two cross-over, yet markedly differ from, the distinction we have employed between epistemic and practical conceptions of rationality. It is the latter non-Weberian distinction, however, that more effectively pinpoints the dividing line between existing methodological treatments of rationality as a tool of social science. Weber is inclined to treat both *zweckrational* action and *wertrational* action as only subjectively rational and hence non-epistemic. And he thinks that most action can be effectively accounted for as *zweckrational*, and that this can be done in a descriptive and non-normative manner (Brubaker, 1984: 53-55). Hollis realizes that this is not possible because he, unlike Weber, pursues the nature of

the subjective self underlying action descriptions (i.e., explanations based on reasons) and the operation of merely practical approaches to the argument from rationality and discovers that in both instances, if the explanatory process is to proceed at all, there is no avoiding normative and epistemic commitments (i.e., what Hollis prefers to call bets). (The full extent of the complexities of Weber's "not... particularly coherent view" of the explanation of action is ably presented in Stephen P. Turner's article "Weber on Action," *American Sociological Review* 48, 1983: 506-19.)

Chapter X

1   See, for example, Ian C. Jarvie, *Concepts and Society*, London: Routledge and kegan Paul, 1972; Russell Keat and John Urry, *Social Theory as Science*, London: Routledge and Kegan Paul, 1975; Richard J. Bernstein, *Restructuring Social and Political Theory*, University of Pennsylvania Press, 1976; Kenneth J. Gergen, *Toward Transformation in Social Knowledge*, New York: Springer-Verlag, 1982; William Outhwaite, *Concept Formation in Social Science*, London: Routledge and Kegan Paul, 1983; and Stanley R. Barrett, *The Rebirth of Anthropological Theory*, Toronto: University of Toronto Press, 1984.

2   The reductionism debate in religious studies parallels or in fact overlaps with the positivism-humanism debate in sociology in two respects. First, both debates centre on two related yet distinct questions: What method of study best explains the phenomena under study (i.e., religious phenomena in the first instance, social in the second)? Are the phenomena in question in fact susceptible to scientific treatment at all? Second, with few exceptions, the anti-reductionists in religious studies look to the humanities for methodological guidance, while the so-called reductionists favour the techniques and concerns of the social sciences.

3   Those familiar with the work of Dr. Wiebe may be surprised by this classification. Wiebe has a reputation as a hardline critic of the nonreductionist agenda. I will argue, however, that his position is more subtle and moderate than most his critics presume.

4   As pointed out by Ivan Strenski in "Reduction and Structural Anthropology," *Inquiry* 19 (1976): 73, in the broadest sense,

"reductionism is a special view about the way scientific knowledge grows." That is, reductionism is a theory of theory change in science, and given the contemporary focus of debates in the philosophy of science on this very issue, it is, then, a philosophy of science itself, complete with its own theory of knowledge. In fact, as their are variant interpretations of the process of reduction, there are actually a number of reductionist philosophies of science.

Historically, however, Ernest Nagel's treatment of reductionism has exerted a pardigmatic influence (1961: Chapter XI). Summarizing this view, C. A. Hooker comments ("Part I: Towards a General Theory of Reduction," *Dialogue, Canadian Philosophical Review* 20, 1981: 38-9):

[For Nagel] the aims of reduction are deductive and explanatory unification. Nagel's treatment of reduction belongs in the positivist-empiricist tradition that dominated philosophy of science in the first six decades of this century. Since in that tradition one has only the resources of deductive logic and sensation with which to capture science ... , it was natural to construe reduction as a purely formal relation (deduction) plus epistemic/operational conditions of some sort. This is what the austerely positivist model of Kemeny/Oppenheim ... provided, reduction becoming merely a deduction relation among sets of observation sentences together with a purely formal requirement of increased systematicity. Nagel's later empiricist model remained true to this tradition, reduction amounting to deduction of the laws and observation statements of the reduced theory from the reducing theory plus connecting principles, provided the latter two are empirically supported and all operational procedures and results can be retained in the process.

Though highly influential, in the philosophy of science this view has been criticized from within the positivist-empiricist tradition itself. Carl Hempel, for example. as argued that "Nagel's conditions (let alone those of Kemeny and Oppenheim) are too weak to ensure the dispensibility of either the reduced theory's conceptual apparatus or its ontology" (Hooker, op. cit., 39). Many other efforts have been made to supply stronger and more feasible conditions (see Hooker's account). However, with the demise of positivism and a revolt underway against empiricism in the philosophy of science. the theory of reductionism has become even more complex and controversial, and certainly too unwieldy to be examined here. For concise overviews of the issues consult K. F. Schaffner. "Approaches to Reduction," *Philosophy of Science* 34 (1967): 137-47; F. J. Ayala and T. Dobzhansky, *Studies in the Philosophy of Biology*, Berkeley:

University of California Press 1974; A. R. Peacocke, "Reductionism: A Review of the Epistemological Issues and Their Relevance to Biology and the Problem of Consciousness," *Zygon* 11 (1976): 307-36; and C. A. Hooker's full three part discussion. "Part I: Towards a General Theory of Reduction," "Part II: Identity in Reduction." and "Part III: Cross-Categorical Reduction,"*Dialogue* 20 (1981): 38-59, 201-36, and 496-529.

5 This situation is divergently represented in, for example, Willam Garrett (1974), Eugene Combs and Paul Bowlby (1974), W. C. Smith (1975), Robert Segal (1980), Charles Davis (1984), Donald Wiebe (1984b), and in addition: H. M. Kuitert 'Is Belief a Condition of Understanding?' *Religious Studies* 17 (1981): 233-43; Margret M. Poloma, 'Toward a Christian Sociological Perspective: Religious Values. Theory and Methodology', *Sociological Analysis* 43 (1982): 95-108; T. Patrick Burke, 'Must the Description of a Religion be Acceptable to a Believer?' *Religious Studies* 20 (1984): 631-36.

6 In other words, they have essentially adopted Nagel's understanding of reduction (see note 4 above).

7 To establish the point would entail too much. Here I will simply note my agreement with Daniel Pals (1986) when he comments: "The surprising thing amid all these endorsements of 'irreducible religion' is that the doctrine has been so seldom subjected to thorough-going analysis."

8 As indicated in Chapter VI, both Hollis and Gellner are self-consciously writing in a post-positivist climate of opinion. They acknowledge the largely conventional nature of science. Yet neither adopts a straightforwardly constructivist view of science (unlike, for example, Paul Feyerabend or Nelson Goodman). In different ways, each postulates the existence of real restraints on the scientific method.

9 Comments like the following might be taken into consideration as well (Otto. 1917: 35):

Everywhere salavation is something whose meaning is often very little apparent, is even wholly obscure, to the 'natural' man; on the contrary, *so far as he understands it*. he tends to find it highly tedious and uninteresting, sometimes downright distasteful and repugnant to his nature, as he would, for instance. find the beatific vision of God in our own doctrine of salvation, or the *henosis* of 'God all in all' among the mystics. 'So far as he understands'. be it noted; but then he does not understand it in the least. Because he lacks the inward teaching of the Spirit, he must needs confound what is offered him as an expression for the experience of salvation – a mere ideogram of what is felt, whose import it hints at by analogy – with 'natural' concepts, as though it were itself just such an one. And so he 'wanders ever farther from the goal'.

The passage, like many others in *The Idea of the Holy*, is itself somewhat obscure in its reference, and Otto's talk of ideograms and natural concepts is as imprecise here as elsewhere in the text. Clearly the passage does suggest, however, that Otto is sceptical about the capacity of scientific observers to pass significant judgements about the nature of religious experience.

10 Passages like the following indicate to me that Otto does in effect identified religious studies with theology (1917: 113-14):

The proof that in the numinous we have to deal with purely a priori cognitive elements is to be reached by introspection and a critical examination of reason such as Kant instituted. We find ... involved in the numinous experience, beliefs and feelings qualitatively different from anything that 'natural' sense perception is capable of giving us. They are themselves, not perceptions at all, but peculiar interpretations and valuations, at first of perceptual data, and then – at a higher level – of posited objects and entities. which themselves no longer belong to the perceptual world, but are thought of as supplementing and transcending it. ... neither are they any sort of 'transmutation' of sense-perceptions. ... The facts of the numinous consciousness point therefore ... to a hidden substantive source, from which the religious ideas and feelings are formed, which lies in the mind independently of sense-experience; a 'pure reason' in the profoundest sense, which, because of the 'surpassingness' of its content, must be distinguished from both the pure theoretical and the pure practical reason of Kant, as something yet higher or deeper than they.

11 In general I would argue that the phenomenological approach to religion is philosophically underdeveloped. For example, in "The Phenomenological Method", *Numen* 1959, Bleeker responds to the criticisms of the philosopher J.A. Oosterbaan by saying: "since 1887 the development of the phenomenology of religion has been such that nowadays nobody confines himself to a mere description of religious phenomena ... the general trend is for an inquiry into the meaning and the structure of these facts" (1959: 104). At no point, however, does he show an appreciation of the hermeneutical problems attendant on this claim. especially in light of the phenomenological bracketing of questions of the truth or falsity of religious beliefs.

12 In "Comparative Religion: Whither and Why?", Smith earlier
expressed this idea as follows (1959: 42):

> For I would proffer this ... no statement about a religion is valid unless
> it can be acknowledged by that religion's believers. I know that this
> is revolutionary, and I know that it will not be readily conceded; but I
> believe it to be profoundly true and important. It would take a good
> deal more space than is here available to defend it at length; for I
> am conscious of many ways in which it can be misunderstood and of
> many objections that can be brought against it which can be answered
> only at some length. I will only recall that by "religion" here I mean
> as previously indicated the faith in men's hearts. On the external data
> about religion, of course, an outsider can by diligent scholarship discover
> things that an insider does not know and may not be willing to accept.
> But about the meaning that the system has for those of faith, an outsider
> cannot in the nature of the case go beyond the believer; for their piety
> *is* the faith, and if they cannot recognize his portrayal, then it is not
> their faith that he is portraying.

By identifying religion with the faith in individual's hearts and
consequently giving the last word on the validity of any explanation to the religious believer, Smith's method implicitly
asserts and builds on the same claim to the *sui generis* nature of
religious phenomena explicitly proclaimed by the Dutch phenomenologists. Accordingly, as this passage also reflects, his
view orients the student of religion to the understanding of
essences (i.e., "the faith in men's hearts") and yet limits the
religious studies enterprise to the descriptive realm (e.g, note
his use of the word portrayal in the last sentence of the quoted
passage).

Now by the end of the same essay, the horizon of Smith's
method has actually been changed and broadened (though no
difference is noted by Smith), as the following passage reveals
(1959: 53). Nevertheless matters remain very problematic.

> In the particular case where |an| encounter is between the academic
> tradition of the West and a particular religion, the statement |about re-
> ligion| that is evolved must satisfy each of two traditions independently
> and transcend them both by satisfying both simultaneously. In the case
> of an encounter between two religious groups, let us say for example
> Christianity and Islam, the scholar's creativity must rise to the point
> where his work is cogent within three traditions simultaneously; the
> academic, the Christian, and the Muslim. This is not easy, but I am
> persuaded that both in principle and in practice it can be done.

I find it difficult to be as sanguine as Smith about the feasibility
of this approach to the study of religion. The examples Smith

provides in the footnotes to his essay do little to bolster my confidence. These notes refer only to the comparatively trivial procedure of using certain very neutral terms in the description of different religious traditions. And one must wonder if this procedure is congruent with Smith's emphasis on understanding every religion in terms of its unique and internal experiential dimension.

13 Smith begins to develop this theme in the closing pages of his 1959 essay (54-58). For example, on page 55 he states:

> The practitioner of comparative religion, then, I am suggesting, may become no longer an observer vis-a-vis the history of diverse religions of distant or even close communities, but rather a participant – in the multiform religious history of the only religious community there is, humanity. Comparative religion may become the disciplined self-consciousness of man's variegated and developing religious life.

14 Cavanaugh cites the following books and articles: Robert Bellah, "Between Religion and Social Science"(1970a), and "The New Religious Consciousness and the Secular University", in *Religion and the Academic Scene*, Waterloo, Ontario: Council on the Study of Religion, 1975; Peter L. Berger (1969 and 1980), and "Some Second Thoughts on Substantive Versus Functional Definitions of Religion", *Journal for the Scientific Study of Religion* 13 (1974): 125-33; William Garrett (1974); Pierre Hegy, "Images of God and Man in a Catholic Charismatic Renewal Community", *Social Compass* 25 (1978): 7-21; David Moberg, "Presidential Address: Virtues for Sociology of Religion", *Sociological Analysis* 39 (1978): 1-18; Ninian Smart, *The Science of Religion and the Sociology of Knowledge*, Princeton: Princeton University Press, 1973.

15 The term refers to Euhemerus of Messene (ca. 340-260 B.C.), author of the *Hiera Anagraphie*, which argues that the gods are nothing more than heroic mortals who have been elevated by mythic embellishment to the rank of dieties.

16 Afterall it is the very tendency of reductionist accounts of religion to prejudge the metaphysical issue of the truth of religious postulates that has precipitated the phenomenological principle of the *epoché* being given a narrow descriptivist reading in the phenomenology of religion. And it is this interpretation of the *epoché*, Wiebe argues, that has led phenomenologists of religion to implicitly introduce a similarly illicit and contradictory metaphysical judgement into their work (1984b: 409).

17 I admit that many of Wiebe's comments, made in different contexts, can be seen as inconsistent. Yet I think that the evidence favours giving a unified cast to his opinions (though the exercise does call for some interpretative generosity). Charles Davis, however, is certainly incorrect in charging that Wiebe simply wishes to reimpose a reductionist framework on religious studies, especially one based on a naive "foundationism" (Davis, 1984: 399). Rather, I would say that Wiebe's psotion is analogous to that of those philosophers of science who restrict themselves to a Humean view of causality, refusing to proceed to the ontological commitments taken-up by Realists.

18 The nearest Wiebe comes, that I know of, to spelling-out a specific conception of science is in a few brief paragraphs of "Theory in the Study of Religion," (1983: 296-97). These comments are more suggestive than conclusive and they need elaboration. In his book *Religion and Truth*, Polanyi's views are discussed in some depth (see Chapter X). But the discussion is focused on his notion of truth and not the method of science per se.

19 Wiebe's use of the term 'transcendence' in his definition runs the risk of creating the terminological confusion discussed at the beginning of this chapter. However, the passage which immediately follows his definition, which I have quoted, shows that his use is meant to be consistent with that adopted here.

20 For the interpretation of the concept of "law" see note 4 to Chapter VI on the views of N. Rescher. For the interpretation of "truth" see Alfred Tarski, "The Semantic Conception of Truth," *Philosophical and Phenomenological Research* 4, 1943: 341ff., and/or Karl Popper's use of Tarski's views (1963: 223-27).

21 Wiebe has yet, to my knowledge, to spell out just what he has in mind.

Chapter XI

1 The term 'strong programme' in the sociology of knowledge was coined by the British philosophers Barry Barnes and David Bloor. See Bloor, *Knowledge and Social Imagery*, London: Routledge and Kegan Paul, 1976 and Barnes, *Interests and the Growth of Knowledge*, London: Routledge and Kegan Paul, 1977 for indepth discussions of the position. For a more limited

but very concise and articulate expression of their position read "Relativism. Rationalism and the Sociology of Knowledge," in M. Hollis and S. Lukes. eds. *Rationality and Relativism* (1982).

2 Support is advanced. calling upon other sources, for a similar epistemological perspective in Derek Layder, "Beyond Empiricism? The Promise of Realism," *Philosophy of the Social Sciences* 15, 1985: 255-274.

3 Some insightful initial formulations of a rationality of degrees have been advanced by Joseph Agassi and Ian Jarvie. Agassi and Jarvie have authored or co-authored with others a series of articles culminated in "The Rationality of Irrationalism," *Metaphilosophy* 11, 1980: 127-33 (the other relevant articles are listed in this article). Constraints of time and space pervent us from properly pursuing their lead here.

Conclusion

1 Compare William Garrett (1974), Paul Heelas (1978), W. Richard Comstock (1981). Karel Werner (1983), and Lucy Dupertuis (1986).

2 Daniel Pals (1986) arrives at a similar conclusion:

The question of whether Eliade (or any one else) has "proved" religion irreducible seems to be badly framed. If it is true, as it seems to me, that such a thesis acts at a high level of abstraction as a kind of disciplinary axiom, directing our attention to a certain aspect of the world and life, then it certainly will not be provable – or refutable – in any simple way. ... Like biology's claim to be autonomous over against the reductions of chemistry and physics, it will have to prove itself over a long run by the quality of its fruits.

References

Abel, Theodore
1948 "The Operation called *Verstehen*."
American Journal of Sociology 54: 11-18.

Abelson, R. P.
1976 "Social Psychology's Rational Man." In S. I. Benn
and G. W. Mortimore, eds. *Rationality and the Social
Sciences*. London: Routledge and Kegan Paul.

Adler, Mortimer J.
1958 *The Idea of Freedom*. New York: Doubleday.

Agassi, Joseph and Jarvie, Ian C.
1980 "The Rationality of Irrationalism." *Metaphilosophy*
11: 127-33.

Austin, John L.
1962 *Sense and Sensibilia*. Oxford: Oxford University Press.

Barnes, Barry and Bloor, David
1982 "Relativism, Rationality and the Sociology of Knowledge."
In Martin Hollis and Steven Lukes, eds. *Rationality and
Relativism*. Cambridge, Mass.: M.I.T. Press.

Bellah, Robert
1970a *Beyond Belief*. New York: Harper and Row.
1970b "Confessions of a Former Establishment
Fundamentalist." *Bulletin of the Council on the
Study of Religion* 1.

Benn, S.I. and Mortimore, G.W.
1976 *Rationality and the Social Sciences*. London:
Routledge and Kegan Paul.

Berger, Peter and Luckmann, Thomas
1966 *The Social Construction of Reality*. Garden City,
New York: Doubleday.

1963 *Invitation to Sociology*. Garden City, N.Y.:
Doubleday.

1967 *The Sacred Canopy*. Garden City, N.Y.:
      Doubleday.
Bernstein, Mark
   1983 "Socialization and Autonomy." *Mind* 92: 120-23.
Bhaskar, Roy
   1975 *A Realist Theory of Science*. Brighton: Harvester Press.
      Harvester Press.
   1978 "On the Possibility of Social Scientific Knowledge and
      the Limits of Naturalism." *Journal for the Theory of
      Social Behaviour* 8: 1-28.
Bianchi, Ugo
   1972 "The Definition of Religion (On the Methodology of
      Historical-Comparative Research)." In U. Bianchi et al.,
      eds. *Problems and Methods of the History of Religions*.
      Leiden: E. J. Brill.
Bleeker, C.J.
   1954 "The Relation of History of Religions to Kindred
      Religious Sciences, particularly Theology, Sociology
      of Religion, Psychology of Religion and Phenomenology
      of Religion." *Numen* 1: 142-52.
   1959 "The Phenomenological Method." *Numen* 6: 96-111.
   1971 "Comparing the Religio-Historical and the Theological
      Method." *Numen* 18: 9-29.
   1975 *The Rainbow: A Collection of Studies in the Science
      of Religion*. Leiden: E.J. Brill.
Brubaker, Rogers
   1984 *The Limits of Rationality*. London: George Allen
      and Unwin.
Campbell, Tom
   1981 *Seven Theories of Human Society*. Oxford:
      Oxford University Press.
Cavanaugh, Michael
   1982 "Pagan and Christian: Sociological Euhemerism Versus
      American Sociology of Religion." *Sociological Analysis*
      43: 109-29.
Christian, William A.
   1964 *Meaning and Truth in Religion*. Princeton: Princeton
      University Press.
Cohen, Percy
   1980 "Is Positivism Dead?" *Sociological Review* 28: 141-76.

Combs, Eugene and Bowlby, Paul
    1974 "Tolerance and Tradition." *Studies in Religion* 4: 315-34.
Comstock, W. Richard
    1981 "A Behavioral Approach to the Sacred: Category
        Formation in Religious Studies." *Journal of the
        American Academy of Religion* 49: 625-43.
Dauenhauer, Bernard P.
    1982 "Relational Freedom." *Review of Metaphysics* 26: 77-101.
Davidson, Donald
    1980 "Psychology as Philosophy." In *Essays on Actions and
        Events*. Oxford: Clarendon Press.
Dawe, Alan
    1970 "The Two Sociologies." *British Journal of Sociology*
        21: 207-18.
    1978 "Theories of Social Action." In Tom Bottomore and
        Robert Nisbet, eds. *A History of Sociological Analysis*.
        London: Heinemann.
Dawson, Lorne L.
    1984 "Determinism in the Social-Scientific Study of Religion:
        The Views of Martin Hollis and Ernest Gellner."
        Religious Studies Review 10: 223-28.
    1985 " 'Free-Will Talk' and Sociology." *Sociological Inquiry*
        55: 348-62.
    1986 "Neither Nerve nor Ecstacy: Comment on the Wiebe-Davis
        Exchange." *Studies in Religion* 15: 145-51.
    1987 "On References to the Transcendent in the Scientific
        Study of Religion: A Qualified Idealist Proposal."
        Religion 17, no.4 (forthcoming).
Dray, William H.
    1957 *Laws and Explanation in History*. Oxford: Oxford
        University Press
Dupertuis, Lucy
    1986 "How People Recognize Charisma: The Case of Darshan
        in Radhasoami and the Divine Light Mission."
        Sociological Analysis 47: 111-24.
Durkheim, Emile
    1895 *The Rules of Sociological Method*. Translated by S.A.
        Solovay and J.H. Mueller. New York: The Free Press,
        1964.

Eliade, Mircea
    1963 *Patterns in Comparative Religion*. New York: Meridian.
    1969 *The Quest*. Chicago: University of Chicago Press.
Ermarth, Michael
    1978 *Wilhelm Dilthey: The Critique of Historical Reason*.
        Chicago: University of Chicago Press.
Feyerabend, Paul
    1975 *Against Method*. London: Verso.
Filmer, Paul et al.
    1972 *New Directions in Sociological Theory*. London:
        Collier-MacMillan.
Follesdal, Dagfinn
    1982 "The Status of Rationality Assumptions in Interpretation
        and the Explanation of Action." *Dialectica* 36: 301-16.
Gadamer, Hans-Georg
    1975 *Truth and Method*. New York: Seabury Press.
Galloway, A. D.
    1975 "Theology and Religious Studies – The Unity of
        Our Discipline." *Religious Studies* 11: 157-65.
Garrett, William
    1974 "Troublesome Transcendence: The Supernatural in the
        Scientific Study of Religion." *Sociological Analysis*
        35: 167-80.
Gellner, Ernest
    1974 *Legitimation of Belief*. Cambridge: Cambridge University
        Press.
Gibson, Quentin
    1976 "Arguing from Rationality." In S.I. Benn and G.W.
        Mortimore, eds. *Rationality and the Social Sciences*.
        London: Routledge and Kegan Paul.
Giddens, Anthony
    1977 *Studies in Social and Political Theory*. London:
        Hutchinson.
Glock, Charles and Stark, Rodney
    1965 *Religion and Society in Tension*. Chicago: Rand McNally.
Goldman, Alvin I.
    1970 *A Theory of Human Action*. Englewood Cliffs. N.J.:
        Prentice-Hall.

Goodenough, Erwin R.
   1959 "Religionswissenschaft." *Numen* 6: 77-95.

Habermas, Jürgen
   1971a *Knowledge and Human Interests*. Boston: Beacon Press.
   1971b *"Vorbereitende Bemerkungen zu einer Theorie der Kommunikativen Kompetenz."* In Jürgen Habermas and Niklas Luhmann, *Theorie der Gesellschaft oder Sozialtechnologie?* Frankfurt.
   1979 *Communication and the Evolution of Society*. Boston: Beacon Press.

Harré, Rom
   1979 Review of M. Hollis, *Models of Man. Mind* 88: 309-12.

Heelas, Paul
   1978 "Some Problems with Religious Studies." *Religion* 8: 1-14.

Heil, John
   1983 "Rationality and Psychological Explanation." *Inquiry* 28: 359-71.

Heimbeck, Raeburne
   1969 *Theology and Meaning*. Stanford, Calif.: Stanford University Press.

Hempel, Carl G.
   1962 "Rational Action." In *Proceedings and Addresses of the American Philosophical Association 1961-62*, Vol. 35. Yellow Springs, Ohio: The Antioch Press.
   1965 *Aspects of Scientific Explanation*. New York: The Free Press.

Hodges, Daniel
   1974 "Breaking a Scientific Taboo: Putting Assumptions about the Supernatural into Scientific Theories of Religion." *Journal for the Scientific Study of Religion* 13: 393-408.

Hollis, Martin and Nell, Edward
   1975 *Rational Economic Man*. Cambridge: Cambridge University Press.

Hollis, Martin and Lukes, Steven, eds.
   1982 *Rationality and Relativism*. Cambridge, Mass.: M.I.T. Press.

Hollis, (James) Martin (works relevant to this thesis only)
   1968 "Reason and Ritual." *Philosophy*. Reprinted in B. Wilson,

ed. *Rationality*. Oxford: Basil Blackwell, 1970 and in
A. Ryan, ed. *The Philosophy of Social Explanation*.
Oxford: Oxford University Press, 1975.

1969 "The Limits of Irrationality." *European Journal of
Sociology*. Reprinted in B. Wilson, ed. *Rationality*.
Oxford: Basil Blackwell.

1972 "Witchcraft and Winchcraft." *Philosophy of the Social
Sciences* 2: 89-103.

1973 "Deductive Explanation in the Social Sciences."
Proceedings of the Aristotelian Society. Supplemental
Volume.

1975 "My Role and Its Duties." In R.S. Peters, ed. *Nature
and Conduct*. London: Macmillan.

1975 "Ideology and Metaphysics." In S. Kroner, ed.
Explanation. Oxford: Basil Blackwell.

1977 *Models of Man*. Cambridge: Cambridge University Press.

1978 "Action and Context." *Proceedings of the Aristotelian
Society*. Supplemental Volume.

1979 "The Epistemological Unity of Mankind." In S.C. Brown,
ed. *Philosophical Disputes in the Social Sciences*.
Brighton: Harvester.

1979 "Rational Man and Social Science." In R. Harrison, ed.
Rational Action. Cambridge: Cambridge University
Press.

1982 "The Social Destruction of Reality." In M. Hollis and
S. Lukes, eds. *Rationality and Relativism*. Cambridge,
Mass.: M.I.T. Press.

1983 "Rational Preferences." *Philosophical Forum* 14: 246-62.

1983 "Categorical Imprisonment." *Grazer Philosophische
Studien* 20: 3-15.

1984 "Behind the Mask." Lecture on B.B.C., Radio 3, 28/1.

1986 "Reasons of Honour." *The Proceedings of the Aristotlian
Society* 87: 1-19 (Presidential Address).

Homans, George
1964 "Bringing Men Back In." *American Sociological Review*.
Reprinted in A. Ryan, ed. *The Philosophy of Social
Explanation*. Oxford: Oxford University Press, 1973.

Horton, Robin
1967 "African Traditional Thought and Social Science."
Africa 37: 50-71 and 155-87. Reprinted in B. Wilson,

     ed. *Rationality*. Oxford: Basil Blackwell.
1979 "Material-object Language and Theoretical Language:
     Towards a Strawsonian Sociology of Thought." In S.C.
     Brown, ed. *Philosophical Disputes in the Social Sciences*.
     Brighton: Harvester.
1982 "Tradition and Modernity Revisited." In M. Hollis and
     S. Lukes, eds. *Rationality and Relativism*. Cambridge,
     Mass.: M.I.T. Press.

James, George A.
1985 "Phenomenology and the Study of Religion:
     The Archeology of an Approach."
     Journal of Religion 65: 311-35.

Johnson, Benton
1977 "Sociological Theory and Religious Truth." *Sociological
     Analysis* 38: 368-88.

Jones, Hugh
1978 "The Spirit of Inquiry and the Reflected Self:
     Theological Anthropology and the Sociology of
     Knowledge." *Scottish Journal of Theology* 31:
     201-16.

Keat, Russell and Urry, John
1975 *Social Theory as Science*. London: Routledge and Kegan
     Paul.

Kitagawa, Joseph M.
1980 "Humanistic and Theological History of Religions
     With Special Reference to the North American Scene."
     Numen 27: 198-221.

Knorr-Cetina, Karin D.
1981 "Social and Scientific Method or What Do We Make
     of the Distinction Between the Natural and the Social
     Sciences?" *Philosophy of the Social Sciences* 11: 335-59.
1981 *The Manufacture of knowledge*. Oxford: Pergamon Press.

Kolakowski, Leszek
1972 *Positivist Philosophy*. Harmondsworth, England:
     Penguin.

Kolb, William
1962 "Images of Man and the Sociology of Religion."
     Journal for the Scientific Study of Religion 1: 5-22.

Kristensen, William Brede (trans. J.B. Carman)
1960 *The Meaning of Religion*. The Hague: M. Nijhoff.

Kuhn, Thomas
    1970 *The Structure of Scientific Revolutions*, 2nd ed.
        Chicago: University of Chicago Press.
    1977 *The Essential Tension*. Chicago: University
        of Chicago Press.

Lakatos, Imre
    1970 "Flasification and the Methodology of Scientific
        Research Programmes." In I. Lakatos and A. Musgrave,
        eds. *Criticism and the Growth of Knowledge*.
        Cambridge: Cambridge University Press.

Langer, Susanne K.
    1942 *Philosophy in a New Key*. Cambridge, Mass.:
        Harvard University Press.

Laudan, Larry
    1977 *Progress and Its Problems*. Berkeley, Calif.:
        University of California Press.

Layder, Derek
    1985 "Beyond Empiricism? The Promise of Realism."
        Philosophy of the Social Sciences 15: 255-74.

Leeuw, van der Gerardus
    1938 *Reiligion in Essnce and Manifestation: A Study in
        Phenomenology*. Translated by J.E. Turner. New York:
        Harper and Row, 1963.

Lemke, James and Shevach, David and Wells, Richard H.
    1984 "The Humanism-Positivism Debate in Sociology: a
        Comment on Tibbett's Reconsideration." *Sociological
        Inquiry* 54: 89-102.

Lévi-Strauss, Claude
    1966 *The Savage Mind*. Chicago: University of Chicago Press.

Lukes, Steven
    1970 "Some Problems About Rationality." In B. Wilson, ed.
        Rationality. Oxford: Basil Blackwell.
    1982 "Relativism in Its Place." In M. Hollis and S. Lukes,
        eds. *Rationality and Relativism*. Cambridge, Mass.:
        M.I.T. Press.

Lundberg, George A.
    1968 *Sociology*. 4th ed. New York: Hargper and Row.

MacIntyre, Alasdair
    1957 "Determinism." *Mind* 66: 28-41.

1962 "A Mistake About Causality in Social Science." In
    P. Laslett and W.G. Runciman, eds. *Philosophy, Politics
    and Society*, second series. Oxford: Basil Blackwell.
1966 "The Antecedents of Action." In *Against the Self-Images
    of the Age*. New York: Schocken, 1971; reprinted from
    B. William and A. Montefiore, eds. *British Analytical
    Philosophy*. London: Routlegde and Kegan Paul, 1966.
1967 "The Idea of a Social Science." *Proceedings of the
    Aristotelian Society*, Supplemental Volume. Reprinted
    in B. Wilson, ed. *Rationality*. Oxford: Basil Blackwell,
    1970 and in A. MacIntyre, *Against the Self-Images of the
    Age*. New York: Schocken, 1971.
1971 "Rationality and the Explanation of Action." In *Against
    the Self-Images of the Age*. New York: Schocken.

Marsh, Cathie
1979 Review of M. Hollis, *Models of Man*. *British Journal of
    Sociology* 30: 128-29.

McCormmach, Russell
1982 *Night Thoughts of a Classical Physicist*. New York:
    Avon.

Melden, A.I.
1961 *Free Action*. London: Routledge and Kegan Paul.

Nagel, Ernest
1960 *The Structure of Science*. Indianapolis: Hackett.

Neurath, Otto
1973 "Empirical Sociology." In O. Neurath, *Empiricism
    and Sociology*, edited by Marie Neurath and R. S.
    Cohen, Boston: Dordrecht and Reidel.

Newton-Smith, William
1981 *The Rationality of Science*. London: Routledge and
    Kegan Paul.

Ogden, Schubert M.
1978 "Theology and Religious Studies: Their Difference
    and the Difference It Makes." *Journal of the
    American Academy of Religion* 46: 3-17.

Otto, Rudolf
1917 *The Idea of the Holy*. Translated by John W. Harvey.
    Oxford: Oxford University Press, 1958.

Outhwaite, William
    1983 *Concept Formation in Social Science.* London:
        Routledge and Kegan Paul.

Pals, Daniel
    1986 "Reductionism and Belief: An Appraisal of Recent
        Attacks on the Doctrine of Irreducible Religion".
        Journal of Religion 66: 18-36.

Peacocke, A. R.
    1976 "Reductionism: A Review of the Epistemological Issues
        and Their Relevance to Biology and the Problem of
        Consciousness." *Zygon* 11: 307-36.

Penner, Hans and Yonan, Edward
    1972 "Is a Science of Religion Possible?" *Journal of the
        American Academy of Religion* 52: 107-33.
    1986 "Criticism and the Development of a Science of
        Religion." *Studies in Religion* 15: 165-75.

Peters, R.S.
    1960 *The Concept of Motivation.* London: Routledge and
        Kegan Paul.

Phillips, D.Z.
    1979 "Alienation and the Sociologizing of Meaning."
        The Aristotlian Society 53: 95-116.

Popper, Karl
    1959 *The Logic of Scientific Discovery.* New York:
        Basic Books.
    1963 *Conjectures and Refutations: The Growth of
        Scientific Knowledge.* New York: Harper and Row.

Quine, Willard V. O.
    1961 "Two Dogmas of Empiricism." In *From a Logical Point
        of View.* Cambridge, Mass.: Harvard University Press.

Rescher, Nicholas
    1969 "Lawfulness as Mind-Dependent." In N. Rescher, ed.
        Essays in Honour of Carl G. Hempel. Dordrecht,
        Holland: D. Reidel.

Robertson, Roland
    1974 "Religious and Sociological Factors in the Analysis
        of Secularization." In Allan W. Eister, ed. *Changing
        Perspectives in the Scientific Study of Religion.*
        New York: John Wiley and Sons.

   1985 "Beyond the Sociology of Religion?" *Sociological
           Analysis* 46: 355-60.

Rorty, Richard
   1979 *Philosophy and the Mirror of Nature.* Princeton:
           Princeton University Press.

Rudolph, Kurt
   1981 "Basic Positions of *Religionswissenschaft.*"
           Religion 11: 97-107.

Schumacher, John A.
   1980 "The Place of Freedom in Life: Some Models of a Human
           Being." *Philosophy of the Social Sciences* 10: 345-77.

Segal, Robert
   1980 "The Social Sciences and the Truth of Religious
           Belief." *Journal of the American Academy of Religion*
           48: 401-13.
   1983 "In Defence of Reductionism." *Journal of the
           American Academy of Religion* 51 97-124.

Shepard, William C.
   1972 "Religion and the Social Sciences: Conflict or
           Reconciliation?" *Journal for the Scientific Study
           of Religion* 11: 230-38.

Simon, Michael
   1982 *Understanding Human Action.* Albany: State University
           of New York Press.

Skinner, B. F.
   1973 *Beyond Freedom and Dignity.* London: Penguin.

Skorupski, John
   1985 "Relativity, Realism and Consensus." *Philosophy*
           60: 341-58.

Smart, Ninian
   1970 *Philosophers and Religious Truth.* London: SCM.

Smith, Wilfred Cantwell
   1959 "Comparative Religion: Whither – and Why?" In
           M. Eliade and Joseph Kitagawa, eds. *The History of
           Religions: Essays in Methodology.* Chicago: University
           of Chicago Press.
   1962 *The Meaning and End of Religion.* New York: Harper
           and Row, 1978.

1975 "Methodology and the Study of Religion: Some
    Misgivings." In Robert Baird, ed. *Methodological Issues
    in Religious Studies*. New Horizons Press.
1976 "Objectivity and the Humane Sciences: A New Proposal."
    In Willard G. Oxtoby, ed. *Religious Diversity: Essays
    of Wilfrid Cantwell Smith*. New York: Harper and Row.

Spiro, Melford
1970 *Buddhism and Society*. New York: Harper and Row.

Taylor, Richard
1963 *Metaphysics*. Englewood Cliffs, N.J.: Prentice-Hall.
1969 "Determinism." In Paul Edwards, ed. *The Enclyclopedia
    of Philosophy*. New York: Macmillan and
    The Free Press, Vol. 1 and 2, pp.359-73.

Tibbetts, Paul
1982 "The Positivism-Humanism Debate in Sociology: A
    Reconsideration." *Sociological Inquiry* 52: 184-99.
1984 "Semantic Grids and a Humanistically Oriented
    Sociology: A Reply to Lemke, Shevach, and Wells."
    Sociological Inquiry 54: 98-102.

Trompf, Gary W.
1980 Review of M. Hollis, *Models of Man*. *Philosophy of the
    Social Sciences* 10: 336-41.

Watkins, J. W. N.
1970 "Imperfect Rationality." In R. Borger and F. Cioffi,
    eds. *Explanation in the Behavioural Sciences*.
    Cambridge: Cambridge University Press.

Weber, Max
1949 *The Methodology of the Social Sciences*. Translated and
    edited by Edward A. Shils and Henry A. Finch. New
    York: The Free Press.
1964 *The Theory of Social and Economic Organizations*.
    Translated by A.M. Henderson and Talcott Parsons,
    edited by Talcott Parsons. New York: The Free Press.

Werblowsky, R. J. Zwi
1975 "On Studying Comparative Religion." *Religious
    Studies* 11: 145-56.

Werner, Karel
1983 "The Concept of the Transcendent." *Religion* 13: 311-22.

Whaling, Frank
1984 "Additional Note on Philosophy of Science and the

Study of Religion." In F. Whaling, ed. *Contemporary Approaches to the Study of Religion, Volume I: The Humanities*. New York: Mouton.

Whorf, Benjamin Lee
1956 *Language, Thought and Reality*. Cambridge, Mass.: M.I.T. Press.

Wiebe, Donald
1979 "Does Understanding Religion Require Religious Understanding?" *Proceeding of the Conference on Methodology of the International Association for the History of Religions, Warsaw, 1979*, (unpublished).
1981 *Religion and Truth: Towards a New Paradigm for the Study of Religion*. The Hague: Mouton.
1983 "Theory in the Study of Religion." *Religion* 13: 283-309.
1984a "Beyond the Sceptic and the Devotee: Reductionism in the Scientific Study of Religion." *Journal of the American Academy of Religion* 52: 157-65.
1984b "The Failure of Nerve in the Academic Study of Religion." *Studies in Religion* 13: 401-22.

Wilson, Warner
1963 "A Brief Resolution of the Issue of Free-Will Versus Determinism." *Journal for the Scientific Study of Religion* 4: 101.

Winch, Peter
1958 *The Idea of a Social Science*. London: Routledge and Kegan Paul.
1964 "Understanding a Primitive Society." *American Philosophical Quarterly*. Reprinted in B. Wilson, ed. *Rationality*. Oxford: Basil Blackwell, 1970.

Wittgenstein, Ludwig
1958 *Philosophical Investigations*. Translated by G.E.M. Anscombe. Oxford: Basil Blackwell.

Young, Robert
1980 "Autonomy and Socialization." *Mind* 89: 565-76.

Index

Akhtar, Shabbir

REASON AND THE RADICAL CRISIS OF FAITH

American University Studies: Series VII (Theology and Religion. Vol. 30
ISBN 0-8204 0451-9   281 pp.   hardback US $ 40.20/sFr. 60.30

Recommended prices – alterations reserved

Is belief in the Christian God intellectually defensible? Is it even morally necessary? In this book, Dr. Shabbir Akhtar, himself a Muslim, examines and rejects one fideist and two reductionist defences of the rationality of Christian conviction in modern industrial society. He identifies another defensive position – «theological revisionism» – which has recently gained popularity with secularized Christian thinkers. Rejecting this as merely a conservative version of reductionism, he emphazises the need for reviving the tradition of natural theology and, in doing so, a religious vision of the world.

Contents: Faith and reason – Feideism – The Christian tradition – Reductionism – Revisionism – Natural Theology – Presupposes some familiarity with philosophical reasoning – Philosophy of the Christian faith in the context of related religious rivals: Judaism and Islam.

«Akhtar undermines this central orthodoxy (among theists in analytical philosophy of religion), and, shows such revisionist views to be evasive and not providing the rational underpinning for religious belief in our secular age ... This is an important book running against the stream ...» (Kais Nielsen, University of Calgary)

«Not only ... erudite and well-researched, but... eloquent and forceful... work of considerable public interest.» (Hugo Meynell, University of Calgary)

«Dr. Akhtar's book stands out from most recent work in the philosophy of religion in being intelligent, clear, direct and forceful.» (C.B. Martin, University of Calgary)

PETER LANG PUBLISHING, INC.
62 West 45th Street
USA – New York, NY 10036

Blasi, Anthony J.

A PHENOMENOLOGICAL TRANSFORMATION OF THE SOCIAL SCIENTIFIC STUDY OF RELIGION

American University Studies: Series VII, Theology and Religion. Vol. 10
ISBN 0-8204-0235-4   205 pp.   hardback US $ 27.85

Recommended prices - alterations reserved

This book develops a theoretical methodology for the scientific study of religion, from the principle of meaning adequacy. Religion is to be understood adequately when the character of its presence in the mind of the religious person is described. This methodology is used to address some major issues in the study of religion in new ways - defining religion, understanding ritual, the connection between religion and morality, religious social morality in the third world, pietism, the value problem in scientific accounts of religion, and types of religious mentalities. These discussions comprise a substantive phenomenology of religion, and a distinctive sociology of religion.

Contents: After developing a phenomenological methodology for the study of religion, the book addresses major issues in the social scientific study of religion. Among these are ritual, morality, and conversion.

PETER LANG PUBLISHING, INC.
62 West 45th Street
USA - New York, NY 10036

Turner, David H.

LIFE BEFORE GENESIS
A Conclusion
An Understanding of the Significance of Australian Aboriginal Culture

Toronto Studies in Religion. Vol. 1
ISBN 0-8204 0244-3   195 pp.   hardback US $ 24.75/sFr. 56.90

Recommended prices – alterations reserved

Turner's 'conclusion' is that the Australian Aborigines, having transcended the problem of incorporation and technology at a Stone Age level of development, achieved what eludes 'modern' society – peace, order and good government. The analysis is based on a comparison of Australian and Canadian aboriginal society and mythology following more than a decade of ethnographic work, numerous publications on the subject and a rhetorical insight into the nature of the human condition. In reading his research findings and his insight into the Book of Genesis. Turner finds that he has gone some way to shattering the silence of the text. What emerges is a Prologue to the Judeo-Christian tradition which also hints at its Conclusion.

Contents: A distinction is drawn between 'incorporative' and 'confederative' historical traditions based on an analysis of Australian and Canadian aboriginal societies. The theoretical articulation of the traditions illuminates the book of Genesis.

PETER LANG PUBLISHING, INC.
62 West 45th Street
USA – New York, NY 10036